Theories of
Industrial Organization

Theories of
Industrial Organization

Gavin C. Reid

Basil Blackwell

Copyright © Gavin C. Reid, 1987

First published 1987

Basil Blackwell Ltd
108 Cowley Road, Oxford, OX4 1JF, UK

Basil Blackwell Inc.
432 Park Avenue South, Suite 1503
New York, NY 10016, USA

British Library Cataloguing in Publication Data

Reid, Gavin C.
   Theories of industrial organization.
   1. Industrial organization
   I. Title
   338.7   HD38

   ISBN 0-631-15172-9

Library of Congress Cataloging-in-Publication Data

Reid, Gavin C.
   Theories of industrial organization.
   Bibliography: p.
   Includes index.
   1. Industrial organization (Economic theory)
   I. Title
HD2326.R45   1987   338.7   86-31007
ISBN 0-631-15172-9

Typeset in 10 on 12pt Plantin
by MHL Typesetting Ltd, Coventry
Printed in Great Britain by T J Press Ltd, Padstow

To
Neil Alexander Reid

Contents

PART V CONCLUSION

Preface

This book is an attempt to differentiate the concept of industrial organization, or industrial economics as it is commonly called in Europe, from the closely related traditional areas of price theory or, more grandly, microeconomic theory. There now exist many good textbooks on the subject of industrial organization, particularly in North America, and it should be made clear that I am not attempting to produce another variation on this well-established theme. The title itself should suggest that I had something else in mind. My original choice was *Approaches to Industrial Organization*, but on the sound advice of those who are doubtless more reliable judges on such matters, I became convinced that a more appropriate and descriptive title would be *Theories of Industrial Organization*. Certainly between these two covers I *am* concerned with various *approaches* to industrial organization – but on a conceptual rather than a technical level. That is to say, this book will not tell the reader how to go about the analysis of a particular problem in industrial organization. This is the sort of advice that I am involved in giving to postgraduate students almost every week of my working life. The view I have reached is that each problem in industrial economics is so distinctive that one would be foolish to attempt to embody such advice in a text which could act as a kind of cookbook. The result would look completely *ad hoc* and would foster a hopelessly unscientific approach to the particular problem with which the student or professional finds himself confronted. However, what may be of use is a book that provides an appropriate framework within which the analysis of industrial organization can take place. This is not the place to digress on the meaning of a paradigm or to probe into the structuralist view that alternative forms of industrial organization are related to cognitive structures. However, I do hope to convince the reader that there are distinct alternative frameworks within which it is fruitful to examine industrial structure, and perhaps even to suggest that some frameworks are potentially more fruitful than others.

A danger with any activity of this sort is that it invites the criticism that the categorization adopted is arbitrary. There is some truth in this view, but I do not feel that the categories suggested are so nebulous that one could seriously contest the core of their contents. To take an example, I do not think that one could legitimately dispute that there are Marshallian and Austrian approaches to industrial organization. In some respects they are similar, particularly in their viewing competition as manifesting itself as a process rather than as an equilibrium state. However, in essential respects the approaches are irreconcilably different. This is particularly important in regard to the attitudes towards the organization of actual industries which proponents of the two views would wish to see fostered. Marshallian and Austrian worlds would be quite different, and immediately recognizable as such. In this context, I am reminded of a seminar that Nicholas Georgescu-Roegen delivered at the University of Glasgow some years ago in honour of the father of thermodynamics, Lord Kelvin. At one stage, Georgescu-Roegen was badgered by a member of the seminar concerning the particular categories of analysis he was adopting in his address. It was pointed out that in fact common elements were shared by what were proffered as distinct categories. Georgescu-Roegen replied: 'Heifetz is a violinist. I am a violinist. We both play the violin. We even play the same music on occasions. But *I* know, *everybody* knows, that I am no Heifetz.' I would not wish to suggest that the categories I have identified go so far as to distinguish the amateur approach from the professional; heaven forbid! Nevertheless, I would hope they provide a basis for exploring industrial analysis by a variety of means. My intention is to provide the reader with sufficient information and comparative analysis that he can form his own view, be it ever so subjective, of the efficacy of one approach over another.

Much of this book was formulated during periods abroad in 1981–82 and 1984 when I held visiting professorships at Queen's University, Ontario and Denver University, Colorado. I should acknowledge the stimulating intellectual climates within these institutions which encouraged me to carry forward this enterprise.

Finally, I should express deep thanks for the moral support of my wife during the busy stages of completing the final draft of this book.

Gavin C. Reid
Edinburgh

Part I
Introduction

1

General considerations

1.1 INTRODUCTION

Industrial organization or 'the organization of industry' is, properly speaking, an empirical subject area. It is to be distinguished from analytical microeconomic theory, which often is concerned with tightly defined theoretical issues that are amenable to abstract mathematical analysis. Such theory need not be informed by specific reference to behaviourally plausible assumptions, and the implications of the theory have no necessary link with practical economic policy-making.

By contrast, the analyst of industrial organization must ground all his work in the reality of the business environment in which firms function. An understanding of actual business behaviour is essential. Further, it may be necessary to conduct such analysis in a framework which is explicitly normative. Gone are the value-free exercises of the microeconomic theorists with their guarded positivist statements of the 'if . . . then' variety; the industrial economist has traditionally had to concern himself with a normative, welfare, or evaluative framework in order to be able to appraise the functioning of an industry.

If industrial organization is, therefore, so rooted in reality, what then is the purpose of an analysis of *theories* of industrial organization? One gets the impression from talking to some industrial economists that they are not at all theory conscious. On further probing, it turns out that they do indeed work within one or more theoretical frameworks, depending on the purpose at hand. Under certain circumstances it might seem appropriate to analyse industries as though they were subject to perfect competition, whilst under other circumstances an oligopolistic form of competition might seem more fitting. For some purposes competition might be viewed as a means of attaining a certain allocational outcome, whilst for others it might best be viewed as a process whose purpose is to enable firms to grow within existing markets and to penetrate, or even to create, new markets.

My point is not that it is undesirable to utilize these different theoretical frameworks under different circumstances, but rather that dangers attend the practice. The most obvious danger is that the industrial economist might end up taking a mutually inconsistent stance. If competition is a process rather than a position, the simultaneous adoption of both standpoints is contradictory. To anticipate the contents of the book, if a traditional structure–conduct–performance industrial economist, who takes the Paretian welfare norm as a performance yardstick, starts to flirt with additional performance yardsticks relevant to the process view of competition (e.g. innovativeness), he is in a strict sense contradicting himself. Part of the purpose of this book is, therefore, by laying bare the bones of various theories, to make it self-evident when contradictions arise.

What other merits are there in paying such explicit attention to *theories* of industrial organization? There are three that immediately spring to mind. Firstly, aspects of certain theoretical schemes which are pervasive but often only implicitly adopted – the Marshallian most readily springs to mind – could with advantage be given an explicit treatment alongside available alternatives. In the Marshallian case a number of basic notions – the distribution of efficiency of firms, the life cycle of the firm, the pervasiveness of increasing returns – are of enormous practical significance. When a single notion is picked up in isolation from the rest, as in Markov chain analysis of the size distribution of firms, the result is attractive but lacks the impact it would have in a broader Marshallian framework. By contrast, in the fuller version it is meaningful to compare the merits of a Marshallian approach with, say, an Austrian. Secondly, the setting out in explicit form of a variety of theories of industrial organization might facilitate the improvement of existing theories. This might occur by mere extension, a prerequisite of this being simply the explicit statement of the theory. It might also occur by cross-fertilization, as interconnections between elements of different theories suggest how one might be improved by taking on broad components of the other. For example, Austrian views on competition might suggest how a new performance component can be logically incorporated into the conventional structure–conduct–performance framework. Thirdly, the method of exposition adopted might expose some industrial economists to entirely new theoretical approaches, or approaches of which they are only dimly aware. Thus whilst most industrial economists are familiar with a static version of Marshall's analysis of industry equilibrium as simplified by Viner (1931), many are unaware of the sophisticated treatment of the topic in the *Principles* (book IV) in terms of a biological or statistical equilibrium.

1.2   AN OVERVIEW

The structure of this book is as follows. The various approaches to industrial organization are grouped under three headings: the dominant schools; rival approaches; and new departures.

Under the heading of the dominant schools (part II) we consider the structure–conduct–performance paradigm, and the case study and structural modelling approaches. All these categories will be very familiar to the industrial economist, but the particular grouping adopted may be more contentious. However, there does seem to be a precise way of characterizing each of the approaches. The structure–conduct–performance approach is normative in intention. We will argue that to some extent it is incidental that the welfare norm adopted is Paretian, that the conduct assumption is usually profit maximization, and that the analysis of structure focuses especially on concentration. The essence of the approach is to establish causal and quantitative links between structure, conduct, and performance, with a view to being able to examine how variations in one of these dimensions will lead to variations in the others.

The case study approach is based on quite different methodological foundations. The view put forward is that the case study method follows what Glaser and Strauss (1967) have called 'grounded theory'. In its initial stages the case study investigation does not operate within preconceived categories. The emphasis is on fact gathering, and facts can be of a qualitative or quantitative nature. Some are concerned with relationships between entities, and others with magnitudes of variables. Qualitative facts include the employer–employee relationship, the stockholder–manager relationship, and the general-office/ operating-division relationships. Quantitative facts include the rate of corporation tax, the level of profit, and the rate of turnover of employees. Obviously both classes of facts interact, and an important aspect of the case study method is to establish the nature of these interactions. As the study evolves, a theoretical structure will be suggested to the investigator, typically in the form of an appropriate set of categories for analysis. Further fact gathering by the case study method proceeds until the categories adopted, or modified variants of the original categories adopted, become 'exhausted'; that is to say, all evidence available points to the suitability of the categories. To use a set of categories made familiar by Williamson (1975), a firm might be examined in terms of the multidivisional hypothesis, the purpose being to fill the categories of 'general office', 'the ith operating division', and 'the ijth functional office' (e.g. sales, finance, etc.). An application of this and other possible sets of categories to a group of eight firms is given in Williamson and Bhargava (1972). They selected their firms from a list of the largest 200 industrial corporations in the US according to the *Fortune* 500 series of 1965. Apart from the multidivisional (M) form, Williamson identifies five other classifications for corporate structures – unitary (U) form, holding (H) form, and so on.

The idea of regarding the structural modelling of an industry as a distinct approach to industrial organization is novel but, we will argue, has some utility. The impetus to adopting this view was the set of studies edited by Lawrence Klein on *Industrial Econometrics* (1969). The purpose behind industrial econometrics is not to discover what goes on within firms (the province of the case study), or to be able to conclude what policy action is appropriate to correct for market failure (the concern of the structure–conduct–performance approach), but rather to construct estimable econometric models of the industry which generate predictions that can be falsified. The stance taken by practitioners of this method is essentially positivist. There are in addition other clear features of this approach: a concern with formulating an underlying optimizing theory of firm behaviour; a desire to follow a procedure that consistently aggregates across firms to the industry level; a wish to take seriously the lag structure which explains delays in decision-making, inertia in habits, and adjustment costs; and finally a determination to discover and appropriately model the mutuality of many behavioural patterns between firms and their market environments. Of course there is no reason in principle why this approach could not be used to illuminate other approaches. Thus it can be carried over to the structure–conduct–performance approach, in part at least, by attempting to establish, free of any normative significance, the relationship between certain structure and conduct variables. In practice, however, the mere fact that the starting point is that of the objective scientist using statistical tools derived from the experimental sciences conditions the way in which industrial econometrics is carried out, and certainly limits the range of issues addressed.

So much then for the established approaches. Under the heading of rival approaches (part III) are considered the Marshallian tradition, the Austrian revival, and workable competition. They are very weighty alternatives to the standard approaches, and have proved highly influential, though in a diffuse fashion. To take the Austrian or workably competitive line on industrial organization nowadays would by some be thought merely unfashionable, but by others might even be regarded as mildly eccentric. Yet there is an enormous amount of sound literature on these approaches, and it may even have been historical accident that they are no longer pre-eminent.

The influence of Alfred Marshall on economic analysis is pervasive, extending from economic history through policy analysis of money, trade, and labour matters into the major branches of theory, including money, trade, business cycles, the firm, the consumer, etc., extending finally to what in their day were the esoteric reaches of mathematical economics. In many senses, Marshall can be said to have founded the analysis of industrial organization with his volume *The Economics of Industry* and book IV of his *Principles*. To some modern industrial economists, Marshall is 'just' another neoclassical economist, and a not very special one at that because of his love of the partial equilibrium method. In fact, the 'free competition' of Marshall (discussed in chapter 5) is *not* perfect competition of the neoclassical type, as so widely thought in the industrial organization literature, but rather a set of trading relationships in which each firm has its special market by virtue of established relationships with customers and suppliers. Far from being a static view of industry equilibrium, Marshall's was dynamic, even biological. This aspect of his theory has been taken up by Newman and Wolfe (1961) who have given rigorous content to the concepts of the equilibrium size distribution of firms and of the representative firm. Apart from this there is the formidable range of practical tools of analysis which Marshall provided for the industrial economist: the theory of joint production; the distinction between external and internal economies; the theory of the life cycle of the firm; and many others. In their totality they provide a coherent model for industrial analysis, but not one which has been adopted in its entirety by many industrial economists. There are notable exceptions, such as Philip Andrews, George Richardson, and Brian Loasby; however, on the whole the importance of Marshallian analysis has been as an indirect but far-reaching influence rather than as a vehicle for expression of a school of thought.

In the case of the Austrian revival, the situation is markedly different. The Austrian School is cohesive and has a small band of influential disciples of whom currently the most influential are Israel Kirzner and Murray Rothbard. They find their inspiration in the writings of Carl Menger, the founding member, and of twentieth-century scholars like Mises, Lachmann, and most notably Hayek. To a considerable degree the Austrian School is impregnable, because it is so aprioristic. It does not brook subversion, and much of its writings involve restatements of previously established positions. Generally speaking, the Austrian School has been opposed to mathematical modes of expression and above all to econometric analysis. More recently there have been signs of some relaxation of this very rigid stance, which was cultivated most strongly by Mises, but even now most Austrian writings are elegant and literary with little appeal to historical data and no use of explicitly mathematical arguments. Possibly its very accessibility to the non-specialist has accounted for its increasing popularity, or revival as we would have it. This, allied to Hayek's monumentally scholarly and extensive treatment of the social, legal, and political context in which an Austrian economy would function, has meant that the revival has had not merely an impact in academic circles, but also a significant effect on prevailing ideology and, through that, on public policy as directed towards the industry. For example, part of the current impetus behind the deregulation movement derives from an Austrian view of industrial organization, which in its policy aspect is markedly non-interventionist. By contrast with the Marshallian influence, which has been pervasive but diffuse, the Austrian influence has been more potent when noticed, but otherwise dormant.

Next, under rival approaches, the workable competition school is considered. It is in many respects a hybrid school. Its origins can be traced from Marshall, through Clark, to its noted practitioners like Sosnick and Markham. Its methods are pragmatic and highly institutional, and often draw on case study techniques without adopting the case study method *per se* as we have presented it. One way of looking at the workable competition literature is as an attempt to define a more useful competitive ideal than that used in the structure–conduct–performance approach. Indeed Sosnick (1958) chose to use the structure, conduct, and performance categories as the basis for his very influential exposition and critique of the workable competition literature. This, however, is to mask the focus of attention on performance. There is a considerable prescriptive content in the writings on workable competition, because their purpose has always ultimately been to give guidance on how practical policy towards firms should be conducted. Unlike the outpourings of the Austrian School, this advice has been not dogmatic but carefully oriented towards the genuine complexity of practical industrial situations. This very pragmatism, and the willingness to be eclectic about theoretical influences, has had the unfortunate consequence of making the views of exponents of workable competition seem imprecise, elusive, and even lacking in rigour to the extent of manifest inconsistency. This is unfortunate, because pragmatism has a great deal to recommend it. More recently, writers on contestable markets have attempted to ally rigour to pragmatism, and in a sense represent the new workable competition school. These are developments which are considered under the heading of new departures.

In part IV, on new departures, we consider natural monopoly analysis, the theory of contestable markets, and the organizational view of the firm, in the scope of two chapters. In the first of these we concentrate on the theory of natural monopoly and contestability, giving some attention in both these contexts to empirical considerations. Natural monopoly analysis enables us to introduce a number of important regulatory issues, building on the more primitive treatment undertaken by Marshall. The contestability theory provides a marvellous link with much more established analysis, and turns up some highly challenging and still controversial results. It has always been suspected by practical industrial economists that 'many' does not have to be 'very large' in order for effective competition to come about. The aim of contestability analysis is to set out rigorously the circumstances under which this can happen, given that 'hit and run' competition is possible. An intention of the contestability literature has been to put forward a set of criteria for effective competition which is at the same time both concise and internally consistent. In this way the conditions for 'workable competition' are set out in a fashion which makes them more acceptable to the rigorously trained industrial economist of today than the older, amorphous workability criteria. This, at least, is the claim of the theory; the extent to which it is exaggerated is explored later.

In the second chapter of this part the organizational view is interpreted in a very wide sense to embrace behaviouralism and managerialism, as well as the organizational approach – as it is generally understood – along Herbert Simon or Oliver Williamson lines. This treatment is the most compressed in the book, partly because it is so extensively dealt with elsewhere, but also because all these approaches have in common the desire to get inside and explore the 'black box' which has conventionally been regarded as 'the firm'. A number of economists, including Solow (1971) and Jensen and Meckling (1976), have furthermore looked at a variety of types of firm and firms' motivations in a general framework, from which theories like growth maximization emerge as special cases. Notwithstanding the plethora of 'alternative' theories of the firm, based on a diversity of insights into the internal workings of firms, it remains true that the simple hypothesis of profit maximization is formidably robust. Therefore, in not treating managerialism or the satisficing theories of the firm in distinct chapters, we have to an extent imposed our own judgement about their relative importance compared with both established schools and new developments.

1.3 APPROACHES TO INDUSTRIAL ORGANIZATION

One approaches the study of industrial organization with many possible purposes. It is essential to realize that no one sort of purpose has logical priority, or methodological superiority, over the other. For this reason it is difficult to make a point by point comparison between alternative approaches, come up with a balancing of merits and demerits, and in this way determine that one approach is superior to another. In holding this view the author is what Caldwell (1982) has described as a methodological pluralist.

If, on reading this book, an industrial economist decides that a particular approach is appropriate to his needs, well and good. The key to his choice is 'his needs' and, as these vary enormously, it is not possible to make choices by proxy for individuals with different needs. On the other hand, choice can be facilitated. Exposition, comparative analysis, and critical commentary all have an important role to play in informing the consumer of theories of industrial organization. Hopefully, this book will offer at least some new perspectives to all industrial economists.

Thus the attitude to be adopted is that different models have different purposes. The Austrian model of the market process is persuasive but very difficult to specify empirically, as the implied dynamic process is so complex. On the other hand, simple statistical models, like the Markov chain model of the evolution of the size distribution of firms over time, are easy to implement empirically but much more difficult to make sense of behaviourally. Each has its own place and each is, in its own way, compelling. What is clearly rejected from consideration is that set of techniques which is purely functional. Thus 'black box' time series models (e.g. exponential smoothing, Box-Jenkins) applied to industrial data like sales have no intellectual rationale, and in this sense cannot be candidates for comparative or critical analysis.

Ultimately there is no decisive test by which a model or theory can be evaluated, and this book is a reflection of that fact. Fortunately we are rarely called upon to make tests of a categorical nature. More often we are required to make judgements about whether one formulation of a model is an advance on an earlier formulation, and whether one line of analysis is different in kind from another when stripped of the overlay of professional presentation. The aim of this book is to be of some assistance in facilitating these deliberations.

1.4   CONCLUSION

The three-part structure of this book has been laid bare: the dominant schools; rival approaches; and new developments. The aim of the book has been explicated: it is concerned with a kind of comparative economic theory as applied to industrial organization. It has been emphasized that the scope of the conclusions reached is circumscribed, for it is not the place of the author to dictate the appropriate choice of models. We now turn to the analysis proper.

Part II
The Dominant Schools

2

The structure–conduct–performance paradigm

2.1 INTRODUCTION

Of the various theories of industrial organization that will be discussed in this book, undoubtedly the most influential has been, and continues to be, that associated with the pioneering work of Edward S. Mason (1939, 1949). Working at the University of Harvard in the 1930s Mason laid the foundations of the structure–conduct–performance (SCP) paradigm. Put simply, the content of this approach is that exogenous basic conditions determine market structure and that there is a unidirectional flow of causality from market structure, through conduct, to performance. Mason also provided intellectual leadership for a group of young scholars who were to develop and extend the SCP approach, including Joe S. Bain, Carl Kaysen, James W. McKie, Jesse Markham, and Morris Adelman.

Following on from Mason's seminal work, major contributions advancing the SCP approach were made by Bain (1959), Clark (1961), and Caves (1972). Today the textbook of Scherer (1979) provides the most extensive and coherent exposition of this approach; and it has been enormously influential in leading industrial economists all over the world to regard SCP as the natural way of proceeding. In achieving this wide acceptance, no doubt an important factor has been that expositions such as those of Scherer use only the standard devices of neoclassical microeconomic theory. Further, in such expositions the main means of arriving at policy prescriptions − the criterion of Pareto optimality − is possibly the only one that would be widely accepted by economists.

Now let us consider, shorn of any technical details of mathematical modelling, the simplest version of the SCP approach. Market structure is assumed to depend upon basic conditions on the demand and supply side. Demand-side conditions include: direct and cross-elasticities of demand; market growth in its trend, cyclical, and seasonal aspects; and purchasing habits of customers.

Supply-side conditions include: location and ownership of raw materials; technology; unionization; product durability; industry history; and the legal, ethical, and political framework within which business activity takes place. Many treatments of the SCP framework assimilate several of these basic determinants into the market structure category. Whatever, the usual attitude is to regard tastes, technology, and institutions as given, and to concentrate on structure, conduct, and performance.

The following characteristics are usually listed under the heading of market structure: concentration, diversification, product differentiation, barriers to entry, and scale economies. Of these, the concentration characteristic, particularly with respect to sellers rather than to buyers, has received by far the greatest attention. A considerable amount of ingenuity has been devoted to finding appropriate statistical measures of concentration. In the final analysis, no single measure is satisfactory, for there is no unique way of summarizing the size distribution of firms by a single statistic. (For a fuller discussion, see Hannah and Kay, 1977.) A few economists, such as Hause (1977), have seen that it is desirable to relate concentration measures to sensible notions in economic theory (he suggests Cournot-Nash equilibrium). However, most have looked at concentration in purely statistical terms, sometimes by simply looking just at numbers of firms, but more often by computing summary measures of concentration such as the Gini coefficient or the Herfindahl index. Structure, however defined, be it by simple concentration indices or something more elaborate involving many characteristics, is assumed to cause but not to be caused by conduct.

In principle many types of conduct can be distinguished, some of which extend beyond the strictly economic. Under conduct, one conventionally looks at: how price is set; the way in which the volume, quality, and range of products are determined; advertising and marketing strategy; research and development planning and implementation; and legal tactics. More often than not, though, conduct is either ignored entirely or else assumed to take some simple form like profit maximization, by quantity variation. Actually, profit maximization can be given a much more general treatment than the elementary theory of the firm might suggest. Following Varian (1984, chapter 1) we can conceive of a neoclassical firm having open to it a set of actions which define an 'action vector' $a = (a_1, a_2, \ldots, a_n)$, with $a_i \geqslant 0$ for all i. The a_i might include production levels, advertising expenditures, level of inventories, and so on. Assuming that revenue R and cost C depend upon this set of actions, the firm's optimization problem may be set up as

$$\max_a \; [R(a) - C(a)] \qquad \text{for } a \geqslant 0 \tag{2.1}$$

By the Kuhn-Tucker theorem, the optimal set of actions $a^\star$ satisfies the following:

$$\partial R(\boldsymbol{a}^\star)/\partial a_i - \partial C(\boldsymbol{a}^\star)/\partial a_i \leqslant 0 \qquad \text{for all } i$$

with the equality holding for the interior solution cases (i.e. when a positive level is assigned, at the optimum, to any action variable). This extended neoclassical framework embraces many conduct variants. When the sole action variable is output, it can lead to the equality of marginal revenue and marginal cost in pure monopoly and monopolistic competition, or to the equality of price and marginal cost in pure or perfect competition. Less traditionally, if advertising expenditure is included as an action variable, it can lead to the Dorfman–Steiner (1954) condition that a firm which is a monopolist and advertises will attain its optimum when the ratio of advertising expenditure to total revenue equals the ratio of the advertising elasticity of demand to the price elasticity of demand. Many other variants are possible. This extended neoclassical framework still falls far short of generating the full repertoire of possible conducts, mainly because it is so unconvincing in a behavioural sense. Satisficing, and a range of institutionally dependent patterns of strategic behaviour, are also possible, though a full discussion of these will be deferred to chapter 9. Conduct, in the rather simple SCP variant that we are currently discussing, is assumed to cause but not to be caused by performance.

As with other categories considered so far, performance too can be measured in many ways. A typical list of performance indicators or measures includes: allocative efficiency, X-efficiency (see Leibenstein, 1973), equity, employment creation, technological progressiveness, and quality of output. To a fair extent, the length and content of this list depend on policy issues of the day. Thus under certain circumstances it would make sense to look at performance in terms of the ability of a firm to absorb costs in a general economic environment of inflation. Despite this fairly full list of performance indicators, the overwhelming emphasis in the traditional literature on SCP is on the extent to which a firm's conduct departs from the Paretian allocative efficiency ideal. The Pareto criterion, involving as it does the simple notion that a change is a welfare improvement if it makes one person better off and no person worse off, is at the heart of the mainstream literature in the SCP vein. Thus it provides the basis for welfare analysis of the misallocation effects of monopoly. Other welfare norms than those implied by the classical Paretian conditions are possible, but are frequently overlooked. A full treatment of these conditions will not be given here, but in brief they are as follows. If $(x_1, x_2, \ldots, x_n)$ is a vector of all goods and factors in the economy, then Pareto efficiency requires that $\partial x_i/\partial x_j$ be the same throughout the economy for i, j distinct. For i, j indices of goods, this implies equality of marginal rates of substitution in consumption across consumers. For i, j indices of factors, this requires equality of marginal rates of transformation in production across firms. Similarly for i, j indices of goods and factors respectively, $\partial x_i/\partial x_j$ should be equalized across firms. Finally, the top-level condition requires that marginal rates of transformation in production and of substitution in consumption should be equal. These are very general conditions and do not apply specifically to a certain type of economy. They are as applicable to a planned economy as to a decentralized market economy. In industrial organization, the conditions are typically applied to the latter, and imply specific conditions for the firm. Price should be set equal to marginal cost for a good. Price should be set equal to the value of the marginal product for a factor. Finally, the marginal rate of transformation in production for factors should be equal to the factor price ratio. Many problems arise in the practical application of these rules. If a number of rules are violated, it does not follow that ensuring that they are progressively satisfied will progressively increase welfare – the problem of 'the second best' (see chapter 7 for a detailed treatment of this problem). The Paretian theory can be extended to a dynamic economy, to environmental uncertainty, and to situations in which markets are not complete (the so-called 'constrained Pareto optimum' theory), but it remains very restrictive as a guide to performance. A possible alternative route is to seek different welfare norms. As we shall see in chapter 6, the Austrian School regard a change as welfare enhancing if it improves the co-ordination of information currently available. In chapter 8, the idea of a contestable market is developed which has most of the attributes of perfect competition, barring large numbers. Despite the extensions noted, and the possibility of alternative welfare norms, the static Pareto rules remain the most widely employed performance guides.

Although the SCP framework is in principle very flexible, it is, as we have seen in its traditional form, somewhat rigid. This is true both of the way in which causality is assumed to operate, and of the factors which are usually considered within each of the three categories used. A stylized version of the SCP framework, and one which is evidently in the minds of some industrial economists with whom one talks, can be represented by the schema in figure 2.1.

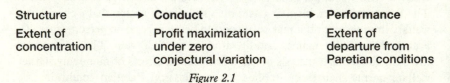

Structure   ⟶   Conduct   ⟶   Performance
Extent of   Profit maximization   Extent of
concentration   under zero   departure from
                        conjectural variation   Paretian conditions

Figure 2.1

This stripped-down version of the SCP framework is attractive in its simplicity. To give an example of its operation, consider the case of the neoclassical monopolist. Structure is characterized by a single seller: the extreme of concentration. Profit maximization is the pattern of conduct, implying the equalization of marginal revenue and marginal cost. The monopolist's performance, evaluated by the Pareto criterion, is inefficient, for price is set above marginal cost. Ways of formalizing this simple schema, and more complex ones as well, will now be considered.

2.2   THE GENERAL HYPOTHESIS

Let us take as our starting point the very general hypothesis that profitability varies across industries as the concentration level varies. This is to take a cross-section approach to the SCP framework with no explicit account being given of the conduct of firms. High levels of concentration are assumed to lead to high levels of profitability, as competition among few firms leads to the possibility of restricting output and raising prices in order to increase profit. A simple way of expressing this hypothesis is by a relationship of the form

$$r = f(C) \qquad f' > 0 \tag{2.2}$$

where $r = \Pi/K$, Π being profit and K a measure of capital. C is a measure of concentration, as yet unspecified. One way of looking at this hypothesis is in structure–performance terms, where the omission of the term 'conduct' is deliberate and significant. If C is a benchmark measure of concentration relevant to some welfare ideal, then $\bar{r} = f(\bar{C})$ is a benchmark rate of profit. Typically $0 \leqslant C \leqslant 1$ is a property of a concentration index, with $C = 0$ being the atomistic competition value of the index, and $C = 1$ being its value under monopoly. Thus $\bar{r} = f(0)$ for most choices of index C, and $f(0) = 0$ is a possibility. The argument embodied in the equation $r = f(C)$ then runs as follows. Firstly, concentration causally determines profitability. This is expressed by choosing r as the dependent variable and C as the independent variable. Secondly, concentration above the benchmark level ($C > \bar{C}$) raises profitability above the benchmark level ($r > \bar{r}$). Formally, profitability is increasing in concentration ($\mathrm{d}r/\mathrm{d}C > 0$). Here we have used the general term 'profitability', though the specific measure chosen is the rate of profit, defined as Π/K. Bain (1951) in his original study, and a number of others since, have used this as the dependent variable in profitability–concentration relationships, but other choices are possible (e.g. the price–cost margin).

In this very simple framework, *structure* is exclusively represented by a single variable C, *conduct* is ignored, and *performance* is judged in terms of the deviation of r from the benchmark value of $\bar{r}$. An important aspect of structure, which has been neglected in the framework developed so far, is the extent of barriers to entry. Bain (1956) distinguished three such barriers. Firstly, scale economies might constitute a barrier in the sense that potential entrants would have to be able to operate at the same output levels as incumbent firms if they were to enjoy the same falling long-run average costs. Secondly, product differentiation barriers might exist as potential entrants face the problem of enticing away customers who are to some extent loyal to incumbent firms. Thirdly, incumbent firms might have absolute cost advantages over potential entrants in terms of: factors which are supplied at relatively favourable prices; knowledge, based on experience, of the technology, which promotes cost reduction; and so on. It is not easy to incorporate factors such as these into a respecified version of equation (2.2). Two possible routes to take are as follows. Firstly, a qualitative evaluation can be undertaken of all aspects of barriers to entry for the given cross-sectional sample. Then various categories of barriers to entry can be postulated (e.g. high, medium, low) and represented by categorical variables (e.g. 0, 1, 2). Alternatively, one can attempt to develop suitable statistical proxies for the various types of barriers to entry. For example, cross-elasticity of demand might be a measure of the extent of product differentiation as a barrier to entry. Mann (1971) chose the former course of action and set up an equation of the form

$$\Pi/K = f(D_{\mathrm{h}}, C) \tag{2.3}$$

where D_{h} is a dummy variable having a value of one for industries with high barriers to entry and a value of zero for those with low barriers. The categories of 'high' and 'low' were subjectively determined by looking at all relevant aspects of the industries in the sample on a case by case basis. Shepherd (1972) and Smirlock et al. (1984) provide more complex examples of the use of dummy variables to represent differing extents of barriers to entry. Comanor and Wilson (1967) by contrast took the latter course of action, and argued that one must directly represent by a statistical variable each of the postulated types of barriers to entry. The presumption was that such variables would be continuous rather than categorical. Thus the effects of advertising might be represented by the ratio of advertising expenditure A to sales S, and equation (2.3) would be modified to

$$\Pi/K = f(A/S, C) \tag{2.4}$$

This framework could then be extended in an obvious way as one developed additional proxies for other barriers to entry.

Opposed to this traditional market concentration doctrine is what has been called the efficient structure doctrine. Brozen (1982), Demsetz (1973), and Peltzman (1977) argue that the supposed relationship between concentration and profitability is spurious, for there are neglected relationships between market share, concentration, and efficiency. If concentration is a product of efficiency – and therefore the superior firms thrive and increase their market shares – the surpluses that accrue to such firms are, strictly speaking, economic rent rather than monopoly rent. To test these hypotheses against one another, Smirlock et al. (1984) proposed a model of the form

$$q = f(MS, C, B_{\mathrm{m}}, B_{\mathrm{h}}, MSG) \tag{2.5}$$

where q is Tobin's q (the ratio of the current market value of the firm to the market value of its productive assets; this is an alternative measure of profitability), MS is market share, C is the four-firm concentration ratio, B_{m} and B_{h} are medium and high entry barrier variables, and MSG is market share growth.

In a linear version of this model it was found that the coefficient on market share was positive and significant, but that on the concentration variable was insignificant. Thus the efficient structure doctrine is favoured over the concentration doctrine. However, as we shall see later in this chapter, if there truly are interrelationships between independent variables, then some sort of simultaneous equations approach is appropriate. Furthermore, equation (2.5), like the preceding equations, lacks any foundation in explicit behavioural assumptions concerning conduct. It is to this issue that we now turn.

2.3   MODELS LEADING TO STRUCTURE–PERFORMANCE RELATIONSHIPS

An influential critique of the sort of approach adopted in the previous section is due to Cowling (1976). The essence of Cowling's argument is that explicit conduct assumptions should be adopted. From his standpoint, an equation such as (2.5) is unsatisfactory, for it is not based on *explicit* behavioural assumptions, though underlying it are certainly *implicit* doctrines of industrial organization. The advantage of his approach is that it leads to quite precise suggestions for the appropriate formulation of structure–performance relationships.

Cowling (1976) takes as his starting point a classical formula due to Kalecki (1939), relating the price–cost margin to the price elasticity of industry demand. This may be written

$$L \equiv \frac{p - MC}{p} = \frac{1}{\eta} \tag{2.6}$$

where η is the price elasticity of industry demand, p is price, and MC is marginal cost. L is the degree of monopoly index due to Lerner (1934). Stigler (1968) developed an important variant of this formula, which may be expressed

$$\frac{p - MC}{p} = \frac{F(H)}{\eta} \tag{2.7}$$

where $F(H)$ is an index of the effectiveness of collusion. This contribution has been followed by a number of other variants, of which one, due to Cowling and Waterson (1976), will be discussed in detail.

Let $p = f(X)$ be the industry demand function, with $X = \Sigma x_i$, where x_i is the contribution of the ith firm to meeting industry demand X. Assume that unit and marginal costs are constant at the level c_i for the ith firm, but that there is a distribution of efficiency in the industry with each c_i being distinct. The ith firm's profit function may be written

$$\Pi_i = px_i - c_i x_i \tag{2.8}$$

The notion of *conduct*, hitherto neglected in the specification of structure–performance equations such as (2.2) and (2.3), may now be introduced. We shall take as our starting point the so-called Cournot–Nash assumption. In keeping with a current resurgence of interest in game theory, it is worth pausing to consider the nature of this assumption in further detail. The Nash solution is applicable to non-co-operative games. To specify a game in so-called strategic form one needs to be able to describe the set of players, the set of strategies, and the payoffs. In this case the n firms, or oligopolists, are conceived of as playing a non-co-operative game and constitute the set of players. Strategies in this case involve choices of output levels by the oligopolists. An obvious alternative to this quantity variation game is a price variation game, which in its simplest form is associated with the model of Bertrand. Finally, in the case under consideration the payoffs are profits. More generally, every player in a non-co-operative game has a scalar payoff function, and this function attains a specific value for any set of strategies deployed by players in the game. To take a simple case, suppose there are just two players with payoffs defined by $P_i(q_1, q_2)$, $i = 1, 2$, where the level of q_i denotes the strategy choice of the ith player. Then the Nash equilibrium $(q_1^\star, q_2^\star)$ has the property that

$$P_1(q_1^\star, q_2^\star) \geqslant P_1(q_1, q_2^\star)$$
$$P_2(q_1^\star, q_2^\star) \geqslant P_2(q_1^\star, q_2)$$

A characteristic of the equilibrium so defined is that no single player can improve his payoff by deploying a different strategy, given the strategy choice of his rival. In the sort of context that we are interested in, P_i is to be interpreted as profit and q_i as output. As Shubik (1984, p. 87) has remarked in his recent definitive volume, the Nash solution concept, whilst apparently simple, has the attraction as applied to oligopoly theory that it requires relatively low information and communication between players.

To determine the relevant Cournot–Nash equilibrium for the oligopoly model under consideration, we require the conditions for profit maximization by the ith firm given the output levels of all rivals. When such conditions have been specified, the Cournot–Nash equilibrium is the set of outputs $(x_1^\star, x_2^\star, \ldots, x_n^\star)$ which solves this set of first-order conditions. For $n = 2$, these first-order conditions give rise to the familiar reaction curve functions $x_1 = R_1(x_2)$ and $x_2 = R_2(x_1)$, first formulated by Cournot. The reaction function R_1 specifies what will be the optimal output chosen by firm 1 given an arbitrary choice of output by firm 2, and vice versa for the function R_2. For a Nash equilibrium $(x_1^\star, x_2^\star)$, clearly $x_1^\star = R_1(x_2^\star)$ and $x_2^\star = R_2(x_1^\star)$, which is to say that the equilibrium is defined where the reaction functions intersect. Such an equilibrium is illustrated in figure 2.2, for the case of quadratic profit functions.

More generally, first- and second-order conditions for maximizing (2.8) are $d\Pi_i/dx_i = 0$ and $d^2\Pi_i/dx_i^2 < 0$. From the first-order condition, assuming the second-order to be satisfied, we get

$$\frac{d\Pi_i}{dx_i} = p + x_i \frac{dp}{dX} \frac{dX}{dx_i} - c_i = 0 \tag{2.9}$$

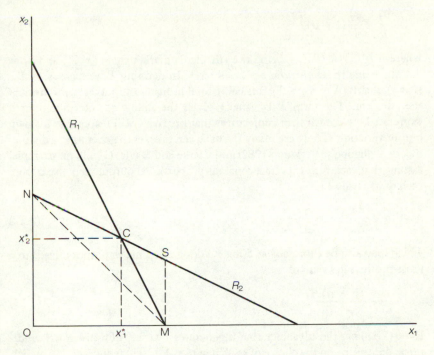

Figure 2.2

Under Cournot–Nash assumptions, the term dX/dx_i is unity. Thus (2.9) can be rearranged to give

$$\frac{px_i - c_i x_i}{pX} = \left(\frac{x_i}{X}\right)^2 \left(-\frac{X}{p}\frac{dp}{dX}\right)$$

Summing over all firms gives

$$\frac{p\Sigma x_i - \Sigma c_i x_i}{pX} = \sum_i \left(\frac{x_i}{X}\right)^2 \left(-\frac{X}{p}\frac{dp}{dX}\right)$$

which implies

$$\frac{\Pi}{R} \equiv \frac{pX - \Sigma c_i x_i}{pX} = \frac{H}{\eta} \tag{2.10}$$

where $H = \sum_i (x_i/X)^2$ is the Herfindahl index of concentration, $R = pX$, and $\eta = -(dX/dp)(p/X)$ is the price elasticity of industry demand. The left-hand side of (2.10) is the ratio of industry gross profits to industry sales. A more general variant of equation (2.10), as developed by Cowling and Waterson (1976) and Waterson (1984), expresses the profits/sales ratio as

$$\frac{\Pi}{R} = \frac{H}{\eta}(1 + \mu)$$

(2.11)

where $\mu = \Sigma s_i^2 \lambda_i / \Sigma s_i^2$, s_i being the ith firm's market share (x_i/X) and $\lambda_i \equiv \mathrm{d}X_i/\mathrm{d}x_i$ being the *conjectural variation* term. In defining λ_i we have $X_i = \Sigma x_i$ $(i \neq j)$, that is $(X - x_i) = X_i$, this being total industry output less the output of the ith firm. The term λ_i is usually given the following interpretation: it expresses how the ith firm conjectures that his rivals will respond to his own output variation. There are many forms λ_i can take, each generating a distinct theory of oligopoly. Cowling (1982) and Clarke and Davies (1982), for example, assume that each firm expects a constant proportional output response α from each of its rivals, i.e.

$$\alpha = \frac{\mathrm{d}x_j}{\mathrm{d}x_i} \frac{x_i}{x_j} = \frac{\mathrm{d}x_j/x_j}{\mathrm{d}x_i/x_i}$$

(2.12)

which may also be expressed as $\mathrm{d}(\log x_j)/\mathrm{d}(\log x_i)$. This assumption leads to a gross-profits/sales ratio of

$$\frac{\alpha + (1 - \alpha)H}{\eta}$$

(2.13)

Ratio (2.13) has the advantage that it generates a variety of well-known conditions, depending on the choice of α. When $\alpha = 1$, (2.13) reduces to $1/\eta$, which is the classical Kalecki ratio and corresponds to complete collusion. When $\alpha = 0$, the case of zero conjectural variation, the Cournot model is implied, giving H/η as the simplified version of (2.13), the ratio already reached in (2.10).

There are many conduct assumptions alternative to Cournot-Nash. For example, there is the von Neumann–Morgenstern conduct assumption of co-operation to jointly maximize profits. In figure 2.2, any point on the line NM is a von Neumann–Morgenstern solution. Clearly, it includes the monopoly points N and M. The Stackelberg variant leads to three possible types of conduct in a duopolistic market. If both firms attempt to become leaders, a disequilibrium emerges. If both firms act as followers, the Cournot solution at C emerges. If one firm acts as leader and the other acts as follower, a new type of stable solution emerges. The follower behaves as in the Cournot model, but the leader maximizes by taking into account the follower's reaction function. If firm 1 is the leader and firm 2 the follower, the Stackelberg solution point is S in figure 2.2. It identifies that pair of outputs which yields firm 1 the highest level of profit consistent with output choices on firm 2's reaction function.

Of the multitude of conduct assumptions, apart from those already discussed, one other has been particularly influential in the industrial organization literature. It is the k-firm cartel (or dominant firm) model. As Reid (1979) points out, the model has a history going back to the work of Karl Forchheimer

(1908). Particularly influential treatments are contained in Stigler (1940), Saving (1970), and Encaoua and Jacquemin (1980). Comparative statics results have been derived by Reid (1975, 1977, 1980). The model may be developed along the following lines.

Suppose there are n firms in the industry, with k firms acting as a cartel and $n-k$ firms in a competitive fringe. When $k = 1$ the model reduces to a partial monopoly, or dominant firm price leadership. Denote industry demand by $D(p)$, with $D' < 0$. The competitive fringe is made up of price-taking firms with marginal cost curves M_i, $i = (k + 1), \ldots, n$. Supplies of these firms, assuming they set price equal to marginal cost, will be given by $M_i^{-1}(p)$. Hence the supply of the competitive fringe $S(p)$ is defined by

$$S(p) = \sum_{i=k+1}^{n} M_i^{-1}(p) \tag{2.14}$$

Assuming increasing inverse marginal cost functions in the neighbourhood of equilibrium for firms in the fringe, $S(p)$ will be increasing in p, $S' > 0$. Then the residual (or net) demand $\tilde{R}(p)$ which the k-firm cartel faces is

$$\tilde{R}(p) = D(p) - S(p) \qquad S' > 0, D' < 0 \tag{2.15}$$

which must be decreasing in p as $\tilde{R}' = D' - S'$. Differentiating (2.15) and dividing by $\tilde{R}/p$ gives

$$\frac{\tilde{R}'(p)p}{\tilde{R}} = \frac{D'(p)p}{\tilde{R}} - \frac{S'(p)p}{\tilde{R}}$$

From this one gets

$$-\eta_{\tilde{R}} = -\eta_D \frac{D}{\tilde{R}} - \eta_S \frac{S}{\tilde{R}} \tag{2.16}$$

where

$$\eta_{\tilde{R}} = -\frac{\tilde{R}'(p)p}{\tilde{R}}$$

$$\eta_D = -\frac{D'(p)p}{D}$$

$$\eta_S = \frac{S'(p)p}{S}$$

are the elasticities with respect to price of residual demand, industry demand, and fringe supply, respectively. By the same reasoning that lead to the classical Kalecki–Lerner formula (2.6), the joint profit maximizing k-firm cartel should set its price–cost margin equal to the reciprocal of the elasticity of its demand curve:

$$\frac{p - MC_k}{p} = \frac{1}{\eta_{\tilde{R}}} = \frac{1}{\eta_D(D/\tilde{R}) + \eta_S(S/\tilde{R})} \qquad (2.17)$$

using (2.16). MC_k is the marginal cost of the k-firm cartel, where the marginal cost function of the cartel is defined as the horizontal sum of the k members' marginal cost functions. A possible variant of the latter assumption is that marginal cost of the cartel be *defined* by the k members, taking into account possibilities like imperfect competition in factor markets. At any given price p, the market share of the cartel, assuming production always satisfies demands, is the ratio of residual demand to total demand, $\tilde{R}/D$. This is, further, the k-firm concentration ratio C_k, assuming members of the cartel are the largest k firms in the industry, for

$$C_k = \sum_{i=1}^{k} s_i = \sum_{i=1}^{k} \frac{r_i}{D} = \frac{\tilde{R}}{D}$$

where the s_i are the market shares of the k largest firms (by output), and r_i is the contribution of the ith cartel member to meeting total residual demand $\tilde{R}(p)$. Using (2.15), $S/\tilde{R} = (1 - C_k)/C_k$. This together with $D/\tilde{R} = 1/C_k$ gives

$$\frac{p - MC_k}{p} = \frac{C_k}{\eta_D + \eta_S(1 - C_k)} \qquad (2.18)$$

Finally, if $\overline{MC}$ is market share weighted average cost for the market as a whole, we get

$$\frac{p - \overline{MC}}{p} = \frac{C_k^2}{\eta_D + \eta_S(1 - C_k)} \qquad (2.19)$$

Let us contrast this with the price–cost margin equation (2.10) derived earlier. An equation such as (2.10) has led Cowling (1976) to argue as follows. Firstly, an elasticity of demand variable should be included as an independent variable in a profit–concentration equation. Secondly, the relevant dependent variable in such an equation is the price–cost margin, rather than the rate of return on capital. Thirdly, the Herfindahl index is the appropriate measure of industrial concentration. Concerning the last point, what Cowling is disputing is the common use in profit–concentration equations of the k-firm concentration ratio. However, as (2.18) and (2.19) make clear, it is quite possible to construct a model (or maybe several models) based on acceptable conduct assumptions which imply a profitability–concentration equation of the form $(p - MC)/p = f(C_k)$, where C_k is the k-firm concentration ratio. Further, it would be difficult to deny the possibility of a model leading to an equation of the form $r = f(C_k)$. All this is to suggest not that C_k is *the* best or most appropriate measure of concentration, but merely that, in strict logic, there *are* reasons for including C_k as a relevant variable in a structure–performance equation.

The merit of Cowling (1976) and Cowling and Waterson (1976) is that they help suggest an appropriate *a priori* specification for a structure–performance equation, based on a coherent conduct model. Their arguments lead to an equation of the form

$$\Pi/R = f(H, \eta) \tag{2.20}$$

with a preference for Π/R as the dependent variable rather than Π/K as in the Bain–Mann framework of equation (2.3), and both H and η as independent variables rather than just C_k. Furthermore, relationships such as (2.10), (2.11), and (2.13) suggest that (2.20) might best be expressed in logarithmic form. Most simple of all, (2.10) can be expressed as

$$\log(\Pi/R) = \log H - \log \eta \tag{2.21}$$

and (2.11) as

$$\log(\Pi/R) = \log(1 + \mu) + \log H - \log \eta \tag{2.22}$$

Both (2.21) and (2.22) involve testable hypotheses on the coefficients of a linear regression of $\log(\Pi/R)$ on $\log H$ and $\log \eta$. Suppose (2.22) were claimed to hold over time, with concentration (measured by H) leading to increased price–cost margins with a τ period lag. Further, suppose that elasticity of industry demand and conjectural variation are relatively constant over time. Then (2.22) can be rewritten

$$\log(\Pi/R)_t = \log(1 + \mu) + \log(H)_{t-\tau} - \log \eta \tag{2.23}$$

with $\log(1 + \mu)$ and $\log \eta$ being constant over time. Then

$$\log(\Pi/R)_{t-1} = \log(1 + \mu) + \log(H)_{t-\tau-1} - \log \eta \tag{2.24}$$

from which, by subtracting (2.24) from (2.23), one gets

$$\log(\Pi/R)_t - \log(\Pi/R)_{t-1} = \log(H)_{t-\tau} - \log(H)_{t-\tau-1}$$

or equivalently

$$\frac{(\Pi/R)_t}{(\Pi/R)_{t-1}} = \frac{H_{t-\tau}}{H_{t-\tau-1}} \tag{2.25}$$

Relationship (2.25) underlies the specification suggested by Cowling (1976). If the Cournot-Nash model is an appropriately specified conduct model, then in an estimation of the unrestricted version of (2.25)

$$\frac{(\Pi/R)_t}{(\Pi/R)_{t-1}} = \left(\frac{H_{t-\tau}}{H_{t-\tau-1}}\right)^{\alpha} + \beta \tag{2.26}$$

it should be found that α is not significantly different from unity and β not significantly different from zero. Clarke and Davies (1982) make the important point that if there is a distribution of efficiencies across firms – a very Marshallian notion, to be revisited in chapter 5 – then both H and Π/R themselves depend upon cost conditions in the industry.

It is also possible to treat the dominant firm model of (2.14) to (2.19) along these lines. Thus Geroski (1982) took as his starting point the simplification that

$$(\Pi/R)^{\star} = \alpha C_k$$

where $(\Pi/R)^{\star}$ is the maximum possible price–cost margin, C_k the k-firm concentration ratio, and α a parameter dependent on industry elasticity of demand, fringe supply elasticity, and concentration, as indicated in (2.19). But, according to Geroski, additional factors like growth and advertising lead to this being an imperfect depiction of the relationship between profitability and concentration.

In truth, both the Cowling–Waterson and Saving–Geroski approaches use conduct assumptions which are highly specialized, involving a very limited set of decision variables for each firm. They are also very abstract, assuming as they do that firms have rich and full information about their economic environments. All the approaches mentioned are stylizations. They may be contrasted in terms of the schema in figure 2.3, which is to be regarded as a generalization of the simpler schema introduced in figure 2.1. Certain measurement problems arise in evaluating performance by the $p > MC$ criterion. In an n-firm industry with each firm having a Lerner index of m_i, it is possible to conceive of a performance index $L(m_1, m_2, \ldots, m_n)$, though L is clearly not unique. Geroski (1983) has indicated ways in which an appropriate L index can be constructed and favours $L = -\Phi/\eta$, where Φ is a weighted sum of market shares – it being possible to parameterize weights by specific oligopolistic forms – and η is the industry elasticity of demand.

	Structure		Conduct		Performance
Bain-Mann	C_k	$\longrightarrow$	Unspecified	$\longrightarrow$	$r > \bar{r}$
Cowling-Waterson	H, η	$\longrightarrow$	Cournot-Nash	$\longrightarrow$	$p > MC$
Saving-Geroski	C_k, η_D, η_S	$\longrightarrow$	k-firm cartel with fringe competitors	$\longrightarrow$	$p > MC$

Figure 2.3

2.4   APPLICATIONS TO VARIOUS MARKET STRUCTURES

In fact, even though the schema in figure 2.3 is a clear advance on that in figure 2.1, both sets of stylizations seriously misrepresent the content of the SCP approach, which is of considerable subtlety and well adapted to encompassing many situations. Now let us consider a more flexible application of the SCP approach to perfect competition and to oligopoly. The following two examples illustrate the possibility of building up a more general SCP framework.

Example 1 *Perfect competition*

Structure
No concentration of buyers or of sellers
No barriers to entry and exit
No product differentiation

Conduct
Independent production-setting strategy (set $q = q^*$ such that $p = MC(q^*)$, assuming that $d[MC(q^*)/dq] > 0$)

Performance
No X-inefficiency
No supernormal profit
No allocative inefficiency (i.e. Pareto optimality prevails)
No innovation
No concern for equity

Notice that under the performance category we have started to look beyond the static Paretian criteria for guidance on performance. Perfect competition only looks compelling as a market structure when confined to a narrow evaluative standpoint – an argument which will be greatly amplified when we come to consider workable competition in chapter 7. The very efficiency of perfect competition in whittling away supernormal profit militates against its providing incentives for innovation in terms of short-term monopoly rentals for entrepreneurs. Hirschman (1970) has emphasized that the competitive market can be, in a sense, *over*-effective in weeding out firms which temporarily fall short of an efficiency ideal. Better than a firm exiting from an industry because it was unfortunate enough to experience a lapse of efficiency, with a consequent social loss in terms of destruction of capital, is perhaps an organization of production in an industry which permits recovery of ailing firms. Pressing further the argument against a narrow concern for allocative efficiency, the neutrality of Paretian welfare economics on issues of equity and distribution is well known. Yet in the policy arena, where to some extent performance norms are established, some concern for equity is likely to be present.

Example 2 *Oligopoly*

Structure
Few firms
Market concentration of sellers, and possibly concentration of buyers (oligopsony)

Barriers to entry, and possible to exit as well (sunk costs)
Either homogeneous or differentiated product

Conduct
Various, depending on conjectural variation. Possibilities include: profit
maximization; constrained profit maximization; utility maximization;
satisficing; and mini-maxing

Performance
Existence of supernormal profits
Allocation not Pareto optimal
Possible X-inefficiency
Probable innovation
Probable quality enhancement

It is to be noted in this second example that the conduct aspects in which
oligopoly is desirable are those in which competition is undesirable, and vice
versa. This emphasizes that the relative evaluation of industries in terms of
performance criteria can be very difficult once many different methods of
gauging performance are admitted. Some would thereby deny the possibility of
making inter-industry, as distinct from intra-industry, comparisons. Geroski
(1983) is more optimistic. He argues that such comparisons are simply subject
to more uncertainty, which must be counteracted by acquiring more information (e.g. on the inter-industry variations in conduct) and/or by imposing
stronger assumptions on the data.

These two examples provide some indication of the ways in which the primitive
SCP approach described earlier can be developed. Note that the examples
adhere to the assumption that causality is from structure to conduct to performance. This is of course debatable. An oligopolist might direct his conduct at
attempting to achieve a change in market structure. By aggressive advertising,
harassment in the courts, or whatever, it might force rivals out of the market
and thus promote an increase in concentration, i.e. a change in structure.
Equally, the attempt to attain performance goals like innovation and product
quality improvement is likely to influence both the way the firm conducts itself
and ultimately the structure of the market in which it operates.

   We thus have the basis for developing a more general structure–conduct–
performance framework in terms of the schema in figure 2.4. Notice that in
this schema many more factors are included under every heading, and furthermore that mutual causation and feedback effects are allowed rather than simple
one-way causation.

   It is clearly facile to argue simply that 'everything depends on everything
else'. The role of model building is to identify the major causal connections
and to establish their quantitative significance. It is important that some

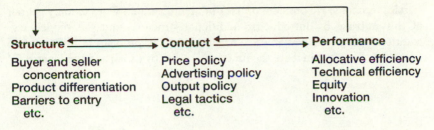

Structure ←————————→ **Conduct** ←————————→ **Performance**

Structure	Conduct	Performance
Buyer and seller concentration	Price policy	Allocative efficiency
Product differentiation	Advertising policy	Technical efficiency
Barriers to entry	Output policy	Equity
etc.	Legal tactics	Innovation
	etc.	etc.

Figure 2.4

simplification be undertaken in order to develop generalizations on which one can get a mental grasp. In this respect the simplest hypothesis of a causal connection from structure through conduct to performance has a lot to recommend it; it conveys more than would the blanket statement that all structure, conduct, and performance variables are mutually related. This simple hypothesis is in a sense, therefore, the most parsimonious. However, as data and computing resources develop, as the power and scope of analytical models of oligopoly increase, so it becomes possible and desirable to depart from the most parsimonious model to contemplate more complex models. This is the purpose of subsequent sections of this chapter.

2.5 PROBLEMS OF CAUSALITY AND SIMULTANEITY

A simple example can be taken as the starting point for a discussion of causality. Suppose that concentration C (an aspect of structure) causes firms to adopt an aggressive advertising policy A (an aspect of conduct) in order to compete successfully with their few rivals. This we might express formally as

$$A = f(C) \quad f' > 0 \tag{2.27}$$

In practice the advertising variable will probably be expressed in 'intensity' terms (e.g. as the advertising/sales ratio), and we already know that concentration may be measured in a variety of ways. However, these are more practical issues which we will pass by here. What is important to observe now is that one could equally well argue for the opposite sort of causation to that suggested above. It may well be that the pursuit of an aggressive advertising policy leads to an increase in concentration in a market sense, as rivals are forced out or lose market shares. Thus the following also holds:

$$C = F(A) \quad F' > 0 \tag{2.28}$$

From a statistical point of view it is a hopeless task trying to disentangle one relationship from the other, at least as they stand. One runs up against the

classical econometric problem of 'lack of identification'. One can only get out
of this impasse by introducing additional structure into the model, e.g.
additional exogenous variables. The nature of the problem is illustrated in
figure 2.5. Graphed in it are the function F given by (2.28) and the inverse f^{-1}

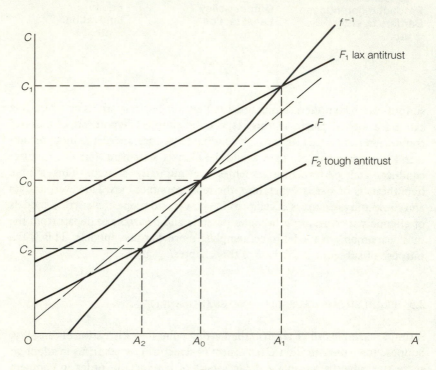

Figure 2.5

of the function given by (2.27). The problem is that any positive association
between concentration and advertising, as represented for example by a linear
regression, will tend to be picked up in the form of the long-dashed line, which
is a hybrid of functions F and f^{-1} and has no causal interpretation at all. Only
advertising and concentration levels of A_0 and C_0 are consistent with the
functions shown. If the function f, and thus its inverse f^{-1}, were subject to
more random variation than F, this would assist the identification of F. If some
factor affected concentration through the function F, but did not also affect
advertising through the function f, this would assist the identification of the
function f. For example, if the antitrust regime were an exogenous influence on
concentration, modifying equation (2.28) to the form $C = F(A, T)$ (where T is
a policy regime variable) but leaving equation (2.27) unaltered at $A = f(C)$,

this would assist the statistical identification of the relationship $f(\cdot)$. Compared with the situation depicted by F, a tough antitrust regime would give rise to the schedule F_2, and a lax antitrust regime to the schedule F_1. The antitrust regime in itself is assumed to have no direct influence on advertising; hence the schedule f^{-1} remains unchanged. Relatively tough regimes are associated with relatively lower equilibrium levels of advertising and concentration (e.g. the pair (A_2, C_2) compared with the pair (A_1, C_1)). Given these variations in policy regimes, concentration/advertising pairs (C_2, A_2), (C_0, A_0), and (C_1, A_1) will be observed, all of which lie along the f^{-1} function, thus facilitating its identification.

As a more general example, consider the advertising–concentration model of D.F. Greer (1971). It is specified as follows:

$$A = f(C, G)$$
$$C = F(A, G, X)$$
$$G = g(A, Y)$$

The variables X and Y are exogenous, and G is a growth rate. For the function $f(\cdot)$ it is expected that growth reduces advertising intensity, and for $F(\cdot)$ that it lowers concentration. What we have here is an exemplar of the view emphasized by Phillips (1972) and later developed in some detail by Geroski (1982) that a simultaneous equations approach is necessary to the setting up of an appropriate structure–conduct–performance model. Even if the focus of attention is on a single equation, like the concentration–advertising relationship, this should be embedded in a simultaneous equations framework to take account of the complex nature of causality.

In the study by Phillips (1972) of structure and performance in UK industry, two aspects of competition are identified: the propensity to attempt price-fixing; and the effectiveness in maintaining price-fixing. The effectiveness of price-fixing both determines, and is determined by, profitability (amongst other variables). The propensity to attempt price-fixing is determined by profitability (amongst other variables) but without reverse causality. In this way, the two different aspects of conduct are determined endogenously, as is performance. The latter is gauged by profitability, measured in this instance by the price–cost margin. Structure is regarded as exogenous and is characterized by variables such as the three-firm concentration ratio, the number of firms, barriers to entry, and market demand. Simultaneous equation estimation (using two-stage least squares) was used to estimate the model and produced a number of useful results, including a negative relationship between output growth and price–cost margins, and a positive influence of effective price-fixing on margins.

When Cowling (1976) initiated a critique of naïve profit/concentration ratios, he made important points about choice of variables, appropriateness of the underlying theory of oligopoly, and restrictions on functional forms. He stopped short of a fully fledged critique, however, in that he failed to address the problem of mutual causality. We have identified, in relatively simple contexts, the nature of this problem. It remains to consider what technical devices are available to the industrial economist to overcome them.

2.6   ECONOMETRIC TESTING

We will explore in some detail in chapter 4 the econometric modelling approach to industrial organization. Here we will briefly anticipate some of the issues in a structure–conduct–performance context. The econometric modelling approach has as a basic tenet the notion that economic structures are best modelled by simultaneous equation systems. This methodological position is quite independent of the particular approach to industrial organization (e.g. SCP as above) that one is adopting. From theoretical considerations it is known that biased and inconsistent estimators will be obtained if one estimates (in isolation) by ordinary least squares an equation which is, properly speaking, part of a *system*. This would apply were one to estimate, for example, the first (advertising) equation $A = f(C, G)$ of Greer's system (described in section 2.5) in isolation from the other two equations explaining concentration and industry growth. Only in one special case – that of a recursive system in which the matrix of endogenous variables is triangular and the system covariance matrix is diagonal – will it be proper to apply least squares to a single equation. Cowling (1976) has argued that this would be appropriate in the case of structure–performance relationships, as substantial lags in adjustment are inherent in market processes. Thus all explanatory variables of the price–cost margin may properly be regarded as predetermined. However, this is to assume knowledge of lag structure that we do not really have. Further, even if we do believe that a recursive system is an appropriate representation of the world, it is useful to know the full theoretical specification, from a purely analytical standpoint, even if equation by equation estimation is appropriate in a statistical sense. In short, there do not seem to be good grounds for ignoring simultaneity. Given the development of econometric techniques in recent years, it is now possible to test for simultaneity, rather than having to depend on highly subjective (and no doubt in some cases highly expedient) judgements.

We will first briefly expound the essential aspects of a test for simultaneity (or, what amounts to the same thing, a test for exogeneity), and then particularize the test to the case of a structure–performance model. Consider an equation which is strictly linear in parameters and variables, where an endogenous variable y is explained by an exogenous variable z and by another variable x which may or may not be exogenous:

$$y = \alpha_0 + \alpha_1 x + \alpha_2 z_1 + u \tag{2.29}$$

Here the α_i are parameters and u is a random (i.e. disturbance) term. If x is in fact endogenous, it is determined by other variables in the system, as well as itself determining other variables. Suppose x is determined in the following way:

$$x = \beta_0 + \beta_1 y + \beta_2 z_2 + \beta_3 z_3 + \varepsilon \tag{2.30}$$

where the β_i are parameters, ε is a disturbance term, and z_2, z_3 are exogenous variables. If (2.29) is estimated by ordinary least squares in the case in which x is endogenous, the estimators $\hat{\alpha}_i$ are biased and inconsistent. However, if the following restricted model holds, with $\beta_1 = 0$ and $\text{cov}(u, \varepsilon) = 0$, then ordinary least squares may be appropriately applied to the first equation:

$$\begin{aligned} y &= \alpha_0 + \alpha_1 x + \alpha_2 z_1 + u \\ x &= \beta_0 + \beta_2 z_2 + \beta_3 z_3 + \varepsilon \end{aligned} \tag{2.31}$$

System (2.31) is a recursive model. If y were a price–cost margin, x an index of concentration, and z_1 the price elasticity of industry demand, this would correspond to the sort of model Cowling (1976) had in mind. In order to distinguish between the restricted model expressed by (2.31) and the unrestricted model expressed by (2.29) and (2.30), an appropriate test of the hypothesis $E(x, u) = 0$ is required. That is, we wish to know whether the x variable is distributed independently of the disturbance term u. Following the writings of Hausman (1978) and Wu (1973, 1974) an appropriate test can be constructed along the following lines. Define x as the sum of a systematic component x^* and a random component v. Thus

$$\begin{aligned} x &= x^* + v \\ x^* &= \beta_0 + \beta_2 z_2 + \beta_3 z_3 + \lambda z_1 \\ v &= \beta_1 y + \varepsilon \end{aligned}$$

The null hypothesis of the test is that (2.31) is true. The alternative hypothesis is that (2.29) and (2.30) are true, in which case $\beta_1 \neq 0$ and/or $E(u, \varepsilon) = 0$. Under the alternative hypothesis, y is certainly not independent of v, whereas it *is* independent under the null hypothesis. The test proceeds by constructing an estimate for v, called $\hat{v}$, using

$$\hat{v} = x - \hat{\beta}_0 - \hat{\beta}_2 z_2 - \hat{\beta}_3 z_3 - \hat{\lambda} z_1$$

where the $\hat{\beta}_i$ are ordinary least squares estimators obtained from a regression of x on z_1, z_2, and z_3. The correlation between v and y is then obtained by using the artificially constructed variable in a regression of the form

$$y = \alpha_0 + \alpha_1 x + \alpha_2 z_1 + \hat{\theta} v + \mu$$

Under the null hypothesis, $\theta = 0$. If $\theta \neq 0$ then the alternative is accepted and x is regarded as endogenous. Note that the model has been *assumed* to be strictly linear. It is possible to confuse non-linearity (another form of mis-specification) with endogeneity. Furthermore, rejection of the null hypothesis implies endogeneity (and hence suggests the need for structural modelling), but failure to reject it may or may not imply endogeneity. However, only under very special conditions (see Geroski, 1982, p. 150) will failure to reject be compatible with endogeneity; hence it is convenient to regard failure to reject as indicative of the exogeneity of x.

Geroski (1982) applies this sort of test procedure to a structure–performance model. Though the term 'conduct' is omitted here, its inclusion would be sensible as an explicit model of the industry is adopted. This model has been developed in equations (2.14) to (2.19) as the dominant firm with a competitive fringe. If k firms act jointly as 'the' dominant firm, and the remaining 'fringe' firms act as competitive followers, then the maximum price–cost margin $M^\star$ is related to the k-firm concentration ratio C_k by the relationship

$$M^\star = \alpha C_k$$

where α is dependent on industry demand elasticity and fringe supply elasticity as expressed by (2.19). However, the desired price–cost margin M does not equal the maximum because of additional factors such as advertising, growth, and diversification. Thus

$$M = M^\star + \text{other factors}$$
$$= \alpha C_k + \beta_0 + \beta_1 X + \beta_2 X_2 + \beta_3 X_3 \ldots + \beta_6 X_6$$

where the other factors are represented by adding on a linear function. In principle a vast number of other factors could be used, but following Geroski (1982) the six X_i will be given the following interpretations: X_1 is the advertising/sales ratio; X_2 is capital stock; X_3 is growth of sales; X_4 is import intensity; X_5 is export intensity; and X_6 is a diversification index. Using single-equation methodology, causality is presumed to run from $C_k, X_1, \ldots, X_6$ to M. However, there are likely to be feedback effects, as our representation of the SCP framework in figure 2.4 suggested. Not only might high profitability (measured by a high M) cause, say, growth; but also, through the profit maximizing conduct assumption, most of the variables $C_k, X_1, \ldots, X_6$ will be linked. Thus potentially all the right-hand variables in this structure–performance relationship are endogenous. The appropriate way to proceed is to use a Hausman–Wu test of the sort briefly described above to test for exogeneity. Proceeding along these lines, using a sample of 52 UK industries for 1968, Geroski investigated the minimally acceptable size of structure–conduct–performance model. He discovered that it was not possible to regard the advertising/sales ratio and the import and export intensity variables as exogenous. The capital stock and diversification variables were regarded as exogenous on *a priori* grounds. Geroski (1982, p. 156) was led to conclude: 'We are left with solid statistical support for thinking that a non-linear profits equation plus two further simultaneous equations involving import and export intensity is the minimum-size model necessary to generate consistent unbiased estimators.'

2.7 CONCLUSION

The SCP framework is very rich – much richer indeed than this chapter has suggested. What we have done is to take the simplest form of structure–performance equation $r = f(C)$, where r is the rate of profit and C is a measure of concentration, as a starting point. No explicit analytical model underpins this relationship and a suitable functional form for $f(\cdot)$ is not naturally suggested. Then the following questions were addressed:

(a)   How can a rationale for a structure–performance equation be developed in terms of oligopoly theory?
(b)   What variables should logically appear in such a relationship, and in what precise form should they be expressed?
(c)   What functional form should a structure–performance equation take?
(d)   Can conduct aspects be explicitly taken into account to fill in the gap between structure and performance?
(e)   What consequences arise from considering issues of causality and simultaneity?
(f)   If simultaneity is to be taken seriously, how might one proceed in a practical sense to gauge its empirical significance for structure–performance modelling?

Pursuing these issues led us to a consideration of work which, at least in a statistical sense, starts to explore some of the full potential of the SCP framework. It takes conduct seriously, is suggestive of appropriate variables and functional form, and takes cognizance of mutual causation. The method also permits one to draw fairly precise conclusions. Of course, much is still omitted, of which perhaps the most important is the propensity of firms to enlarge their scope of conduct into the legal and political arenas. These possibilities are probably not sensibly explored by statistical means. However, a shrewd combination of legal and political insight with sophisticated structural modelling have the potential to revivify what, in terms of the literature of the past twenty years, was beginning to look like a depressingly naïve interpretation of the structure–conduct–performance framework.

3

The case study approach

3.1 INTRODUCTION

The case study approach has been extensively employed in industrial organization. In a number of classical cases it has led to the development of new schools of analysis. Thus Mason (1939) was an advocate of the use of the case study method to illuminate structure, conduct, and performance. Ideas on workable competition were derived from case studies of particular industries and so also were behavioural theories of the firm. And, of course, an enormous amount of case study work is done on behalf of government agencies to investigate abuses of monopoly power. In a loose sense these are all methods oriented towards case studies, meaning by this methods that involve gathering detailed data on particular firms or industries. The collection of such data might proceed 'at arm's length' using published sources available for public consumption, such as annual accounts, and perhaps also documents internally circulated by firms if availability is not restricted. Usually, however, more than this is required; the investigator needs to get into the field and gather primary source data himself if his case study is to have any depth.

Is there a distinction to be made between the approaches described above, and what is to be analysed in this chapter as the case study approach to industrial organization? We shall argue that it is possible, and indeed potentially very fruitful, to look at the case study as a distinct method in its own right, rather than as an adjunct to established methodologies – structure–conduct–performance, behavioural, workably competitive, or whatever. This distinction is made feasible, because it is possible to regard the case study as a detailed fact-gathering activity which can lead to the construction of theoretical systems. Such systems are not posited and then subjected to falsification tests based on samples of data, but are generated by the process of data collection itself. The approach advanced is very much influenced by the writings of Glaser and Strauss (1967) on grounded theory, and by the structuralist approach, of which the work by Kay (1982) provides an example as applied to industrial organization.

3.2 CASE STUDY ANALYSIS AS A SCIENTIFIC METHOD

Glaser and Strauss advance the case for *theoretical sampling*, a slightly misleading term coined by themselves to describe what is most assuredly an empirical
process. It has as its special feature the requirement that sampling should be
organized to suggest, develop, and make precise a theory about relationships in
the universe. Such samples are certainly non-probabilistic, and are also judge-
mental. The initial position of the industrial economist about to start an
empirical investigation should, according to this line of reasoning, be free from
preconceptions about the appropriateness of any particular theoretical model.
Data are collected initially using a very general economic perspective. The
investigation proceeds by suggesting tentative hypotheses and then modifying
them in the light of the unfolding evidence. As a general position, Glaser and
Strauss maintain that relationships established by this method are essentially
qualitative, there being an insufficiently defined structure to facilitate
quantitative conclusions.

It will be noted that theories in the sense used here are generally about
categories and relationships between categories. The work of Kay (1982) is
helpful in displaying the sorts of categories and relationships which might be
relevant to the industrial economist. The basic theoretical construct favoured
by Kay is that of 'synergy', a term due to Ansoff (1965, p. 75), who defines it as
'the effect which can produce a combined return on the firm's resources greater
than the sum of its parts'. What Kay advocates is the construction of 'synergy
maps', these being essentially qualitative or relational schemas for representing
synergy links in the activities of the firm. For an attempt to make this framework
operational, see Diamantopoulos and Kay (1986). His racquet/ski example is
illustrated in figure 3.1. A firm produces for markets A, B, and C, these being
for tennis racquets, skis, and boat fittings, all made in aluminium. The relative
size of activities (measured possibly by value added) is indicated by the extent
of the bounded areas. Thus C is a relatively unimportant market to the firm.
There are close technological links between the production of tennis racquets
and skis, and this is indicated by the thick operating synergy line connecting A
and B. By contrast, sales synergy is weak between A and B, denoted by the
relatively thin connecting line. Kay (1982, p. 51) suggests that 'accurate
synergy maps would require detailed investigation of each firm' – a plea for
the case study method.

The aim of Glaser and Strauss's theoretical sampling, if the theory is about
categories as in Kay's example, is to collect data until the categories are
exhausted. It is possible for falsification to occur when practising this
methodology; it consists in detecting unexplained exceptions, anomalies, or
counter-examples. The theory, in its final form, should have no counter-
examples.

In achieving this final form for a theory, no precise guidelines are offered. It

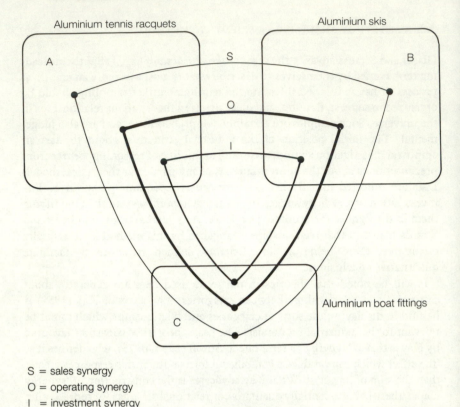

S = sales synergy
O = operating synergy
I = investment synergy

Figure 3.1

should be stable in the face of new data, and rich in detail. In achieving such detail, the collection of different 'slices of data' is favoured. This is to argue in favour of using diverse methods for collecting data, with the purpose being to get different perspectives on categories. Just by comparing slices of data, it is hoped that new perspectives can be generated. Rather than dismissing 'anecdotal comparison' out of hand, as economists are often inclined to, Glaser and Strauss regard such activity as useful for starting a new research direction and developing categories. They dispute the criticism that theoretical sampling leads to 'unbounded relativism'. Indeed, the very strength of taking slices of data is that it tends to offset the biases of methods and the misrepresentations of respondents against one another.

In standard statistical sampling more data are generally better than less. Thus we know that the distribution of the mean has a variance σ^2/n, where σ^2 is the variance of a large population and n is the sample size. Thus the variance of the sampling distribution can be reduced by increasing the sample size. In theoretical sampling, merely increasing the sample size is not necessarily useful. Such data gathering could be redundant if relevant categories are already exhausted, or could be inefficient in the different sense that it adds information on 'full' categories but none on others yet to be exhausted. Theoretical sampling is deliberately directed at filling categories. If they are 'core' categories they should be filled as completely as possible; but with less significant categories, the requirements are not so stringent. In fact the Glaser and Strauss procedure is not too far conceptually from any one of a variety of extensions of standard sampling theory. For example, if we require to know the sample size needed to ensure an error of less than E in our estimate of the population mean, with probability 0.95, it is given by $n = (1.96 \sigma/E)^2$. To take another example, in acceptance sampling used in industrial quality control, a certain attribute of a good is being monitored. A limited number of lots is examined and, on the basis of this, entire lots are accepted or rejected. The acceptance of a lot as having a certain attribute (e.g. tensile strength, elasticity) is analogous to the filling of a category, and the acceptance of all lots on this basis is tantamount to regarding the exhausted categories as providing a basis for a validated theory. Clearly, like all analogies, this is imperfect. In theoretical sampling, the data are highly qualitative and there is no single attribute that one is looking at. Many qualities one is examining are in fact relationships (e.g. employer/employee) which could not readily be accommodated within a classical statistical quality control framework.

3.3 METHODS OF INVESTIGATION

Let us look at methods firstly in terms of scientific instruments, and secondly as applied to concrete examples.

There is no universally recognized set of instruments for conducting a case study investigation. Broadly speaking, methods can be divided into the qualitative and quantitative. The data of qualitative investigations are prose. The words gathered from qualitative methods may be obtained by observation (including participant observation), interviews (conducted at a variety of levels of formality), and documents (ranging from official publications, through memoranda, to personal diaries). An increasingly widely used technical accessory to data collection is the tape recorder, and transcribed tapes are an important source of qualitative data. Given the large volume of textual material that can emerge from an extensive gathering of qualitative data, a variety of data reduction techniques are often deployed, even to the extent of using numeric coding devices. There is, however, a more common tendency to use matrices, graphs, networks, and charts as devices for data reduction.

Quantitative data can, of course, be dealt with in a somewhat similar way. Corresponding to the data reduction process referred to above in a qualitative context, we find the computation of summary statistics like means, variances, and indices in a quantitative context. Display methods common in qualitative methods (networks, matrices) are paralleled by histograms, scatter diagrams, and other devices in quantitative methods. There is available for dealing with quantitative data a huge array of highly developed statistical methods alongside which the representational schemas of qualitative analysis look naïve and unsophisticated. It is certainly true that industrial economists have very much favoured the use of quantitative data when conducting case studies. This can be obtained using postal or administered questionnaires. A half-way house to the qualitative approach is to use the semi-structured interview, which generates data that can be readily coded but are in a strict sense textual.

Let us now turn to some examples of the use of case study methods in actual investigations into industrial organization. We will consider three cases: firstly, the analysis of the economic effects of mergers, due to Cowling et al. (1980); secondly, the detailed case studies of West German transnational corporations by Fröbel et al. (1980); and thirdly, a set of general firm-level case studies by Mackintosh (1963), Boswell (1973), and Reid (1986).

Cowling et al. (1980) report on a set of case studies into industrial mergers scrutinized by the UK Mergers Panel between 1965 and 1970. In approaching this subject matter they had open to them a variety of approaches. Broadly speaking, choices are amongst theories which look at stockholders' interests, managers' interests, and the public interest. Cowling et al. (1980) concentrate on the last of these. Their concern is with the welfare implications of mergers. Put simply, merger activity can be seen to lead to potential gains in terms of increased efficiency, and potential losses in terms of an increased degree of monopoly power. Indices of both these effects can, of course, be computed, but to a considerable extent the weighing of costs and benefits is a qualitative exercise as conceived in a case study framework. The actual indices favoured by Cowling et al. are the ratio of profits to sales as a measure of potential monopoly power, and total factor requirement per unit of output as a measure of potential efficiency gain. Some considerable attention has already been given in chapter 2 to the former measure, so let us confine attention to the latter.

Suppose a single output y is produced using n factors $x_1, x_2, \ldots, x_n$, with p and $q_1, \ldots, q_n$ being output and factor prices. Suppose factors are related to output by the following technological relationship:

$$x_i = ka_i y \qquad k, a_i > 0$$

Then the profit function can be written

$$\Pi = py - \sum_{i=1}^{n} q_i x_i = py - \sum_{i=1}^{n} q_i ka_i y = py - ky \sum_{i=1}^{n} q_i a_i$$

The term $\Sigma q_i a_i$ is a price index for input prices using the fixed weights a_1, $a_2, \ldots, a_n$. Denote this index I_q. Then the profit function becomes

$$\Pi = py - kyI_q$$

which implies

$$k = \frac{p}{I_q}\left(1 - \frac{\Pi}{R}\right)$$

where $R = py$.

In the multiproduct case, the single price p is replaced by a price index of outputs, say I_p. Thus k may be expressed

$$k = \frac{I_p}{I_q}\left(1 - \frac{\Pi}{R}\right)$$

It is simple to show that, so defined, k is average cost deflated by an index of factor prices. It is described by Cowling et al. (1980) as 'total unit factor requirement'. In computing k before and after a merger, a post-merger fall in k implies an efficiency gain. In Cowling et al. (1980) some discussion of possible biases in k is undertaken, the conclusion being that it may tend to overstate the efficiency gains from mergers.

The welfare framework adopted involves applying a cost–benefit analysis to a series of case studies. However, clearly the ratio of profits to revenue and the k index are imperfect measures of losses and gains, and are highly restrictive. For this reason, each case study takes a broader approach, and no uniform method was adopted. Thus it is reported by Cowling et al. (1980, p. 72) that 'a variety of approaches and a variety of stresses' were deployed, with 'each investigator in his search for effects being conditioned by the feel of the evidence and the nature of the important questions in each case'. In terms made familiar by Glaser and Strauss (1967), different 'slices' of data were used. Material consulted included Monopolies Commission reports, trade journals, commercial market intelligence reports, trade association reports, official government business statistics, company reports and other such company documentation, and, of course, scholarly publications. No systematic attempt was made to collect data in the field, which must necessarily have involved a certain loss of insight into the merger process. One must therefore interpret with caution the general finding of Cowling et al. (1980) that in the cases studied mergers were generally not beneficial as evaluated by their welfare trade-off method.

A quite different sort of case study is that of Fröbel et al. (1980). The general frame of reference is Marxian, and the object of examination is the transnational corporation. In Marx's *Capital*, it is argued that the motivation behind the movement of capital is the compulsion to accumulate. Potential limits on accumulation can be overcome by two principal methods – the division of labour and the introduction of new machinery. The application of these methods in capitalist production increases firms' power over the labour force and lowers the supply price of labour. A so-called 'new international division of labour' comes about which has the characteristic that it undermines the traditional distinction between the industrialized and the less developed countries, and encourages the development of the division beyond the work-place itself to the subdivision of a manufacturing process into several partial operations taking place in distinct host economies. There are held to be three prerequisites for this: the extension of a domestic reserve army of the unem-ployed to a world-wide reservoir of potential labour power; the deskilling of the existing employed labour force by the decomposition of complete produc-tion processes into simpler sub-operations; and the development of technologies whose feasibility is independent of the site in which production takes place. It is argued that this world-wide reservoir of labour is characteristically over-worked, because labour can be cheaply replaced. Deskilling arises because the division of labour is so advanced that individual operations are sufficiently elementary to require no craft abilities. The independence of technology on any particular site has been facilitated by the development of transport and communications.

It is clear that a general theoretical framework was adopted as a starting point and that it was Marxian. As Miles and Huberman (1984) have argued, it is strictly impossible to start with no preconceptions whatsoever at the commence-ment of research. However, the specific way in which the Marxian theory was developed to construct a novel theory of the new international division of labour was made possible by permitting the data to suggest an appropriate contingent theory, and by attempting to let the data gathered exhaust the categories of this emergent theory.

Three case studies were undertaken to develop and test the emergent theory of the new international division of labour: firstly, West German textile and garment production; secondly, the employment and production activities of West German guest workers in non-textiles manufactures; and thirdly, the growth of free production zones. Fröbel et al. (1980, p. 16) concede that each case study looks at only part of the overall picture, but suggest that 'taken together they provide adequate empirical information to allow an empirical assessment and elucidation of the fundamental forms in which the international division of labour is appearing'. In other words, sufficient information has been gathered by theoretical sampling to exhaust the newly evolved theoretical category of 'the new international division of labour'.

The evidence upon which this category was exhausted was voluminous, and it is only possible to look at the three case studies in the briefest manner. The first case study looked at 214 textile and 185 garment manufacturers in West Germany. It was found that between 1966 and 1975 foreign employment by these manufacturers more than doubled. The second case study examined 602 manufacturing companies in West Germany engaged in other than textile and garment production. Of these, 335 were found to have 709 subsidiaries in industrialized countries, and 444 had 1051 subsidiaries in developing countries. Clearly, there is a tendency for feasible production to be independent of site. The number of foreign subsidiaries was found to increase fourfold between 1961 and 1976, and the number of employees abroad fivefold between 1961 and 1974. These data lend support to the notion of a new international division of labour. The third case study looked at free production zones in 103 countries in Asia, Africa, and Latin America. In these zones it was found that the labour employed was cheap, fresh but expendable, and relatively unskilled. Young women were particularly important in this workforce. One can draw a variety of normative conclusions from these findings, but this is perhaps best left to the contemplation of the reader. One cannot rule out the possibility of other emergent theories arising from similar case studies, but undoubtedly the new international division of labour is a compelling theory, given that one started from a Marxian position.

Finally, let us look at a variety of case studies conducted on a firm by firm basis using approaches that are eclectic compared with those considered so far. A vast array of case studies could be considered, particularly if one takes into account work conducted for consultancy purposes or for government agencies. Important early empirical works, which embody certain aspects of the case study method, include Hall and Hitch (1939), Saxton (1942), Andrews (1949), Barback (1964), Heath (1961), Kaplan et al. (1958), Adams (1961), Fog (1960), Edwards et al. (1961), Hague (1971), and Swann et al. (1974). A more recent sophisticated textbook treatment of the case study method is due to Shaw and Sutton (1976).

As our concern here is with the purpose and method of the case study approach, we shall concentrate on examples which illuminate the methodology. The chosen area for further examination is the set of firm-level case studies due to Mackintosh (1963), Boswell (1973), and Reid (1986).

The avowed intention of Mackintosh (1963) was to investigate a proportional stratified random sample of manufacturing enterprises in the area of Birmingham, UK. In practice 123 firms were approached, of which 36 co-operated fully and provided the main evidence upon which the study was based. Mackintosh had a particular interest in the firms' investment policies.

It seems that Mackintosh did not himself carry out very much of the field work, which can lead to methodological difficulties. It means that the field worker (in this case, one research assistant only) would need to have been particularly well briefed in the purpose of the investigation. There is an inevitable loss of information in communicating field experiences through the mouth of a non-specialist assistant to a non-field-working expert. In short, the evolving theory is likely to be less well 'grounded'. Ideally the expert or group of experts should be sufficiently fully involved with the field work to have traversed the steep part of the 'learning curve' invariably attached to the cultivation of field expertise.

Mackintosh's orginal ideal of a stratified sample was not realized, partly because of the low response rate overall, and the skewed distribution of response rates across strata. Ultimately constrained by the need to get co-operation from firms, and to have data collected within a reasonable time frame, he departed from the hope of getting a strict statistical sample, and instead attempted to get at least reasonable (if not proportional) representation in each size class. Mackintosh (1963, p. 59) argued that 'from such tests as it has been possible to make and from general observation, these firms seem to be fairly representative in character of manufacturing firms in this area and range of size'. Such an attitude is supported by Glaser and Strauss's (1967) conception of 'theoretical sampling'. One aims to get sufficient information in a category that the potential of it for theory generation becomes exhausted.

The exact instruments used for the investigation are reported on in a sketchy fashion. Three 'slices' of data were apparently collected. Firstly, given the particular focus on investment policy, business accounts for the seven to ten years prior to the inception of the study were copied and analysed. It is not reported whether firms were apprised of this intention at the beginning of the study, but clearly such wholesale accommodation could be regarded as threatening. The 36 firms which fully co-operated represent just a 30 per cent response rate, which is low for a field study investigation which is not concerned with a highly sensitive or socially taboo question. A more selective approach to information acquisition might well have greatly improved the response rate. If one simply wants to know about return on capital employed, this being the ratio of profit before interest and tax to net assets, one can ask for this figure directly, perhaps requiring no more than the determination of a range within which it falls. This is a useful piece of information from an economic standpoint, much more so than profits and assets *per se*, though the latter two statistics might be regarded as much more sensitive pieces of information from the firm's standpoint.

In this study, a questionnaire was apparently used at some stage, though it is not clear who filled it in and whether respondents were guided through it. Mackintosh (1963, p. 60) described it as 'a rather daunting document of 40 foolscap pages and 100 or more questions'. Unfortunately, the questionnaire schedule was not provided with the study – a serious neglect in a methodological sense. For 36 firms, interview data were also obtained, though again information on the instrument is woefully lacking as only four of the nine sections of the interview schedule were reproduced. The interview schedule covered the development of the firm in question since 1945, with an emphasis on investment decisions and finance. These then were the three ways in which 'slices' of data were obtained: by transcription of accounts; by questionnaire; and by interview. An unfortunate feature of the Mackintosh study is that these data were not used to their fullest effect. Individual case studies were given, but no attempt was made to undertake comparative analysis between cases, using these 'slices' of data. It was reported by Mackintosh (1963, p. 61) that some attempt at systematic statistical analysis across cases, looking at variables such as growth rates, earnings, and capital, was contemplated but looked unfruitful and was abandoned.

More satisfactory as an example of the case study method is the work of Boswell (1973), which concentrated on small private manufacturing enterprises. Boswell's appendix 2 on field work methodology provides information on the criteria which guided sampling. According to Boswell (1973, p. 204) the manufacturing sectors chosen had to be 'relatively homogeneous, localized, reasonably amenable to research and also representative of small firm weaknesses and strengths'. All enterprises selected were engaged in engineering, hosiery, and knitwear activities in the East Midlands, UK. Directories of engineering firms were used as the initial point of departure, with firms being ruled out if they were too big, were branches of larger concerns, and so on. Advice obtained from the regional office of the (then) Ministry of Technology was used to prune this list further, invoking additional criteria. From this final list a random sample was chosen. The sample really should be viewed as a judgement sample, given the qualitative considerations that surrounded the early sifting. Lacking a strict statistical sample, Boswell was nonetheless able to confirm that representation by strata was reasonable in relation to 1963 census data.

The so-called 'gatekeeper' to the case study site was the chief executive of the company concerned. He was approached by a 'pre-letter' – an important initial letter of considerable strategic significance to the ultimate nature of the research. This was individually typed and signed, and laid stress on the independence of the research, its confidentiality, and its practicality. The pre-letter aimed to state the purpose of the enquiry sympathetically and to suggest only a limited commitment of time. Boswell (1973, p. 208) explained that 'these minutiae were developed from a pilot study', and, small though the points may seem, a proper regard for them is important to field work success.

The questionnaire used has three sections: (a) company background; (b) personal background; and (c) progress, plant, and problems. Section (b) had a purpose which was largely sociological, and contained some questions which seemed rather far fetched (e.g. 'Where do you see the firm in twenty years time?', p. 213). Whilst the field work methodology of Boswell seemed sound, the instrumentation appeared deficient.

The principal instrument was a questionnaire, but in a number of respects it had weaknesses. Very little precise numeric information was required, such as one would normally expect from a questionnaire. Many questions could probably have been tightened up quite simply. For example the question 'What kind of education did you have?' can be readily broken up into primary, secondary, and higher education, and so on. Others were so open ended that some bounds would have to have been put on the range of possibilities and perhaps some vocabulary provided to the respondent to help him formalize his views. As another example, consider the question 'As compared with your direct competitors, what would you say are your main disadvantages (advantages) as a company?'. Broad areas would need to be defined (e.g. production, sales, marketing) and criteria for evaluating advantages enunciated (e.g. cost effectiveness). Boswell himself conducted all the interviews, which could explain the open ended nature of the questionnaire, for the investigator might have had in mind an implicit framework of greater coherence and precision. One advantage of having at least a limited number of co-workers is that the framework adopted has to be made explicit, even if it evolves as the field work progresses. Rather than making the areas of questioning very vague, to accommodate the possibility of shifts of perspective in the course of the study, a probe structure can be devised which naturally leads questions along different paths, depending on a variety of broad contingencies.

Finally, as an example of the case study method, let us consider the work undertaken jointly by Jacobsen and Reid, as described in the thesis of Jacobsen (1986) and the working paper of Reid (1986). The case study employed two principal instruments of investigation – the questionnaire and the semi-structured interview. A prelude to the deploying of these instruments was the qualitative field work conducted by Jacobsen. Figure 3.2 indicates in a schematic

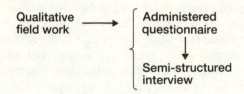

Figure 3.2

form the general nature of the study. The initial qualitative field work influenced the design of both the administered questionnaire and the semi-structured interview, but there was no overlap in the samples used for the qualitative field work and for the questionnaire and interview instruments. By contrast, all the semi-structured interviews were applied to respondents who had previously participated in the administered questionnaire. The instruments were first tested in a pilot study; this led to substantial revisions to the administered questionnaire schedule, but few to the semi-structured interview agenda.

Miles and Huberman (1984) provide a detailed and balanced set of arguments for and against prior instrumentation. In the full spirit of Glaser and Strauss's 'grounded theory', one should avoid exact prior instrumentation. In the study reported, a shift from this extreme position was taken, with the initial qualitative field work being used to suggest possible appropriate forms of instrumentation, and the instruments *per se* being very precisely formulated after appropriate pilot work in the field. The general position adopted followed that advocated by Reid (1981), where arguments were advanced in favour of gathering primary source data in industrial organization. The administered questionnaire took as its point of departure the work conducted by Nowotny and Walther (1978) and Wied-Nebbeling (1975) who had developed a framework which involved the examination of general characteristics, pricing, costs, sales, and competition. This framework was completely redesigned both to put it into an administered questionnaire format and to orient it towards the context of small owner-managed firms rather than large corporate enterprises. To it was added a new section on finance, due to Jacobsen (1986), which adopted the same pattern of instrumentation. The form taken by the semi-structured interview was what Lofland (1971) in his classical study of field work methods described as an 'intensive interview with an interview guide'. A general principle of design with such interviews is that no more than ten topics should be covered, with eight being the normal upper limit. In the study reported upon here just three main topics were introduced, using a framework suggested by Porter (1980, 1985). This was found to be a sensible practical limit, given the attention spans of interviewer and respondent alike, and the (not unrelated) need to keep the interview length within a two-hour limit. The areas investigated covered competitive forces, competitive strategy, and defensive strategy. These constitute but a part of the Porter framework; however, it was felt that they were most readily adapted to the analysis of small owner-managed firms. Over 100 interviews were conducted, leading to very detailed data on more than 70 firms. These data were set up on the SIR database, and included both numerical data from the administered questionnaire and textual data from the semi-structured interviews. This permits relatively sophisticated data handling of the sort that entails linking qualitative textual material with numerical statistics. The analysis of such combined data sets is still in its infancy, but is no doubt indicative of future trends in case study analysis.

3.4 THE PROBLEM OF GENERALIZATION

Suppose one has gathered case study data, ideally by field work. How does one proceed to generalize from the data so obtained to the wider population of firms? Indeed, is such generalization even possible? One way to proceed, as exemplified by the study of Boswell (1973) reported in section 3.3, is to set up a statistical sampling frame for the case studies. In his case, this procedure failed through the patchiness of the response rate, though there is some reason to hope that Boswell's sample is at least not too far removed from a statistical sample.

However, this case is perhaps untypical. Opportunistic, snowball, and theoretical sampling are much more common. Such methods were used, for example, by Barback (1964) and Hague (1971). One gets what one can, and at the margin always tries to edge towards acquiring especially informative data. Redundant, irrelevant, or overdetermining data are not worth collecting, given the highly labour-intensive nature of field work. Having acquired information in such a fashion it is probably best to accept the wise counsel of Miles and Huberman (1984, p. 232) concerning possibilities for generalization: 'We suggest that you *assume* you are selectively sampling and drawing inferences from a weak or non-representative sample of "cases", be they people, events, or processes. You are guilty, until you prove yourself innocent.'

It has more recently been realized in statistical sampling theory that so-called 'outliers' are often particularly informative. That they may not lie in the population is one possibility; however, another is that they may actually be a true part of it, though subject to some special combination of forces at the time of sampling. To reject such outliers is to discard the possibility of probing further the true forces acting on the population. Now field work analysis has traditionally taken the view that one need not sample simply for representativeness, but should also take account of the range or richness of the population. In terms of standard statistical terminology there is amongst field workers frequently a tendency to oversample the tails and to undersample around the centre of gravity of the distribution of attributes. This limits the scope for generalization, but is really more informative about the population. Take the case of a profitability distribution across firms in an industry. Suppose many firms cluster around the mean profitability level. How informative is it to sample proportionately highly from such firms, simply because they are most numerous? As industrial economists we are very often interested in why firms fail or in why firms are unusually successful, but less so in why firms are of merely average profitability. The field worker interested in case studies oriented towards causes of profitability might therefore seem justified in over-sampling from firms lying in the tails of the profitability distribution. In terms of theory construction and verification, close examination of such relatively deviant firms is probably more informative about what makes for average or typical profitability than simply confining the bulk of attention to average firms.

3.5   CONCLUSION

A resurgence of interest in the case study method, and related techniques, has become evident in economics. Thus Lawson (1985, p. 926) has recently advocated that 'more resources should be allocated, and attention paid, to the results of forms of case study, to personal histories, and to the study of primary sources. At the very least a re-evaluation of research priorities and methods may be in order'. Such an attitude is in sympathy with the drift of this chapter.

One could embrace the case study method in a way which simply puts new wine in old bottles. This approach entails selecting stratified statistical samples, and using detailed secondary source data to construct each case study. Such is the method recently advocated by Oughton (1985) and Davies (1985) in a proposed study of UK multinational enterprises. What is proposed here is much more radical. It advocates using primary source data gathered in the field as the main basis for analysis. The collection of such data is not guided by the conventional canons of statistical sampling, but by the more subtle promptings of theoretical sampling. Thus what will be looked at in the field is determined by what has been examined so far, and by the shape of an evolving theory. The case study method so conceived does not advocate any theory; rather it generates and validates theories.

4

The structural modelling approach

4.1 INTRODUCTION

We have already seen in the discussion of structure–conduct–performance models that the drift in the advanced literature on industrial organization is to regard any single behavioural relationship (e.g. the advertising–profitability one) as but part of a larger set of behavioural relationships. Usually this makes sense in an *a priori* context, for few economic relationships are simple. One must take account of simultaneity, and the pattern of causality. Further, each relationship itself might have a more complex form than the linear variety one would like to adopt as the simplest hypothesis available. Non-linearities might take unusual forms; as well as the more obvious examples of higher-order terms, there could be 'on–off' and 'threshold' types of non-linearity. This is all to say that a satisfactory model in industrial organization should ideally be expressed in terms of a set of non-linear simultaneous equations. However, this is clearly to set very high standards for the investigator.

At the one extreme one finds model building of the most naïve sort, involving bivariate correlations between what are regarded as two 'key' variables. At the other, one finds a model of an industry embedded in a much larger, highly disaggregated, economy-wide model. The former approach ignores causality, simultaneity, functional form, and much more besides. Except for performing exploratory data analyses, such procedures have no place in modern investigations into aspects of industrial organization. The latter approach is too ambitious for specific purposes such as those of concern to the industrial economist. There is a pragmatic intermediate course of action, such as is currently being pursued in some of the literature, which takes seriously the issue of setting up an appropriate simultaneous equations (structural) model of the industry, but stops short of investigating *all* the linkages that the industry has with the rest of the economy. Where one draws the dividing line is unclear, and differs, no doubt, from one case to the next. However, one is comforted by the widespread finding amongst model builders that an industry model developed independently of a larger economy-wide model usually is very easily integrated at a later stage into the larger model, without the need for substantial respecification.

Phillips (1976), in a far-reaching critique of structure–conduct–performance models of the sort discussed in the early part of chapter 2, focused on: the lack of sound behavioural theory; the poor quality of the data and their imperfect correspondence with theoretical categories; and, above all, the inadequacy of econometric methods. His position was that policy would be best guided by case study methods of the sort explored in chapter 3, until industrial economists became willing and able to set up statistically identifiable simultaneous equation models. This attitude was echoed by Hart and Morgan (1977) who were also concerned with discovering what policy guides could be derived from appropriate econometric work on the industry. Even if a suitable simultaneous equation model were set up, with adequate statistical attributes, they were cautious about what could be concluded from average relationships of the sort these methods give rise to. Hart and Morgan (1977, p. 118) remained convinced that even with substantial advances in econometric modelling, it would still be necessary to engage in detailed analysis of specific industry effects, saying 'such case studies are labour-intensive and hence unfashionable, but they will probably provide more reliable information than regression analysis'. It is not now our intention in this chapter to destroy the foundations of the methods expounded in the previous chapter. Structural modelling is an approach which can coexist with the case study method, and typically its theoretical basis will be different. The former has an emphasis on *a priori* specification, and the latter is more inductive or 'grounded'; both have their place.

Let us take as our starting point, therefore, the position that the structural modelling approach is worth pursuing. One must then seek guidance on how to go about the activity. In recent years the favourable attitude to structural modelling that had once been the exclusive preserve of the econometrician has been taken on board by industrial economists. Representative of this new approach is the work of Gabel (1979), which reports on a structural model of the US petroleum refining industry. His position appeals to the views of Weiss (1969) and Almarin Phillips that large-scale cross-sectional industry studies of the sort reported on in chapter 2 should give way to time series studies of a more detailed sort, directed at individual industries. Gabel argues for the use of identifiable, dynamic, simultaneous equations models of individual industries. This focus on industry-specific responses, it is claimed, is more satisfactory both from a policy standpoint – for most policy problems at the microeconomic level are directed at individual industries – and from a scientific standpoint. The latter is our major concern here. Gabel (1979) specifies a five-equation dynamic simultaneous equations model with the following endogenous variables: the number of refineries; the Herfindahl index; the annual percentage change in refinery capacity; refinery capacity utilization; and the percentage mark-up on total production cost. Exogenous variables included: minimum efficient scale; sales; and the mix between refining and production. Two- and three-stage least squares simultaneous equations estimates are reported upon, and it is interesting to note that the profitability–concentration relationship, which is normally quite robust in cross-sectional studies, does not emerge as significant in any test applied to this time series model. Gabel (1979, p. 90) also argues against using reduced form methods, saying that 'when simultaneity is acknowledged, one must acknowledge that single-equation, semi-reduced form coefficients indicate only partial effects – total derivatives relating endogenous and exogenous variables will be different in magnitude and possibly even sign'. As an example, he contrasts the following partial and total derivatives:

$$\partial(MKP)/\partial(MES) = 8.39$$
$$\mathrm{d}(MKP)/\mathrm{d}(MES) = 7.90$$

where *MKP* is the percentage mark-up on production cost and *MES* is minimum efficient scale. The difference is not dramatic, but is clearly illustrative of Gabel's point. Actually the issue of whether to choose a structural form or a reduced form is more complicated than this single point indicates.

We have seen in chapter 2 that Cowling (1976) argued in favour of single-equation ordinary least squares estimation, because lag structures were claimed to be such that simultaneous equations systems, if they did exist, were likely to be recursive. For such systems, no bias arises in the application of ordinary least squares to each equation in turn. Such systems exhibit exclusively one-way causation and are exactly identified. Thus it is always possible to infer structural coefficients from reduced form coefficients. In a strict sense recursiveness is associated with a lack of simultaneity – here interpreted as a lack of *mutual* causality. Strotz (1960) argued that simultaneity, in the sense of mutual causation, was often imposed on models out of convenience. Such models were, properly speaking, the equilibrium analogues of dynamic disequilibrium systems. Recursive modelling is thus particularly appropriate to disequilibrium systems. Unfortunately, theories of industrial organization are rarely specified in disequilibrium form, though in chapter 6 on the Austrian revival an important exception to this will be noted. But worse, even when they *are*, the systems implied are either too vaguely specified to be capable of empirical implementation, or else so complex that they are only amenable to simulation methods, along lines particularly associated with Nelson and Winter (1982).

Sawyer (1982) has favoured the use of single-equation or reduced form estimation for quite different reasons, his emphasis being on equilibrium rather than disequilibrium states. His analysis also has important implications for the *a priori* specification of models in industrial organization. Sawyer's view is that too often alternative and conflicting theories are appealed to in specifying equations. Thus the variables used and the functional form adopted are more a reflection of a literature search rather than a coherent theory.

Sawyer looks at three modelling possibilities: heterogeneous oligopoly as expounded by Cowling and Waterson (1976); oligopoly with advertising as expounded by Martin (1979); and dynamic limit pricing as expounded by Encaoua and Jacquemin (1980). Using the Cowling–Waterson (1976) model of differentiated oligopoly, the optimizing conditions of the model lead, as noted in chapter 2, to a relationship between the price–cost margin as the dependent variable, with elasticities and a conjectural term as independent variables. In this model, barriers to entry variables such as economies of scale and advertising intensity should *not* appear, whereas factors influencing elasticities (e.g. import penetration, export/sales ratio, growth rate) should appear. To include both sets of variables is, in Sawyer's view, both inconsistent and incoherent. Using a model of advertising oligopolists, first-order conditions for profit maximization lead (Sawyer, 1982, p. 300) to equations of the form

$$M = f(A/S, CR, \mathbf{Z})$$
$$A/S = g(M, CR, \mathbf{Z})$$

where M is the price–cost margin, CR is a concentration ratio, A/S is the advertising/sales ratio, and $\mathbf{Z}$ is a vector of exogenous variables. Now Sawyer points out that as the vector $\mathbf{Z}$ is common to the functions $f(\cdot)$ and $g(\cdot)$, the system is not identified. He concludes that either there is no simultaneous equation problem, or, if there is, it consists of an intractable lack of identification. The above first-order conditions have no causal interpretation in his view, so no appeal can be made to a recursive model. Both M and A/S are clearly jointly determined, so the application of ordinary least squares to $f(\cdot)$ and $g(\cdot)$, possibly using linearized approximations to these functions, would be inappropriate. What Sawyer suggests is solving the above to get the reduced form

$$M = h(CR, \mathbf{Z})$$
$$A/S = i(CR, \mathbf{Z})$$

and then applying ordinary least squares to these equations. Finally, Sawyer looks at a dynamic generalization of the k-firm cartel model first introduced in static terms in chapter 2. In a variant due to Encaoua and Jacquemin (1980) the maximum problem is

$$\max V = \int_0^\infty e^{-rt} \{ [F(p, S) - q_c] [p - c] - S \} dt$$
$$\text{subject to} \quad \dot{q}_c = R(p, S, q_c)$$

where demand is $q = F(p, S)$, S is sales promotion, and q_c is the size of the fringe. The control variables are p and S, and q_c is the state variable. Using the maximum principle, it can be shown that on the path to the stationary state the price–cost margin is related to the level of concentration and to the ratio of sales promotion to sales revenue. This is a direct generalization of the static optimality conditions referred to earlier. Actually, in the stationary state, three equations characterize the optimum. It would be possible to solve these in terms of three variables, though in this case there are no unique choices for endogenous variables. Sawyer's critique may be summarized by three points. Firstly, many simultaneous equations models developed by industrial economists have no coherent theory. Secondly, those approaches which are coherent lead to equations for estimation which are highly non-linear. These are typically non-linear first-order conditions for maximizing some form of net revenue function. Thirdly, in his view, the simultaneous equation approach should not be pursued: either because it is not implied by the model; or because reduced form estimation will suffice.

Whilst the first two points have some force, the third is more contentious. A model of even a moderate degree of complexity typically will involve several equations, so this is a problem that must be tackled. If, for a simultaneous system, lack of identifiability is indeed as pervasive as Sawyer suggests, then reduced form estimation is not appropriate, as there is then no way of going uniquely from the reduced form estimates to the structural equation estimates. He is able to reject causality, because his systems of equations generally involve equilibrium conditions, with no account given of processes of adjustment. Once such factors are considered (e.g. inventory adjustment) the implied lag structure makes a causal interpretation more reasonable. This, however, need not go so far as in recursive modelling. Ultimately, even if all equations in a structural model involve contemporaneous variables, and one has no clear notion of causality, there is some merit in using simultaneous equation estimation. Referring back to Sawyer's advertising–concentration example, one might write the structural equations as

$$\phi(M, A/S, CR, Z_1) = \varepsilon_1$$
$$\psi(M, A/S, CR, Z_2) = \varepsilon_2$$

where ε_1 and ε_2 are appropriately well-behaved random variables, and Z_1 and Z_2 are vectors of at least partially distinct sets of exogenous variables. Identifiability (typically *over*-identifiability) is achieved here by the introduction of additional exogenous variables. Typically, the functions ϕ and ψ will be approximated in a local way by linear functions, but in these days of advanced econometric packages capable of non-linear estimation this is by no means strictly necessary. The appearance of the random variables ε_1 and ε_2 might be regarded as reflecting inaccuracies on the part of economic agents in fulfilling the optimality conditions embodied in $\phi(\cdot)$ and $\psi(\cdot)$. It should be noted that in terms of a simultaneous equations model derived from an optimizing framework there is no reason why the functions ϕ and ψ should emerge from the solution to the same optimizing problem; hence the legitimacy of introducing variables in ϕ which do not appear in ψ.

Many notable attempts at structural modelling in industrial organization use cross-section data. Examples include Intriligator (1978), Intriligator et al. (1975), Strickland and Weiss (1976), Golbe (1986), Lunn (1986), Pagoulatos and Sorensen (1981), and Chou (1984). However, here we favour the application of structural modelling to the industry using time series data, as proposed by Gabel (1979). In doing so, our enthusiasm for this approach is by no means novel. It has been used by econometricians for decades. Unfortunately, only recently has an awareness of this work penetrated the consciousness of the typical industrial economist.

This approach is based on eight important principles:

1   The object of analysis is the industry. Industry-specific analysis typically involves using time series data, but the pooling of time series and cross-section data has more recently become a feasible proposition given the availability of detailed intra-industry data (e.g. on company accounts).

2   Leading on from 1, aggregation must be taken seriously. Thus an explicit procedure for moving from firm-level to industry-level conduct must be devised.

3   Explicit behavioural postulates must be adopted about the firm's behaviour. Typically this will involve some sort of maximizing behaviour, but bureaucratic and satisficing modes of behaviour are two of the alternative possibilities.

4   Functional form must be taken seriously. In empirical modelling general functional relationships subject to loose qualitative restrictions are not useful: explicit functions must be utilized. Going hand in hand with this, one requires explicit measures of theoretical concepts (e.g. profitability, concentration).

5   Dynamics must be taken seriously, which will usually entail some consideration of disequilibrium adjustment.

6   The formation of expectations, and attitudes to risk, should be explicitly considered.

7   Stochastic specification should be regarded as an integral part of the model building process.

8   Finally, simultaneous equation estimation techniques should be applied to the model adopted.

Even today, very few studies adhere to the demanding requirements of these eight principles. By and large one must refer to the econometrician, rather than the industrial economist, in seeking examples of this rigorous methodology. It turns out to be the case that a remarkable attempt to meet these standards has been available — largely unrecognized by industrial economists — for over thirty years in the shape of the work by Klein (1950). There, a rigorous microeconomic theory of the firm is developed leading, via an appropriate aggregation procedure, to a set of stochastic equations which are estimable and provide a statistical representation of the industry. The approach is that of the econo-metrician – but it would do well to be that of the specialist in industrial organization.

4.2   AN ECONOMETRICIAN'S VIEW OF THE FIRM AND THE INDUSTRY

The starting point of Klein's approach is that entrepreneurs maximize antici-pated profits. The operator 'an' is introduced to convey the sense of an antici-pated variable. It would be possible to be more mathematically precise than this and introduce the mathematical expectations operator E, and talk about expected profit $E(\Pi)$ rather than anticipated profit an(Π). However, this gain in precision is bought at the cost of strengthening the assumptions of the model, for now it is necessary to postulate a probability density function $\phi(\Pi)$ for the distribution of profit. Adopting an anticipated profit maximization formulation, the objective of the firm can be stated as being the maximization of a finite horizon discounted profit integral of the following sort:

$$
\text{an}(\Pi) = \int_0^T \{ \text{an}[p(x - \dot{h})] - \text{an}(wn) - \text{an}(q\varkappa)
$$
$$
+ \frac{\text{d}[\text{an}(ph)]}{\text{d}t} - \delta(h, \varepsilon) \} \, e^{-\rho t} \, \text{d}t \tag{4.1}
$$

The symbols have the following meaning: Π is profit, p is output price, x is output, h is inventories (and a dot above this symbol indicates a time derivative), $x - \dot{h}$ is sales, w is the wage rate, n is labour hours, q is the price of capital services, $\varkappa$ is capital hours, δ is the storage cost of inventories, ε is a random disturbance, T is the planning horizon, and ρ is a risk-adjusted interest rate. Regarding equation (4.1) as a function of n, $\varkappa$, and h, the demand functions for labour, fixed capital, and inventories can be derived from standard maximization theory. The explicit dependence of (4.1) on output is removed by substitution into it of the production function relationship

$$
x = f(n, \varkappa, t, v) \tag{4.2}
$$

where t is time (representing technical change and other dynamic factors) and v is a stochastic disturbance term. In the case of perfect competition, the terms p, w, q, and ρ can be regarded as given, in which case the factor demand equations have the form

$$
\frac{\partial x}{\partial n} = \text{an}\left(\frac{w}{p}\right) \qquad \frac{\partial x}{\partial \varkappa} = \text{an}\left(\frac{q}{p}\right) \qquad \frac{\partial [\delta(h, \varepsilon)]}{\partial h} = \text{an}(\dot{p}) \tag{4.3}
$$

Diminishing marginal productivities for factors $\varkappa$ and n are assumed, and so is an increasing marginal cost of storage. Capital hours is assumed to depend on current and lagged values of gross investment v and a disturbance term μ:

$$x = g(v, v_{-1}, v_{-2}, \ldots, \mu) \tag{4.4}$$

Were we to assume instead that the firm faces a downward-sloping demand curve having an elasticity of η, the factor demand equations of (4.3) would be modified to

$$\frac{\partial x}{\partial n} = \text{an}\left[\frac{w}{p(1 - 1/\eta)}\right] \qquad \frac{\partial x}{\partial \varkappa} = \text{an}\left[\frac{q}{p(1 - 1/\eta)}\right] \tag{4.5}$$

So far no mention has been made of estimation, and the theory has been formulated in very general terms. In order to put the theory into a form which makes econometric analysis possible, functions have to be given explicit expression, and a method of handling unmeasurable variables like an(Π) must be devised. Typically one adopts an explicit functional form which is linear in the variables in question, or can be transformed into such a linear relationship. There are many ways in which one could proceed in order to develop appropriate proxy variables for anticipated magnitudes. A simple operational device which Klein (1950) uses extensively is to express anticipated variables as functions of lagged values of the actual variables to which the anticipations refer. Suppose that the production function, the capital hours function, and the storage cost function have the following forms:

$$x = An^{\alpha_1} \varkappa^{\alpha_2} e^{\alpha_3 t + \alpha_4 t^2} v \tag{4.6a}$$
$$\varkappa = \beta_1 + \beta_2 k_{-1} + \beta_3 v + \mu \tag{4.6b}$$
$$\delta(h, \varepsilon) = \gamma_1 + \gamma_2 h + \gamma_3 h^2 + \varepsilon \tag{4.6c}$$

where A and the α, β and γ terms are parameters, and v, μ, ε are disturbances. Here k_{-1} is fixed capital at the end of a period prior to the planning period; it is related to net investment i by

$$k_t = \int_{-\infty}^{t} i(\tau) d\tau \tag{4.7}$$

Assuming perfect competition, the factor demand equations for the system of equations (4.6a)–(4.6c) may be written

$$\frac{\partial x}{\partial n} = \alpha_1 \frac{x}{n} = \text{an}\left(\frac{w}{p}\right) \tag{4.8a}$$

$$\frac{\partial x}{\partial \varkappa} = \alpha_2 \frac{x}{\beta_1 + \beta_2 k_{-1} + \beta_3 v + \mu} = \text{an}\left(\frac{q}{p}\right) \tag{4.8b}$$

with the marginal storage cost equation being

$$\frac{\partial [\delta(h, \varepsilon)]}{\partial h} = \gamma_2 + 2\gamma_3 h = \text{an}(\dot{p}) \tag{4.8c}$$

By simple rearrangement, (4.8a)–(4.8c) can be expressed as

$$\text{an}(wn) = \alpha_1 \text{an}(px) \tag{4.9}$$

$$\text{an}\left(\frac{px}{q}\right) = \beta_1' + \beta_2' k_{-1} + \beta_3' v + \frac{\mu}{\alpha_2} \tag{4.10}$$

where $\beta_i' = \beta_i / \alpha_2$, and

$$h = -\frac{\gamma_2}{2\gamma_3} + \frac{1}{2\gamma_3} \text{an}(\dot{p}) \tag{4.11}$$

Two tasks now remain if (4.9) to (4.11) are to be suitable for econometric estimation. Firstly, an appropriately specified lag structure must be found for determining the anticipated variables. Secondly, these relations, which refer to the single firm, must be aggregated across firms.

Concerning lag structure, the terms $\text{an}(px)$, $\text{an}(px/q)$ and $\text{an}(\dot{p})$ of equations (4.9), (4.10), and (4.11) can most simply be modelled as linear functions of the actual (as distinct from anticipated) variables in current and lagged form, plus a disturbance term. Thus we can now write

$$wn = \alpha_1' + \alpha_2'(px) + \alpha_3'(px)_{-1} + \varepsilon_1 \tag{4.12}$$

$$v = \beta_1'' + \beta_2''(px/q) + \beta_3''(px/q)_{-1} + \beta_4'' k_{-1} + \varepsilon_2 \tag{4.13}$$

$$h = \gamma_1' + \gamma_2' \Delta p + \gamma_3' \Delta p_{-1} + \varepsilon_3 \tag{4.14}$$

In deriving (4.12) to (4.14) we have set $\text{an}(wn) = wn$ and regarded $\Delta p = p - p_{-1}$ as the empirical counterpart of $\text{an}(\dot{p})$. The coefficients α_i', β_j'', and γ_k' are of course equal to products and quotients of coefficients, and the disturbance terms ε_1 are likewise modified from their original form. This system of equations relates to an individual firm, whereas typically, in industrial organization, data are presented to the investigator in aggregate industry-level form. An appropriate procedure is therefore required to move from the firm to the industry level.

Fortunately the linear specification above greatly simplifies the process of aggregation. In the simplest case, where all variables are measured in the same units, the aggregated relation is a linear relationship in variables which are sums of the micro-variables, where the coefficients are weighted averages of the micro-coefficients. If the variables of the micro relationship have different units of measurement, we must perforce use indices for the macro-variables. Fortunately, Klein (1950, p. 20) provides evidence that this is an empirically satisfactory procedure.

Proceeding to aggregate (4.12)–(4.14) from the firm to the industry level, we get

$$W = \alpha_1'' + \alpha_2'' PX + \alpha_3''(PX)_{-1} + \varepsilon_4 \tag{4.15}$$

$$V = \beta_1''' + \beta_2'''(PX/Q) + \beta_3'''(PX/Q)_{-1} + \beta_4''' K_{-1} + \varepsilon_5 \tag{4.16}$$

$$H = \gamma_1' + \gamma_2'' \Delta P + \gamma_3'' \, ' \Delta P_{-1} + \varepsilon_6 \qquad (4.17)$$

The symbols for the aggregated variables have the following interpretation: W is the industry's wage bill; PX is the value of output in the industry; V is the industry's gross real investment; K is the real value of capital stock in the industry and H its real stock of inventories; Q is an industry price index for capital goods; and P is a price index for the output of the industry.

A few remarks on the system of equations (4.15) to (4.17) are in order. This is really a partial 'reduced form' rather than the full structural model. We have, by a process of substitution, eliminated the profit equation and the marginal productivity equations. Some substitution was necessary in order to develop suitable proxies for the anticipated variables; no data are generally available on the storage cost of inventories δ, and hence this variable has been eliminated from the system; and so on. In the context of a particular study one may wish to set a limit to the extent to which equations are eliminated from the full structural system. Eliminating equations reduces the amount of information, and this should only proceed as far as is compatible with the aims of the study. The interpretation of a partial reduced form can also be troublesome, as it is several steps removed from the familiar *a priori* conceptions that one incorporates in the structural model. The linear form of the equations, which we have already mentioned as facilitating aggregation, is also of great convenience when it comes to statistical estimation.

The economic theory which led to the formulation of the system (4.15) to (4.17) was of the simplest sort, assuming as it did perfect competition in both goods and factor markets. There are several ways in which this treatment can be extended in the direction of greater realism, without detriment to the formulation of a model suitable for statistical estimation. Rather than assume that firms face an infinitely elastic demand curve, one can assume a curve of finite elasticity η. When it comes to the selection of a specific functional form, the constant elasticities demand curve has found much favour in practice. One might in addition consider the possibility of the firm making capital gains from inventory speculation – a matter to be seriously considered if the firm has a price-setting capability. Klein (1950, pp. 24–5) has shown that this leads to a problem in the calculus of variations because both time derivatives and levels of variables appear under the profit integral. The solution to such a variational problem leads, after a process of elimination of equations, to a set of relationships somewhat similar to (4.15) to (4.17). They do, however, entail the additional complexity of involving ρ, the discount rate. This poses a problem for estimation, as satisfactory data on ρ are hard to obtain. If ρ is itself permitted to vary, the formulation becomes yet more complex. Kalecki (1937) propounded 'the principle of increasing risk', according to which the risk of asset loss increases as the amount borrowed for expansion increases, relative to the size of the firm. Klein has investigated the way in which this principle can be incorporated into a structural model and found that its main consequence was to introduce into the system a new variable, the value of current assets minus current liabilities, though it should be added that the form of the structural equations was also altered.

So far, attention has been confined to traditional models of profit maximization. In our discussion of structure, conduct, and performance in chapter 2, we saw that this still remains the most widely adopted conduct assumption, though it can take many forms. However, as later chapters will confirm, there are many alternative view of the firm that one might adopt. Various forms of utility maximizing conduct, entrepreneurial behaviour, and satisficing are possible. Though little attempt has been made in the literature to derive the corresponding structural equations for estimation, this is a failure on the part of theorists and industrial economists, rather than an intrinsic weakness of alternative theories of the firm.

A very general utility maximizing framework postulates that the preferences of the firm are defined over different types of assets and profit. Following Klein (1950, pp. 27–32), an anticipated utility functional over the time horizon $(0, T)$ can be defined, having as its arguments anticipated profit an(Π), capital k, inventories h, cash balances m, and the net value of securities s:

$$\mathrm{an}(u) = u \begin{bmatrix} T & T & T & T & T \\ \mathrm{an}(\Pi), & k, & h, & m, & s \\ 0 & 0 & 0 & 0 & 0 \end{bmatrix} \tag{4.18}$$

The firm can then be assumed to maximize this utility functional subject to a number of constraints, including balance sheet constraints (e.g. previous period's assets + interest + earnings = current period's assets). An obvious refinement of equation (4.18), when referring to the corporate sector, would be to decompose profits into corporate savings and dividends. The detailed procedure by which a simplified variant of (4.18) is maximized will not be considered here, and the reader is referred to Klein (1950, pp. 27–32) for the full process. He develops, for the firm, a set of eight equations which are to be regarded as structural demand equations. The analogy with the system of consumer demand equations is complete. When aggregated across firms, industry-level equations may be obtained which explain anticipated profits, labour hours, capital hours, net investment, the stock of real capital, cash balances, the net value of securities, and the aggregate stock of real inventories in terms of the same list of variables: price, lagged price, the wage, the price of capital, the rate of interest, and initial values of the 'stock' variables of capital, cash balances, and securities. Expressed in this way we have a set of conditions similar, in a logical sense, to those derived by Sawyer (1982) for a variety of optimizing frameworks. By contrast, Klein (1950, p. 32) does not regard such a system as hopelessly unidentifiable:

All the market variables need not appear in each equation. Some may be more sensitive than others to changes in wages or prices. In one equation lags may be of higher order than another; even higher-order lags than we have written may appear for some of the variables. We can tell the quantitative importance of the general variables in particular equations only after we have examined the relevant data. Only a few of the variables will appear in any single equation.

So far, emphasis has been on starting from an extended neoclassical profit function, and thus proceeding to a set of structural equations. However, this is not the only possible approach to adopt in constructing structural models of industrial organization. Another possible approach is to concentrate on entre-preneurial behaviour. The detailed possibilities that may emerge from this will be explored more fully in chapter 6. Here we will look at the simple hypothesis that investment is a non-decreasing function of anticipated profit. This is to postulate an elementary rule of entrepreneurial conduct, namely that when expectations of profit are low, firm size will be contracted, and when high, firm size will be increased. Thus investment is an increasing function of anticipated profits. (A variant of this would make investment dependent on *rates* of profit rather than *levels* of profit.) Such intuitively appealing rules make sense if the firm is conceived of as being adjusted in size by the entrepreneur to achieve the largest profit possible, consistent with the market rate of return. If anticipated rate of return is an(ρ), the size of fixed capital k, and the anticipated profit an(Π), then

$$\text{an}(\Pi) = \text{an}(\rho)k \qquad (4.19)$$

Now this relationship leads to indeterminacy because, given that firm size as measured by k can be freely varied, anticipated profit is unbounded. By appealing to Kalecki's (1937) principle of increasing risk, this indeterminacy can be removed. The anticipated profit function can be modified from (4.19) to the form

$$\text{an}(\Pi) = \text{an}(\rho)k - f(i) \qquad (4.20)$$

where $f(i)$ is convex and monotonically increasing in investment i. Kalecki's principle is embodied in the specification of the risk function $f(i)$. Maximiza-tion of (4.20) leads, by an appropriate choice of functional forms, to an invest-ment function which is linear in the current and previous period's rate of return on capital. If risk were made to depend not only on investment but also on the value of the stock of liquid assets, the latter variable would also appear in the investment function.

Finally, rather than adopting maximizing assumptions (be it maximization of profit, utility, risk-adjusted profit, or whatever) it might be more realistic in behavioural terms to consider rules of thumb. Klein (1950) considers two ostensible rules of thumb, but is inclined to regard both as approximations to an appropriate profit maximizing rule. The first is the 'rule' that entrepreneurs set price at a mark-up on average variable cost, and sell all they can at that price. If average variable cost AVC is constant (and much empirical evidence suggests that it *is*) then the 'optimal' mark-up is equal to $AVC/(1 - 1/\eta)$, where η is the elasticity of demand. It should be said that the adoption of a mark-up rule *per se* by a firm does not in itself imply an 'optimal' mark-up determined according to this formula. The second rule of thumb is that businessmen set aside a certain proportion of the value of output to meet the wage bill. If the firm produces according to a Cobb–Douglas technology, then profit maximization under perfectly competitive assumptions implies an optimal wage bill which is related to the value of output by a proportionality factor. The rule of thumb, for an appropriate choice of proportionality factor, becomes equivalent to profit maximization. Of course, one could take another line in remarking on rules of thumb, rather than adopting the above 'revisionist' interpretation. Once one takes into account ignorance, uncertainty, limited cognitive ability, etc., it may be that rules of thumb are sensible, but yet are not in any sense approximations to profit maximizing conduct. Such issues will not be pursued here, but will be left for consideration until chapter 9.

4.3   AN EXAMPLE OF STRUCTURAL MODELLING IN INDUSTRIAL ORGANIZATION

There are many examples available of structural modelling in industrial organization, including contributions by Chou (1984), Lunn (1986), Pagoulatos and Sorensen (1981), Gabel (1979), Golbe (1986), and Schroeter (1983). However, these studies appear *ad hoc* in comparison with a number of classical econometric works. For this section, we have chosen to illustrate the method of 'industrial econometrics' by reference to an example, due to Tsurumi (1969), which is concerned with modelling the US automobile industry. The general structure of the model is illustrated by the schema of figure 4.1, which is based on Tsurumi (1969, p. 53).

Tsurumi's model is one of oligopolistic interdependence between five firms: the price leader, General Motors; two others making up with GM the 'Big Three', Ford and Chrysler; and the small independents, American Motors and Studebaker. A simultaneous equation model was set up for each company, each one including the following relationships: distinct demand functions for cars, buses, and trucks; capacity production functions; investment functions; labour requirement functions; price determination functions; wage rate determination functions; cost functions; target profit, profit, and dividend functions; tax functions; and industrial aggregation relationships. Each company was described by 30 equations, implying a complete structural model of the US

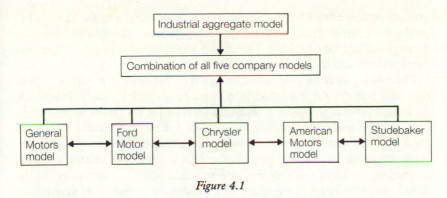

Figure 4.1

automobile industry composed of 150 equations. Two-stage least squares estimators were obtained for this model using annual data from 1947 to 1965.

The demand for GM's cars was assumed to be determined by the price of GM cars relative to rivals' prices (as measured by a price index), an increment in advertising expenditure, and the rivals' market share. The demand for cars produced by the other oligopolists was assumed, in each case, to depend upon the expected relative price, the actual relative price of the previous period, the rivals' market share, real income, and, in certain cases, advertising expenditures. Expected price was modelled using a partial adjustment mechanism. Thus a principal difference between the demand function of General Motors, as compared with that of its rivals, was that for GM, the price leader, there was no discrepancy between desired and actual price. For the larger firms, desired price elasticities of demand tended to be higher than for smaller firms, with the GM elasticity being greatest in absolute value. This implies that, should price cutting by rivals occur, GM would have more leverage in regaining demand were it to match rivals' prices. The strength of this potential retaliatory action would buttress GM's price leadership.

Capacity production functions were introduced for GM, Ford, and Studebaker. Capacity production was made a linear function of last year's capital stock. The investment functions were hybrids of a modified accelerator principle and a profit principle. A typical investment function made investment dependent on desired demand, profit, and lagged investment. Price determination by the leader, General Motors, was based on a target rate of profit principle. The desired level of net profits after taxes was at a fixed percentage of net worth (20 per cent in this case), which implied setting a price which was a mark-up on the ratio of the payroll to output. This target profit principle is akin to Baumol's (1958) constrained sales revenue maximization hypothesis. It was found that the larger the rivals' market share the higher was its cross-price elasticity of demand. Larger companies are apparently more sensitive to price differentials. On the labour market side, labour requirements were given by a production function. The price leader, General Motors, was also assumed to be the wage leader. Dividend functions were specified in a fashion suggested by the work of Lintner (1956). The model was completed by simple cost and tax functions, and industrial aggregation relationships.

The model clearly has descriptive uses; it is in that sense an elaborate form of economic history. But more than this, it can be used for simulation exercises. Tsurumi (1969) reports on a forecasting exercise for his model from 1966 to 1969. In the study, the entire 150-equation system was divided into three blocks. In the first, exogenous variables were fixed. In the second block – market determination – variables such as prices, production of cars, etc. were determined simultaneously by the interactions of the five companies. In the third block – company – variables such as labour and costs were determined in terms of the behaviour of each company. The inequality coefficients were computed to test the simulation in a controlled way over the sample period, and were found to be satisfactory. The forecasting exercise for 1966–69 predicted no major shift in market shares for these (then) four existing automobile companies. These predictions were reasonable in 1966 and 1967. Less successful were the predictions which overestimated production levels for all companies. These in turn could be attributed to an overestimate of production for the industrial aggregates.

However, perhaps more impressive than the forecasts as such is the great inspiration that this exercise provides for industrial econometrics. It meets many of the criteria laid down earlier in this chapter for structural modelling in industrial organization. It is a sobering thought that, seventeen years after its development, this 150-equation model should still seem awesome in its scope and detail compared with many models developed by industrial economists today.

4.4 CONCLUSION

Most of the structure–conduct–performance modelling developed in chapter 2 was concerned with inter-industry analysis. By contrast, the approach here is concerned with intra-industry analysis – with the analysis of the industry as composed of a set of firms. The programme for research in this area of industrial economics is well defined, but underdeveloped. However, with the richness of today's data banks, the power of contemporary supercomputers, and the better understanding on the part of economic theorists of how to formulate models of the industry in a form which may be empirically implemented – with all these factors being most auspicious – it is perhaps reasonable to predict that from now on the star of industrial econometrics will be in the ascendancy. (A significant step in the right direction is the 'micro to macro' modelling of Goudie and Meeks, 1985.)

Part III
Rival Approaches

5

The Marshallian tradition

5.1 INTRODUCTION

We introduce this third part of the book, on rival approaches, by considering aspects of the work of the founder of industrial organization, Alfred Marshall. For insight into how Marshall came to formulate his position, see Pigou (ed.) (1925). It used to be said with reverence that 'it is all in Marshall', but with the passage of a century this phrase would no longer meet with the approval of all industrial economists. Slowly, Marshallian methods have had a lesser influence on mainstream industrial organization, though many of his technical devices are in universal use. But Marshall was much more than the inventor of elasticity, the theory of joint production, and so on. He made a distinctive contribution to industrial organization which offers important perspectives on the subject. This view has been fostered by writers such as Andrews (1951), Robertson (1959), Richardson (1960), Wolfe (1964) and Loasby (1978), and the purpose of this chapter is to amplify their mutual standpoint.

The point of departure is with what went wrong. This is associated with the celebrated simplification of Marshall's analysis of the industry and the firm by Viner (1931). We then examine a more refined and sympathetic view of Marshall due to Andrews (1951), which focuses on the essential attributes of 'free competition'. We turn our attention next to the opposite end of the spectrum – to monopoly analysis, a Marshallian theme which has been neglected but is illuminating from a regulatory perspective. This is followed by an examination of the extended Marshallian analysis of the industry in the Frisch–Blaug tradition. Finally, a particularly important theme is treated – the analysis of industry equilibrium in statistical or biological terms.

In his *Economics of Industry* Marshall first put forward his biological and evolutionary views of the development of firms. He made an analogy between industrial organization and the physical organization of higher animals. He talked of the struggle for survival in which firms engaged. All this is relatively crude, though undoubtedly suggestive. His more refined analysis of the

Principles emphasized the life cycle of the firm and the biological nature of industry equilibrium. This approach has influenced writers on the theory of the growth of the firm, like Penrose (1952), but our emphasis will be on those who drew the implication from Marshall's analysis that what is required is a theory of statistical (rather than deterministic) equilibrium at the industry level.

Some Marshallian themes of importance are, regrettably, passed over. Thus his analysis of joint production, which has been influential in the formulation of the distinction between economies of scale and economies of scope in contestability theory (see chapter 8) is neglected. Further, his significant contribution to the development of a managerial theory of the firm (see chapter 9) is ignored. Miyazaki (1982, 1984) has more recently explored this territory. This is all to suggest that the Marshallian tradition is not yet exhausted, and offers a fuller research agenda than this chapter alone can describe.

5.2   VINER'S STYLIZATION OF MARSHALL

Viner (1931) is regarded as having provided the economics profession with what is widely accepted as a convenient encapsulation of Marshall. Every student who undertakes a conventional training in economics is initiated into the ritual of Viner's charts. Somewhere along the line a passing reference to Alfred Marshall is made, and in this way a bowdlerized version of Viner becomes regarded as 'the Marshallian tradition'. The devices of Viner are themselves of considerable merit but have suffered from having been over-simplified in the subsequent literature. However, as we shall argue here, even the original version of Viner (1931) seriously misrepresents Marshall, except perhaps in the very final paragraph of that famous article, where Viner writes:

> Long-run equilibrium would apply only to the industry as a whole, and would be a sort of statistical equilibrium between rate of output and rate of consumption. None of the individual producers under this theory need be in long-run equilibrium at any time. At any moment, some producers would be enjoying exceptional profits, and others incurring heavy losses ... There would be ... an equality in rate of withdrawal of producers from the industry through bankruptcy or otherwise, on the one hand, and of entrance of new producers into the industry, on the other hand. A theory of this sort would leave room for pure profits even in a static sense.

In this paragraph Viner came closest to the intention of Marshall, but the article is remembered for what we shall here characterize as a 'stylization of Marshall'. This stylization has three essential features. Firstly, all firms face an infinitely elastic demand curve. Secondly, in characterizing the equilibrium of a typical firm, one has characterized the equilibrium of *any* firm. Thirdly, in long-run equilibrium, every firm has the same average costs. These three conditions will later be contrasted with a more thoroughgoing Marshallian approach, but will in the meantime be used as a point of departure.

Costs are divided into fixed and variable in the short run, with the former being interpreted as a parameter which in principle is continuously variable. Such variations of fixed costs represent different possible choices of the scale of operation. Average variable (or direct) costs are assumed by Viner to be everywhere increasing, though in interpretative texts nowadays a U-shaped form is usually postulated. The good is assumed to be homogeneous, and competition is atomistic, with each producer assuming that variations in his scale of production will have no effect on price. The producer is a profit maximizer, and will set price equal to marginal cost to achieve this. At the selected optimal output the quasi-rent on fixed plant per unit of output will be equal to average fixed costs. This $p = MC$ rule for profit maximization implies that the firm's marginal cost curve is its short-run supply curve. Then short-run industry supply is simply the sum of these individual firms' short-run supply curves. So much is familiar. In the long run, when the scale of operation can be freely varied, all costs become variable, and cost differences between firms will be evened out by appropriate remunerations to those factors which might cause inter-firm variations in efficiency. In long-run equilibrium all firms have the same long-run average cost curves and produce at minimum average cost, at which point price is also equal to marginal cost. It was an equilibrium position such as this which was used as the basis for the discussion of Pareto optimality in chapter 2 on structure, conduct, and performance. It provides a convenient geometrical device for illustrating but one of the many conditions which make up a full Walrasian general equilibrium, but misses a number of important Marshallian nuances.

Let us now return to the three key assumptions. In Viner, the firm faces an infinitely elastic (horizontal) individual demand curve. In Marshall, the individual firm's demand curve is not necessarily horizontal. An infinitely elastic demand curve is a limiting case which he did discuss, and which he did consider important; but is not the generic case. More typically, every firm has a price-setting capability, because of established trade connections with principal customers. This is not quite the same case as that captured by models of product differentiation. There may not be branding or packaging differences between goods coming from the various firms in the industry. Perhaps the simplest way of suggesting Marshall's intentions in a formal sense is by use of a market share model, where each firm's share is determined by the extent of customer loyalty. Thus the ith firm's demand curve is

$$k_i D(p) \qquad 0 < k_i < 1 \qquad \sum_{i=1}^{n} k_i = 1 \qquad\qquad (5.1)$$

where k_i is an index of loyalty, there are n firms in the industry, and $D(p)$ is the industry demand curve. If a dispersion of prices is to be permitted, p could be treated as a vector of n prices rather than a scalar, but this is to complicate matters more than is necessary for the current illustration. Clearly, if there is no reason for customers to be more loyal to one firm than to another, then $k_i = k$ for all i and therefore $nk = 1$ or $k = 1/n$. That is, each firm gets an equal share of $1/n$ of the market. Further, even if the number of firms becomes large, the elasticity of $(1/n) D(p)$ remains unchanged and the limiting infinitely elastic demand case is not achieved. Secondly, consider Viner's device of examining the equilibrium of a typical firm and then imputing this to all other firms. In Marshall, it is not possible to treat any one firm as essentially like the rest, because each firm will generally be at a different point in its life cycle. At one stage in its life cycle a firm may enjoy increasing returns, and at another stage decreasing returns. Neither situation is 'typical', and which is more important depends on the stage of evolution of the firm. Thirdly, let us look at the long-run equilibrium of Viner, in which each firm has identical long-run average costs and is producing at an output where these unit costs are minimized. In Marshall, even in the long run, there remains an 'efficiency distribution' of firms in the industry. Because the industry is made up of an evolving population of firms, there is no tendency for this distribution of efficiency to collapse to a unique long-run value. This Marshallian picture is best viewed in a statistical fashion, as Viner hinted at the very end of his famous article. Steindl (1965) has made the most important contribution in this direction, though earlier (Steindl, 1945) he had been rather critical of the Marshallian view. Later we suggest another approach, due to Newman and Wolfe (1961), for embracing at least more of the complexity of Marshall's concept of long-run equilibrium than did Viner's static analysis.

5.3   ANDREWS'S REINSTATEMENT OF THE MARSHALLIAN FIRM

The partial eclipse of the Marshallian view was due to the writings of a number of influential economists including Robbins (1928), Shove (1930, 1942), and, perhaps most devastatingly, Sraffa (1926, 1930). There was dissatisfaction with the logical tightness of the concept of the representative firm, an uneasiness over the possibility of competitive equilibrium under increasing returns, and, most important of all, dissatisfaction with Marshall's analysis of the equilibrium of the individual firm in relation to the equilibrium of the industry. It was argued that the latter analysis involved a logical flaw: that Marshall's analysis of individual and industry equilibrium was internally inconsistent.

Andrews, in a number of writings in a general sense (for example, Andrews, 1964; Andrews and Brunner, 1975), but most particularly in his 1951 paper 'Industrial analysis in economics – with especial reference to Marshallian doctrine', was the most influential post World War II economist to attempt to reinstate the Marshallian analysis of the industry and the firm. Others were to follow, bringing to bear on the Marshallian analysis both a greater receptivity to his ideas, and the technical equipment necessary to explain to the modern mathematically trained economic theorist the content and further implications of the sophisticated Marshallian theory. Some notable contributions along these lines are the papers by Frisch (1950), Newman (1960), Wolfe (1955), Newman and Wolfe (1961), and Loasby (1978) and the books by Steindl (1945, 1965) and Richardson (1960).

Andrews's view was that it was not necessary in a logical or practical sense to abandon the concept of the industry. Provided the framework of analysis was couched in terms of the long period, within which profitable entry by firms was possible, an internally consistent Marshallian theory could be constructed. There is no pure or perfect competition in Marshall, and his form of competition embraces a variety of market imperfections. The key aspect of Marshallian competition is that a firm, to be competitive with a rival, should be able to produce a good to the same technical specification as its rival's and be able to sell that commodity to the same customers. If some impediments to trade, such as a franchise or patent, prevent these conditions from being satisfied, monopoly is said to exist. Marshall's monopoly analysis is then essentially that of Cournot's. A maximum is determined for the net revenue function using calculus methods, and optimality conditions are expressed in what is essentially a statement of the condition that marginal cost equals marginal revenue (*Principles*, note XXII).

However, Marshall did not regard monopoly as an especially important category of analysis, though as we shall see later he made some significant contributions to the theory of monopoly. In a fashion which is reminiscent of the Austrians and close in theoretical terms to the later contestability literature, Marshall was inclined to argue that it was unlikely that the forces of competition would be sufficiently absent that the simple pure monopoly model would be the appropriate vehicle of analysis. The essential attribute of the competitive market is that some measure of entry should be possible. Marshall's treatment of entry is incomplete but has been filled out by Andrews himself using the following argument. Businesses in the industry should be regarded as having the necessary equipment, knowledge, and experience to be able to direct production to any range of commodities in their market. Andrews proffers the example that the producers of electrical motors might be regarded as constituting an industry and goes on to argue that producers of light electrical products in general might sensibly be regarded as within the same industry. It is for this reason that the possibility of entry is so pervasive in Marshallian competition, for firms within submarkets of a given industry can fairly readily direct their production to other submarkets should it appear profitable to do so.

Unlike the equilibrium attained in the purest of pure competition where all firms end up operating the same plants of the same efficiency, essential to the Marshallian view as we have hinted in section 5.2, is the notion that even in the long run a distribution of efficiency will exist in an industry. In the case of proprietorships or private companies a systematic influence leading to this is the variation in the acumen of a businessman over a lifetime. Further, it was argued that businesses which passed on into family hands would eventually decline, as sons who had been reared in a less demanding environment than their fathers would not display the vigour necessary for business success. In the case of a joint stock company, Marshall saw that the separation of ownership from control implied a more sluggish competitive response from this type of firm, and was aware that the actual demise of a joint stock company was less likely than in the case of a proprietorship. However, the managerial team that organizes a joint stock company is likely to have its own cycle of growth and decline in efficiency, and for this reason too the fortunes of large corporations will vary, with some rising and some declining, some even disappearing, and some being born. In Andrews's interpretation of Marshall the representative firm is taken to be the target towards which entrants to the industry direct their efforts. Marshall in his *Principles* (p. 317) himself defined the representative firm as 'one which has had a fairly long life, and fair success, which is managed with normal ability, and which has normal access to the economies, external and internal, which belong to that value of production'. As we shall see, if we look at a statistical distribution of firms by attributes, the representative firm may be defined as the modal firm. Potential entrants will not know their actual efficiencies until they enter an industry, but, in Andrews's view, will use the efficiency of the representative firm as a benchmark. Thus the long-run supply price will cover the costs of the representative firm with a normal return and provide an inducement for the entry of new firms who hope that in the long term they too can at least aspire to a niche such as that occupied by the representative firm. The long-run supply price for an industry such as that described above will have a determinate relationship with the average costs of firms in the industry, this relationship varying across firms as their efficiencies vary.

Turning now from the industry to the individual firm, it is Andrews's view that Marshall's treatment is rather unsatisfactory. To him, Marshall's analysis of the actual individual firm, rather than the possibly notional representative firm, is unsatisfactory on two counts. Firstly, in its tentative effort to explain an individual firm's short-run equilibrium, it emphasizes the increasing cost case. This is best applied to primary products rather than to manufactured goods. Secondly, it is, strictly speaking, an indeterminate analysis, for Marshall's analysis of the increasing cost case is expressed in terms of the marginal short-run supply of the *industry*, rather than the individual business, and his analysis of the decreasing cost case, as developed in chapter 12 of book V and appendix H of his *Principles*, really side-steps the issue. We are referred back to the life cycle theory of the firm and 'a position of balance or equilibrium between the forces of progress and decay'. It seems that what Andrews had hoped for from Marshall could not be delivered, for the notion of a falling supply curve was essentially dynamic. Indeed, in his appendix H Marshall receives with sympathy the suggestion of a critic that should a new point further along a falling supply curve be achieved, the form of the supply curve for lesser levels of output would no longer represent accurately the conditions of supply. Having increased supply to this new level, weaker competitors would have been forced out of business, and the supply curve at lower levels of output should be beneath the original supply curve. Expressed simply, the argument is that the falling supply curve is not reversible. Marshall was vague in a deliberately studied fashion about the appropriate method of analysis in this case and took refuge in the view that such 'economic problems are imperfectly presented when they are treated as problems of statical equilibrium, and not of organic growth'.

The approach that Andrews would have preferred to see taken, and which he himself regarded as an appropriate interpretation of Marshall, would be to emphasize the limitation on an individual firm's demand resulting from custom or goodwill. Each firm will thus get a share of the market, this being dependent on trade connections, personal contact, etc. As Professor Loasby (1978) has put it, 'Marshall's industries are information structures.' Realistic considerations like this, when taken alongside the pervasive tendency to increasing returns, are incompatible with marginalism – a notion which Marshall was understandably reluctant to abandon. Having once decided that marginalism should be abandoned, which was very much Andrews's view, one is free to draw attention to the pervasiveness of falling costs. For Andrews, the norm in manufacturing firms is increasing returns. Even in the short run he regards it as typical that short-run average total costs decrease up to the limit of short-run capacity. In the long-run analysis of costs he is at one with Marshall in emphasizing decreasing costs.

Of course it is now well known that an appropriate *marginalist* analysis of equilibrium for a competitive system is impossible if all firms are subject to increasing returns. In such a case, the profit maximizing output level for an individual firm is unbounded. Firms will thus grow without limit (those with the more rapidly decreasing costs having the stronger prospects of survival) until concentration reaches such a level that one can no longer sensibly maintain the assumption that a firm can ignore the consequences of its actions on the prices and outputs of its rivals. The suggestion made by Sraffa (1926), and subsequently analysed in greater detail by Robinson (1933), Chamberlin (1933), and Harrod (1930), was that a determinate solution would be attained if the individual firm's demand curve was negatively sloped, and not horizontal, because of the product differentiation achieved by advertising and other selling costs. To some extent these conclusions were based on Marshallian premises.

Firstly, it was accepted that in both the short run and the long run, decreasing costs were common in manufacturing industry. Secondly, it was recognized that the Marshallian producers supplied to their various customers a differentiated rather than a homogeneous good. This was the import of Marshall's discussion of goodwill and business contacts. Chamberlin (1933) with his *dd'* and *DD'* curve analysis, was able to analyse the short- and long-run implications of a market such as this. By adopting the Marshallian assumption of free entry, provided a normal profit could be earned, he was able to derive his famous tangency solution – or what Andrews calls 'a Marshallian equilibrium' – in which a long-run determinate equilibrium was attained by the firm at an output at which costs were falling and normal profit was being earned. The modification which Andrews undertook of the Chamberlinian system was not so trivial as Andrews himself suggested. It was to take but a part of each of Chamberlin's *DD'* and *dd'* curves, and thus to construct a kinked demand curve. This construction, and its relation to Chamberlin's analysis, has been discussed in considerable detail by Reid (1981). However, Chamberlin's analysis is essentially that of a large-group case, in which tastes are uniformly distributed over product varieties; and the analysis cannot be carried over without modification to the case in which there are few sellers, some of which may have greater market power than others. More problematic, if some sort of 'full cost' or 'normal cost' theory is to be incorporated into the kinked demand curve analysis, it is important that the determinants of full cost should be specified. It has been generally observed that such an account is not clearly given in the study of Hall and Hitch (1939).

What Andrews hoped to provide was a basis for price determination. His starting point was the static analysis of a single-product firm, with certain fixed overheads, and variable costs incurred by purchasing variable factors of production at given prices. Empirical evidence suggests the pattern of firms' costs. Average direct costs will be approximately constant over a large range of output, and average total cost will fall as output increases. A distinct limit of production exists, given fixed factors, but planned capacity will fall short of the maximum level of production possible, it being desirable to always have a certain reserve capacity. If, by choice, output were permanently to exceed current planned capacity, the business would deliberately expand, and it is assumed that such a larger, newly organized business would incur lower average costs for its greater levels of output. In this way, Andrews argues, the business enterprise experiences falling average costs in both the short and the long run, though the effect is more marked in the short run. Costs themselves will be prone to fluctuations, and any reorganization of the firm to extend production will generally imply a temporarily higher level of costs than can eventually be achieved. A good indicator of costs for larger levels of output than that which is presently being produced is therefore current costs.

Passing from costs to demand, Andrews retains the Marshallian emphasis on goodwill, but magnifies its importance because of his emphasis on firms' demands for goods as distinct from final consumers' demands. Marshall himself had emphasized the latter, and the goodwill relationship he referred to was really that between households and firms. Andrews recognized the great importance of inter-firm transactions and saw that the Marshallian emphasis on goodwill applied *a fortiori* to this case. Clearly, no business would be able to set a price above that of its rivals for a technically identical product in the long run, though in the short run such a strategy is possible. However, though possible, the short-run strategy is unlikely. Businessmen know that goodwill has to be built up slowly and patiently, and would not be willing to pursue a pricing policy that would eventually be thwarted in any case by the forces of competition, and would in the meanwhile destroy the customer–supplier relationship. The strategy of holding price below that level which the market could immediately bear and establishing a strong goodwill relationship with customers will lead to an increase in orders from existing customers and new orders from customers who have heard of the sound reputation of the supplier. Given the pervasiveness of increasing returns, this enlarged range of customers, and increasing average size of each customer's orders, leads to benefits to the firm which are by no means confined to the long run, and which do not involve a vigorous price-setting policy.

It will be noticed here that the emphasis has been on price-setting *by the firm*, rather than on the firm taking price as given. This tendency will be even more marked than is apparent from the above argument when one recalls that customers frequently have particular requirements for the goods they are purchasing and that prices are therefore quoted for a particular specification.

A matter which must naturally be investigated if we are working in a competitive structure in which firms are price-setters is the fashion in which price is set. Chamberlin's analysis of the price-setting firm involves marginal cost being set equal to marginal revenue, where the latter curve is marginal to the *dd'* average revenue curve. In this light, the analysis looks very conventional and marginalist. Despite his general approval of Chamberlin, this is not what Andrews had in mind with respect to pricing policy. To Andrews, prices were determined according to a costing-up procedure, with the price quotation being based on a detailed calculation of all costs, to which was added a net profit margin. Alternatively, and perhaps more crudely, price was determined as a gross profit mark-up on average direct costs. In each case, the price set would to some extent deter entry; it would regulate or limit rivalry.

If prices are indeed determined as a mark-up on costs, the question arises as to how they will be revised in the face of cost variations. Of course there are costs involved in making frequent minor adjustments. These are not our concern, for such flexible pricing policies are not typical of manufacturing. It is convenient to break down cost variations into those that are consequential on changed factor market conditions, and those that are 'autonomous' in the sense of deriving from changes in the scale of operation of the firm or in the efficiency with which production is organized. Of course this distinction – adopted by Andrews – will not always be clear cut, particularly if the firm is an oligopsony. Given well-informed customers and firms, changes in raw materials and wage costs will fairly rapidly be reflected in changes in price. Customers will expect this type of flexibility, and thus firms will not be concerned that acting in this way might affect the strength of the market. It is one matter to raise prices when the market is buoyant and demand is rising, but quite another to do so in the face of falling demand. This might suggest to customers that the firm is not operating as efficiently as it should, and such an attitude could be self-fulfilling in the sense that a withdrawal of further custom will force a firm on to a higher point on its long-run average cost curve. Firms in this situation can be victims of a vicious circle of declining custom and rising costs. By contrast, a virtuous circle is also possible, with a growing firm achieving higher levels of output, efficiency gains, and enlarged custom. The latter type of firm, which can generally pursue a policy of price reduction as growth takes place, was regarded by Andrews as being one of the major forces of competition in manufacturing markets. Such a firm enjoys enlarged revenues (which can provide the funds for further growth and innovation), an enhanced long-run position in the market, and a competitive edge which will enable it to weaken its rivals. The author, in Reid (1975, 1979), has developed a formal model along these lines in which the enterprise pursuing this aggressive pricing policy is a dominant firm price leader. Andrews himself noted the existence of such market structures, but gave more emphasis to the price leadership of vigorous medium-sized firms.

It will be noted that an important implication of Andrews's interpretation is that the firm in competitive conditions is determining *price* rather than output. Once price is set, the firm sells all the market will take. This approach has been taken up and made the centrepiece of the post-Keynesian analysis of price determination. Firms following such a policy will typically be prepared to take short-run losses and, should they be new entrants, they will not continue to produce unless they have optimistic views of future prospects. Perhaps more important than new, optimistic entrants are existing firms with an established base in other markets who are contemplating diversification of their product range. They can more easily experiment than single-product new entrants, and have the resources to sustain losses on at least a portion of their product ranges for substantial periods.

It is apparent that if existing businesses are likely to be the principal source of competition to any firm, it is difficult to have a theory of the firm without also having a notion of the group within which that firm conceives its potential rivals as lying. Andrews defined an industry very broadly, as being any grouping of firms which is relevant to the study of any one member of such a group. The term 'relevant' is somewhat question begging, but clearly its intent is to have as

flexible a concept of the industry as possible. More important than the definition of an industry itself is the methodology being advanced, namely that no
meaningful theory of the firm is possible if it involves abstracting from the
particular type of industrial grouping within which the firm is operating.

The proposal that Andrews put forward amounts to a hierarchical view of
industrial groupings. At the base of this hierarchy are firms producing goods of
identical or very similar technical specification, which are sold at identical
prices or prices which are only very slightly varied, such variations being a
reflection of cost differentials among firms. In the short run, such firms constitute the effective competitors for the particular product group under examination. In the longer run, it has been argued, the pool of potential competitors is
wider, for it includes firms not yet operating in the product group, who nevertheless have the technology and know-how to do so. Thus a narrower definition,
used for short-run purposes, might look at the markets for electrical generators,
or for leather gloves. A broader definition, taking into account the possibility
of firms changing their product lines, would look at the electrical engineering
market or the leather goods market.

On the purely theoretical level, or for pedagogic purposes, Andrews favoured
retaining the Marshallian concept of an industry, for which all firms were
regarded as producing an identical product at a uniform price. Andrews
employed the assumption that the demand curve for the industry was inelastic
in the neighbourhood of the prevailing price, with this total demand being
decomposable into individual firms' shares of industry demand, such shares
being determined by goodwill relationships. Such an assumption is characteristic of the post-Keynesian theory of oligopoly pricing, such as that expounded
by Eichner (1976). At this juncture, it should be sufficient to point out that this
assumption of an inelastic demand must imply that firms are operating at
outputs beyond the profit maximizing level, and indeed beyond the sales
revenue maximizing level. This is obviously inconsistent with any neoclassical
account of monopolistic or competitive pricing, including the Chamberlinian
construction.

A characteristic of Andrews's industrial equilibrium is that the price prevailing
is based on the normal cost of producing the good, and that industrial capacity
is more than sufficient to meet demand at this price. Short-run increases of
demand can thus be met from existing capacity, at an unchanged price. Long-
run increases of demand would provide firms with the opportunity to reorganize
the methods of production and to enlarge capacity, with the general consequence
being a lowering of price. This is very similar in reasoning to the Marshallian
analysis of long-run increasing returns. In the longer term, expansion of
industrial output will be attained both by the enlargement of the capacity of
existing firms and by the entry of new firms. Essential to Andrews's view is the
notion that competition is a cost-reducing activity which takes place over real
(historic) time where such cost reduction involves a reorganization of produc-

tion. Here, he is entirely Marshallian. Antithetic to both their views is the neoclassical notion that competition will involve cost reduction taking place instantaneously in analytic (logical) time, with minimum unit cost being achieved for a given technology of production.

5.4   THE MARSHALLIAN ANALYSIS OF MONOPOLY

The centrepiece of discussion in the previous section was Marshall's analysis of competition. It was concerned with a kind of imperfect competition in which customer loyalty played a significant role. Marshall placed less emphasis on pure monopoly analysis as he felt it was of less empirical significance. However, it would be a mistake to ignore his monopoly analysis, because it treats welfare considerations in an illuminating fashion.

Marshall postulates that the objective of a monopolist is to maximize net revenue. He perceives difficulty in defining the net revenue schedule, not because of the demand side, which is quite uncomplicated, but because he chooses to treat the cost side in terms of the supply schedule. Included in the supply price of a commodity should be normal profit, but in the case of a private business the monopoly rental element may not be distinguished from managerial reward. In the case of a public monopoly, however, this difficulty is largely absent because managerial payments are itemized as expenses of production.

In such a case, the supply schedule represents the normal expenses of production for the good under consideration, where such expenses include interest payments and the salaries of directors and permanent officials. The 'monopoly revenue schedule' or perhaps more descriptively the 'net revenue schedule' is constructed by deducting the supply price from the demand price at every possible level of output. Bearing in mind that the supply curve in this case should be interpreted as a unit or *average* cost of production schedule rather than a *marginal* cost schedule, Marshall's monopoly revenue curve is what we would today call an average net revenue curve or, more simply, an average profit curve. This may be written

$$p = f_1(x) - f_2(x) \tag{5.2}$$

where f_1 and f_2 are demand price and supply price, respectively. Then the firm aims to maximize

$$xf_1(x) - xf_2(x) \tag{5.3}$$

which is achieved when

$$x\frac{df_1(x)}{dx} + f_1(x) = x\frac{df_2(x)}{dx} + f_2(x) \tag{5.4}$$

that is, when marginal revenue equals marginal cost. This, however, is deliberately to cast the analysis in familiar terms. There are a number of distinctive aspects to the Marshallian approach to the analytics of a net revenue maximizing monopolist. Most obvious of these is his desire to investigate monopoly equilibrium using no more than familiar supply and demand schedules. Rather than deal with *total* revenue and cost schedules, as did Cournot in characterizing monopoly equilibrium, Marshall deals with average curves. The optimum of the firm cannot therefore be directly represented as a maximum on the net revenue schedule. Instead, Marshall introduces a family of constant revenue curves, which are rectangular hyperbolae of the form

$$xp = C \tag{5.5}$$

where C is the parameter representing different total revenues for amounts x and unit revenues p. Then the optimizing problem of the monopolist may be expressed as

$$\max C = xp \quad \text{subject to } p = f_1(x) - f_2(x) \tag{5.6}$$

for which the Lagrangian may be written

$$L = xp + \lambda [p - f_1(x) + f_2(x)] \tag{5.7}$$

where λ is the Lagrange multiplier. First-order conditions for maximizing (5.7) are

$$\frac{\partial L}{\partial x} = p - \lambda \frac{df_1}{dx} + \lambda \frac{df_2}{dx} = 0$$

$$\frac{\partial L}{\partial p} = x + \lambda = 0$$

from which one gets

$$p = -x \frac{df_1}{dx} + x \frac{df_2}{dx}$$

This implies that

$$f_1(x) - f_2(x) = -x \frac{df_1}{dx} + x \frac{df_2}{dx}$$

or

$$f_1(x) + x \frac{df_1}{dx} = f_2(x) + x \frac{df_2}{dx} \tag{5.8}$$

where expression (5.8) is again the marginal revenue equal to marginal cost condition $MR = MC$. In terms of geometry, this condition can also be derived from observing that the optimal output is attained when the net revenue function is tangential to the highest constant revenue curve. This condition of equality of the derivatives is expressed by

$$- \frac{p}{x} = \frac{\mathrm{d}f_1(x)}{\mathrm{d}x} - \frac{\mathrm{d}f_2(x)}{\mathrm{d}x} \tag{5.9}$$

which is easily rearranged to give the $MR = MC$ condition of (5.8).

Another notable feature of Marshall's monopoly analysis is that it always runs in terms of a falling expenses of production (i.e. supply) curve. We would generally expect a falling unit cost curve to be associated with a falling marginal cost curve, though of course what is strictly implied is that marginal cost should be below average cost. This introduces the possibility of the implied equilibrium being unstable in a Hicksian sense. Cournot had recognized the decreasing marginal cost case, and thought it typical of manufacturing enterprises. Hicks (1935) provided a detailed statement of many monopoly results which are now regarded as standard, including the stability requirement that the derivative of the marginal revenue curve should be less than that of the marginal cost curve in the neighbourhood of equilibrium. With the downward-sloping marginal cost and marginal revenue curves which are typical of the Marshallian case, this requires that the marginal revenue curve should cut the marginal cost curve from above.

Marshall, in his analysis of monopoly, is aware of other analytical subtleties, such as the possibility of multiple equilibria, and undertakes two further important investigations to which we shall now direct our attention. Firstly, the comparative statics properties of the monopoly model are investigated with considerable thoroughness. Notably, there is an analysis of the general bounty/tax function $F(x)$. Secondly, a welfare analysis of monopoly is undertaken, with particular emphasis on the public utility case.

The general case of a tax or bounty (subsidy) which varies with the output level can be dealt with by introducing the function $F(x)$ into the monopolist's maximand. A necessary condition for net revenue maximization can then be written

$$\frac{\mathrm{d}}{\mathrm{d}x} \left[xf_1(x) - xf_2(x) - F(x) \right] = 0 \tag{5.10}$$

which implies that

$$f_1(x) + x\frac{\mathrm{d}f_1}{\mathrm{d}x} = f_2(x) + x\frac{\mathrm{d}f_2}{\mathrm{d}x} + \frac{\mathrm{d}F}{\mathrm{d}x} \tag{5.11}$$

This is to say that marginal revenue equals marginal cost plus the marginal tax, or minus the marginal subsidy.

In two simple cases, the root or roots of equation (5.11) are unaffected by the form of $F(x)$. The first of these is the case of a lump-sum tax $F(x) = k$ where k is a constant, and the second is the case of a profits tax m for which

$$F(x) = m\,[\,xf_1(x) - xf_2(x)\,] \qquad 0 < m < 1 \qquad (5.12)$$

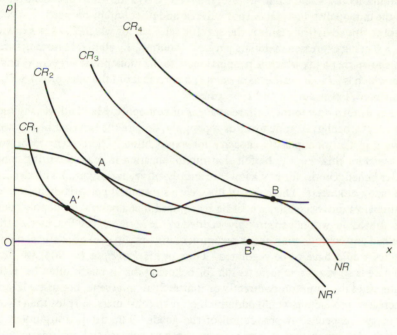

Figure 5.1

Should there be multiple equilibria (i.e. several roots to (5.11), the first-order equation for a maximum), it is possible for substantial jumps in the optimum to occur for small variations in a shift parameter. Figure 5.1 illustrates this sort of phenomenon. Curve *NR* indicates the initial net revenue function $xf_1(x) - xf_2(x)$, and curve *NR'* represents the function $xf_1(x) - xf_2(x) - F(x)$ for some general tax function $F(x)$ which has in effect raised the expenses of production curve and thus lowered the net revenue curve. There are initially local optima A and B on the constant revenue curves CR_1 and CR_2 which are relatively close. Point B, being on the higher constant revenue curve, clearly is the global optimum. The effect of taxation is to make A' the only admissible optimum. There is a marked fall in output, which would be associated with a substantial increase in the monopolist's price. It is worth noting in passing that this *jump* behaviour of the economic model in the face of *continuous* variation in one of the determinants of equilibrium (in this case the tax schedule) gives a result which is analogous to that discussed much more recently in the literature of mathematical economics under the heading of catastrophe theory.

If the tax function has the general property that $dF/dx > 0$, then the monopolist will reduce output and increase price, provided that the usual stability condition is satisfied. Contrariwise, if $dF/dx < 0$ as the result of subsidization of the monopolist, optimal output will rise and price will be reduced. A special case of this analytical result is the specific sales tax for which $F(x) = kx$, with $k > 0$ being expressed in dollars per unit of output. By similar reasoning it can be shown that a tax which is proportionate to the monopolist's revenue, and a tax which is *ad valorem* (i.e. expressed as a percentage of the sales price), will, if increased, lower output and raise price.

Let us turn now to the welfare analysis of monopoly. Marshall was inclined to adopt a benign attitude towards monopoly, despite the fact that he was well aware of the monopolist's capacity for exploitation. There seem to be two reasons for this. Firstly, he felt that monopolization in manufacturing could offer benefits in the form of a lowered supply curve, as compared with the case of many producers. There was in his view a substantial potential benefit from rationalization. Secondly, whilst he recognized that a natural monopoly could be abused, he was not so strongly wedded to the notion of the free market that he had any compunction about recommending that, in general, natural monopolies would have to be regulated. Thus in his *Principles* (p. 503) we find: 'There is strong *prima facie* reason for believing that it might often be in the interest of the community directly or indirectly to intervene, because a largely increased production would add much more to consumers' surplus than to the aggregate expenses of production of the goods.' The detailed argument by which the conclusion is reached can be best understood by reference to Marshall's notion of 'compromise benefit' – a concept to which we now turn our attention.

Expressed briefly, Marshall's welfare analysis of the monopolist can be captured by the relationship

total net benefit = monopoly net revenue + consumers' surplus

In order to elaborate his ideas in greater detail, there are three additional functional relationships which need to be introduced, apart from the net revenue function already encountered. These may be represented geometrically by the consumers' surplus curve, the total benefit curve, and the compromise benefit curve. The net revenue curve NR will be represented by the function $f_3(x)$, where

$$p = f_3(x) = f_1(x) - f_2(x) \qquad (NR) \tag{5.13}$$

Consumers' surplus, essentially a Marshallian device (although originating with Dupuit) may be represented by the area under the average revenue curve above any given demand price. For such a price p, consumers' surplus is defined by

$$\int_0^x f_1(\alpha) \mathrm{d}\alpha - x f_1(x) \tag{5.14}$$

where $f_1(x)$ is the average revenue (inverse demand) function. Then Marshall's consumers' surplus curve CS has the property that the product of the co-ordinates of a point on it yields a value equal to consumers' surplus as defined by (5.14). The equation for the CS curve, $f_4(x)$, is clearly given by

$$p = f_4(x) = \frac{1}{x} \int_0^x f_1(\alpha) \mathrm{d}\alpha - f_1(x) \qquad (CS) \tag{5.15}$$

with the desired property that $xp = x f_4(x)$, this being the value of consumers' surplus. The total benefit curve has as its equation $f_5(x)$, where

$$f_5(x) = f_3(x) + f_4(x) \qquad (TB) \tag{5.16}$$

this being the sum of the monopoly net revenue and consumers' surplus functions. Clearly $x f_5(x)$ measures total net revenue plus consumers' surplus. If the monopoly were run for the benefit of society as a whole, it is this which should be treated as the maximand. In this case, the benefits to consumers are treated on a par with the benefits to the monopolist. More realistic, however, is the case in which the monopolist gives lesser weight to consumers' surplus than he does to the net revenue that accrues to himself. In attaining this compromise on benefits, we may regard the simple additive definition of $f_5(x)$ in (5.16) as being modified to a new function $f_6(x)$, which when graphed may be described as the compromise benefit CB curve. It has the form

$$f_6(x) = f_3(x) + n f_4(x) \qquad 0 < n < 1 \qquad (CB) \tag{5.17}$$

By subtracting (5.17) from (5.16)

$$f_5(x) - f_6(x) = (1 - n) f_4(x) > 0$$

and (5.13) from (5.17)

$$f_6(x) - f_3(x) = n f_4(x) > 0$$

one obtains by implication the following inequalities:

$$f_3(x) < f_6(x) < f_5(x) \tag{5.18}$$

or

$$NR < CB < TB$$

Expressed geometrically, the compromise benefit curve must lie between the net revenue and total benefit curves. Consumers' interests are clearly reflected in the weighting parameter n in the expression for compromise benefit.

Two analytical results follow directly from the theoretical framework established. Firstly, comparing the case in which the monopolist is mindful simply of his own interest ($n = 0$) with the case in which he also looks to the interests of his customers ($n > 0$), we find that price is higher, and output lower, in the former case compared with the latter. Secondly, the greater is the desire of the monopolist to promote the interests of his customers, as measured by a larger rather than a smaller n, the greater is output and the lesser is the price set. More precisely, what needs to be established is that the optimum on the compromise benefit curve is attained at a higher output than the optimum on the net revenue curve. We proceed to prove this.

The total compromise benefit may be expressed as

$$xf_6(x) = xf_3(x) + nxf_4(x)$$

Then, using the definitions of the net revenue and consumers' surplus functions,

$$xf_6(x) = xf_1(x) - xf_2(x) - nxf_1(x) + n \int_0^x f_1(\alpha)d\alpha$$

$$= (1 - n)xf_1(x) - xf_2(x) + n \int_0^x f_1(\alpha)d\alpha \tag{5.19}$$

The first-order condition for maximizing (5.19) is

$$\frac{d}{dx}[xf_6(x)] = (1 - n)x\frac{df_1}{dx} + (1 - n)f_1(x) - x\frac{df_2}{dx} - f_2 + nf_1(x) = 0$$

or

$$(1 - n)x\frac{df_1}{dx} + f_1(x) - f_2(x) - x\frac{df_2}{dx} = 0 \tag{5.20}$$

By contrast, the first-order condition for a maximum to total net revenue is

$$\frac{d}{dx}[xf_3(x)] = x\frac{df_1}{dx} + f_1(x) - x\frac{df_2}{dx} - f_2(x) = 0 \tag{5.21}$$

Suppose function (5.21) attains a maximum at $x = a$, implying

$$a\frac{df_1(a)}{dx} + f_1(a) - a\frac{df_2(a)}{dx} - f_2(a) = 0 \tag{5.22}$$

Then, if $d[af_6(a)]/dx$ can be shown to be positive, the required result is proven. Substituting in expression (5.20) for $d[xf_6(x)]/dx$ gives

$$\frac{d}{dx}[af_6(a)] = (1 - n)a\frac{df_1(a)}{dx} + f_1(a) - f_2(a) - a\frac{df_2(a)}{dx}$$

$$= -na\frac{df_1(a)}{dx}$$

using expression (5.22) for $d[af_3(a)]/dx$. Now we can generally assume a downward-sloping average revenue curve, that is $df_1(a)/dx < 0$, from which $d[af_6(a)]/dx > 0$, the required result. When $n = 1$, we have

$$f_6(x) = f_3(x) + nf_4(x) = f_3(x) + f_4(x) = f_5(x)$$

Thus

$$\frac{d}{dx}[af_5(a)] = -a\frac{df_1(a)}{dx} > 0$$

proving the total benefit curve too attains a maximum at a greater output than the total net revenue curve. Finally, one would generally expect the maximum on the total compromise benefit curve to be attained at an output greater than that level of output at which the total net revenue curve (beyond that point at which it reaches a maximum) attains a value of zero. At such a point, say output level b, supply price is exactly equal to the demand price, i.e. $f_1(b) = f_2(b)$. Looking at the derivative of the compromise benefit curve at this output level, we get

$$\frac{d}{dx}[bf_6(b)] = (1 - n)b\frac{df_1(b)}{dx} - b\frac{df_2(b)}{dx} \qquad (5.23)$$

by using $f_1(b) = f_2(b)$. For this expression to be positive, given $b > 0$, we require

$$(1 - n)\frac{df_1(b)}{dx} - \frac{df_2(b)}{dx} > 0$$

For $n < 1$, and a downward-sloping average revenue curve $df_1/dx < 0$, the first term is negative. Thus a necessary condition for positivity is $df_2/dx < 0$, that is a downward-sloping supply curve; this is the increasing returns case on which Marshall placed so much emphasis. To ensure the satisfaction of the condition we require that the absolute value of the slope of the supply curve should exceed $1 - n$ of the absolute value of the slope of the average revenue curve:

$$(1 - n)|df_1/dx| < |df_2/dx| \qquad (5.24)$$

In the special case that the monopolist regards customers' interests as no different from his own (formally $n = 1$), the simple requirement is that

$$-df_2/dx > 0 \quad \Rightarrow \quad df_2/dx < 0 \qquad (5.25)$$

that is, a negatively sloped supply curve. The altruistic monopolist will therefore, if increasing returns prevail, produce beyond that point at which supply price equals demand price.

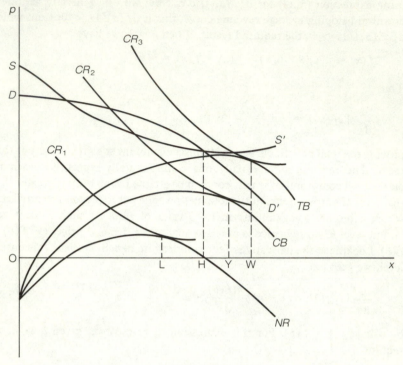

Figure 5.2

All of these analytical points can be illustrated by Marshallian geometry, as in figure 5.2. Constant revenue curves are represented by CR_1, CR_2, and CR_3. Supply and average revenue curves are given by SS' and DD'. The average net revenue, compromise benefit, and total benefit curves are denoted NR, CB, and TB respectively. The optimum for the net revenue curve is attained at output level OL. Necessarily the optima for compromise and total benefits are attained at higher output levels. Furthermore, in this particular case OY > OH, that is the optimum on the compromise benefit curve is attained at a higher output than that at which supply price is equal to demand price. A downward-sloping demand curve is, as we have seen, a necessary but not a sufficient condition for this to hold. In fact in Marshall's own illustration of these analytical devices we have OY < OH. He does not, however, side-step the issue of whether monopolies should be operated if they run losses. Even if a monopoly should make a loss at all output levels, there may be social arguments for continuing production. More precisely if, after taxation of consumers to meet the necessary subsidy, the compromise benefit curve still attains its optimum for a positive output level, production should be continued. Marshall generally felt that the interests of consumers had been neglected, to some extent because information was so poor, but looked forward to a period in which some attempt would be made to measure consumers' surplus when contemplating new courses of public or private action.

Let us now turn from the analysis of monopoly to a further Marshallian analysis of the industry and the firm. We develop the ideas in a fashion which leads to what Gee (1983) has recently described as 'the Frisch–Blaug position'.

5.5 SOME FORMAL DEVELOPMENTS OF THE MARSHALLIAN SCHEMA

The cornerstone of Marshall's analysis of the industry and the firm is of course his recognition of the various types of equilibria which emerge, depending on whether one considers the immediate, the short or the long run (see Whitaker, 1982). Let us now consider these three in turn.

Immediate period   His temporary equilibrium related to a very short run, which he illustrated by reference to a daily market within which a price must be established. The period might at most extend to a few weeks for some commodities in which trade is not very brisk; but would normally be a few days or a day. Temporary equilibrium established what he called 'the market price'. In this first situation, no production is taking place to augment or diminish market supply and price is essentially demand determined, though expectational factors can affect the willingness of holders of the stock to disburse it onto the market.

Short period   In the short period, some but not all costs vary with the volume of production and these were described by him as special, direct, or, more usually, prime costs. Those costs that do not vary with the volume of production are described as supplementary. Frisch (1950), in his masterly encapsulation of the Marshallian analysis, which we adopt as our model in this section, substitutes for the Marshallian terms 'prime' and 'supplementary' costs the now more familiar 'variable' and 'fixed' costs. This is not entirely faithful to Marshallian analysis, but here we shall follow Frisch.

Long period   Finally, there is equilibrium in the long period, in which the cost analysis is complicated by the possibility of internal and external economies. All factors are variable in this period, and the firm has open to it a choice of productive capacity.

These different periods are distinguished for analytical reasons only, and Marshall was aware that one tends to shade into another. A useful pendulum analogy is given by Frisch (1950, p. 497) where he elaborates on a rather similar analogy in the *Principles* (p. 346). Consider a cord to which are attached three pendula, one beneath the other, with the smallest pendulum at the bottom and the largest at the top. Even this relatively simple construction — simple, that is, compared with the social cosmos — is difficult to analyse in mathematical terms. A possible route, which is approximate and no more, is to analyse the behaviour of each pendulum in its own right. Thus we can analyse the motion of the lowest pendulum under the assumption that the middle pendulum is stationary. In this way we can build up a picture of the overall motion of the pendulum; this is admittedly an approximation, but nevertheless probably the best one available. In the same way, Marshall's approach is an attempt to provide a means of understanding the evolution of firms and the industry by the device of recognizing distinct analytical periods.

Let us pass by as understood his analysis of temporary equilibrium and direct attention to his analysis of normal equilibrium with reference to short periods. In his famous analogy of the trees in the forest, Marshall recognizes that a life cycle for the individual firm implies a distribution of efficiency within the industry. Another way of expressing these efficiency differences is to say that the extent of internal economies differs across firms. Thus unit total and average variable costs will attain different minima for different firms, at different levels of output. So much is familiar from expository accounts of the Marshallian analysis, such as that of Viner (1931). Firms will set price equal to marginal cost, and thus the marginal cost and supply schedules will be coincident. Let us hold in reserve for the moment a consideration of whether the individual firm's demand curve really should be regarded as horizontal, and examine the 'theorem' that supply and marginal cost coincide. A typical caveat to this is that price should be above average variable cost. Marshall himself has a more subtle analysis, which distinguishes between cases in which the product price is high or low in relation to cost. He would accept that *above* average total cost price should equal marginal cost, but would deny that in the region of cut-throat competition between average variable cost and average total cost the firms would follow marginal cost pricing. He held that the businessman would fear spoiling the market by this strategem, and that more likely was a sharper curtailment of output at a price above marginal cost. Consider the case in which fixed costs are large, implying a considerable gap between average variable and average total costs, and hence a large region of potential cut-throat competition. It is especially likely, Marshall argued, that supply would be limited to support price. Thus in the *Principles* (p. 375) we find that:

> In a trade which uses very expensive plant, the prime cost of goods is but a small part of their total cost; and an order at much less than their normal price may leave a large surplus above their prime cost. But if producers accept such orders in their anxiety to prevent their plant from being idle, they glut the market and tend to prevent prices from reviving ... they

might ruin many of those in the trade, themselves perhaps among the number.

The practice of supporting price in these circumstances is described by Frisch (1950) as a *restrictive strategy*. In a market with a distribution of efficiency, different firms enjoy different levels of quasi-rent. Those of lower efficiency, already earning low quasi-rents, would be unlikely to follow a restrictive strategy. The more efficient firms, however, would be more likely to favour this strategy, having a greater vested interest in their own survival and that of the industry. Finally, let us explore the meaning of Marshall's 'true marginal supply price for short periods'. When Marshall talks of the 'marginal supply price' he does not refer to a point on a supply schedule with the characteristic that the area beneath it represents the total cost of producing the amount which firms bring to the market at that price. Marshall's supply curve defined between price p and quantity x axes has the characteristic that any point (p, x) on it represents the total value of goods sold, that is the product of p and x.

Let us turn now to a matter of the greatest importance in view of Andrews's disenchantment with this part of Marshallian analysis, namely normal equilibrium with reference to long periods. Crucial to an understanding of this is the distinction between normal and actual profits. Normal profit is one of the costs which determine long-run supply. Normal profit should be identified with the gross earnings of management, where these arise from 'the supply price of business ability and energy ... and the supply price of that organization by which the appropriate business ability and the requisite capital are brought together' (*Principles*, p. 313). In standard perfectly competitive analysis, the firm is regarded as changing its scale of output if actual profit is above normal, and further this provides an inducement to entry. In Marshallian analysis, the important point is that a profit above the normal changes the life cycle of firms in the industry. Firms that are already growing will enjoy an acceleration in their expansion, and those that are declining will experience a diminution in their decay. It is in this way that an increase in aggregate output for the industry is achieved, rather than by firms moving to new static positions on their long-run cost curves. An ingenious modelling of this process by Newman and Wolfe (1961), using Markov chain analysis, will be discussed later. The next question that arises concerns the extent of the increase in output. Considering the stationary situation, in which the volume of production actually gets sold at a price, it is evident that the requirement for stationarity is that the market, whenever presented with that price, will in a unit period produce a certain amount of output, some of which comes from growing firms and some from declining firms. This will require a distribution of firms earning both above and below normal profit, with stationarity implying a more or less equal representation of these types. In the process of a larger volume of production being attained, firms will have access to both internal and external economies.

Marshall's analysis embraced the possibility of internal economies that arose out of the adaption of existing knowledge, though it excluded substantive inventions. Working against this cost-reducing tendency was the possibility of expansion leading to a rising supply price of factors.

The analysis is obviously potentially highly complex, and Marshall attempted to facilitate its development by introducing the device of the representative firm. We have already seen that under Andrews's interpretation this firm has the characteristic that it is earning a level of profit which a potential entrant would regard as a target level. Frisch (1950) expresses another characteristic of the representative firm as being that it produces a volume of output which varies in parallel with the aggregate volume of output. It is described as a miniature representation of the market which is characterized by two variables: x, its short-period volume of production; and y, its long-period volume of production. The supply curve of this firm, with an appropriate rescaling of the axis, may be looked upon as the market supply curve. It is important not to confuse this artificial construction with a simpler device commonly employed in mathematical treatments of perfect competition. There it is sometimes argued that, with perfect information, full factor mobility, and no specialized factors of production, all firms will employ the same technique and hence be subject to the same long-run average costs. The optimal output for any firm i, say S_i, is the same as that for any other firm, and hence may be represented simply by S. Thus industry supply, if there are n firms, will be nS. The typical firm may then be represented on a diagram, and what is true of this firm (e.g. were a tax on a factor of production to be imposed) would be true of other firms in the industry. A similar device was used by Chamberlin in his analysis of monopolistic competition, and we have already seen that Viner (1931) used it in his exposition of Marshall. However, the representativeness of a firm in this sense is trivial, for all firms are the same. When a delegate is said to have represented the views of a body of people, it is not implied that all views in that group were identical, and that one member might as well have been chosen as another to act as the delegate. It may also be that a group cannot decide on who an appropriate representative should be. Similarly, the Marshallian representative firm is not a carbon copy of other firms, and indeed for an industry at any time it may not be possible to discover a representative firm in a concrete sense. One would expect that, in the history of the industry, at different times distinct firms would reach that stage in their life cycle when they could be regarded as representative.

The representative firm, as a technical device to facilitate thought rather than as an empirical entity, will have a number of attributes. The most important of these is that in the stationary state associated with long-run production, in which some firms are growing and some declining but aggregate output remains constant, the output of the representative firm itself should be constant. In this sense it is not subject to the same laws as actual firms. The representative firm will continue to be subject to the *same* internal and external economies as long as external conditions do not alter. Another important attribute of the representative firm is its level of profit. This firm, if it is appropriately to represent the market as a whole, should in the short run decrease, maintain, or increase its output according to whether actual profit is below, equal to, or above normal profit. In the long run, when the stationary state is reached, it should earn normal profit. It is in this sense that the level of profit of the representative firm should provide an aspiration level for the potential entrant as suggested by Andrews. Clearly, normal profit will become a long-run cost to the firm, in the sense that supply will only be maintained if full cost, including this component, is covered by market price. To each of the stationary situations that bring forth a given volume of aggregate output there will correspond an average cost for the representative firm, which itself is a function of this firm's output. It is this relationship which defines the long-period average cost curve. This curve may rise *or* fall with an increase in production.

We are now in a position to examine long-period equilibrium. Marshall's analysis of costs as related to different periods is subtle; by comparison, his treatment of demand is cavalier, a point emphasized by Loasby (1978). Frisch (1950, p. 516) concludes that the Marshallian demand curve is conceptually the same for all markets. This is clearly an oversimplification, for one finds in Marshall the suggestion that demand is more elastic in the long run than in the short run, and further that demand is regarded as endogenous in the long run – for tastes in his view should not be regarded as immutable. What is clear is that the demand curve will generally continue to be downward-sloping. Long-run equilibrium is attained when the long-run demand curve intersects the long-run supply curve, where it is understood that the latter construction is an *average* cost curve showing what the long-run cost would be for a certain long-run volume of production. Frisch (1950, pp. 517–18) insists that long-run adjustment takes place along the demand curve. He is correct that the path to equilibrium is attained by quantity rather than price adjustment. When output is less than the long-run industry equilibrium level of output, price will be higher than the long-run average cost of the representative firm. Thus most firms will be encouraged to increase output because they are earning above normal profits. Newman (1960, p. 592) insists that long-run adjustment takes place along the long-run supply curve. In fact there is no inconsistency between the views; it is simply that Frisch has lapsed into an informal discussion of shorter-run dynamics. Newman is correct to insist that the long-run cost curve cannot be used to examine the path to equilibrium, for by definition equilibrium is assumed for every point on it. Long-run equilibrium then involves the selection of one point in this set of equilibria.

5.6 INDUSTRY EQUILIBRIUM IN MARSHALLIAN ANALYSIS

It was the notable contribution of Newman (1960) and Newman and Wolfe (1961) to see that the real problem with Marshall's long-period analysis was not with its intention, but with its execution. Marshall himself (*Principles*, p. 809) had said that 'The unsatisfactory character of these results is partly due to the imperfections of our analytical methods, and may conceivably be much diminished in a later age by the gradual improvement of our scientific machinery.' The 'scientific machinery' proposed by Newman and Wolfe is the theory of Markov chains. Few before them had seen the merit of Marshall's concept of a statistical equilibrium. Shove (1930) to his credit was aware that, for Marshall's approach to be valid, it was necessary that there be a constant size distribution of outputs, and that increases in output for the industry as a whole would imply a different distribution of businesses within size groups. Before long his insight was lost, and Kaldor (1934, p. 61) was soon to say dismissively:

> Marshall and Professor Pigou appear to argue that an industry can be in equilibrium without all the firms composing it being simultaneously in equilibrium ... But if the growing output of young firms is to cancel out the declining output of old ones on account of something more than a lucky coincidence, it is necessary to assume that all firms are in equilibrium.

Such a view involves the complete destruction of the Marshallian approach. In industry equilibrium as depicted by Kaldor (1934) all firms are in equilibrium as well. Gone are the increasing returns enjoyed by growing firms, and gone is the notion that a stable aggregate output is consistent with an *evolving* population of firms, some growing and others declining. We have seen earlier in this chapter that the classical article by Viner (1931) did at one point subscribe to a view similar to this, but had the saving grace of finally recognizing in its last few lines that Marshall's conception of industry equilibrium was statistical in nature. Conceptually its foundation was biological rather than mechanical. As such its expression in theoretical terms presents formidable analytical problems.

This section is concerned with looking at one – not entirely successful – attempt, by Newman and Wolfe (1961), to undertake the appropriate modelling of Marshall's conception of long-run equilibrium. The basic mathematical idea used by Newman and Wolfe is that of the Markov chain. As a preliminary to looking at the economic analysis proper, a few mathematical terms and theorems must be mentioned. Suppose a random experiment leads to one of r possible outcomes. The basic Markovian assumption is that the probability of a particular outcome on any given experiment is *at most* dependent on the outcome of the immediately preceding experiment. In more colloquial terms such a Markov process is described as 'having no memory'. The probability of the jth outcome on any experiment, given that the ith outcome occurred on the preceding experiment, is denoted Π_{ij}. It is common to regard Π_{ij} as denoting the probability of moving from the ith to the jth *state* in one period, where a certain outcome is regarded as a state, and the experiments are conceived of as taking place over a sequence of periods. The entity Π_{ij} is known as a *transition probability*, and the $(r \times r)$ matrix of such probabilities as the *transition matrix* Π. Suppose the initial state of the process is given by an r-element vector t_0, each component of which defines the probability of being in a particular state. Then the state of the process after one period t_1 is defined by $t_1 = t_0 \Pi$, and in general $t_n = t_{n-1} \Pi$. Using the initial t_0 and the latter recursive relationship, the state of the process after n periods may be written $t_n = t_0 \Pi^n$, where Π^n is the nth power of the transition matrix obtained, by analogy with the scalar process of multiplication, by post-multiplying Π by itself n times. Π is defined as a *stochastic matrix*, this being a matrix with non-negative components and row sums of unity. Then a stochastic matrix is said to be *regular* if some power of it has only positive components. Finally, the probability vector t is described as a *fixed point* of the linear transformation Π if $t = t\Pi$. We are now in a position to state the relevant theorems. Firstly, if Π is a regular stochastic matrix, then: (a) the powers Π^n of Π approach a matrix Π^* as n tends to infinity; and (b) each row of Π^* is the same probability vector t. Secondly, for Π regular and stochastic: (a) for *any* probability vector h, $h\Pi^n$ tends to t as n tends to infinity; and (b) the vector t is the unique fixed-point probability vector of Π. More informally, whatever the initial probability vector, there is a unique probability vector t towards which the process tends. Rather than taking successively higher powers of n to determine this probability vector t, one can simply use the fixed-point relationship $t = t\Pi$. As the row sums of Π are unity, this set of equations is linearly dependent. To solve for the elements of t, one has to use the additional relationship $\Sigma t_i = 1$. This technique has been used by Adelman (1958) to determine the equilibrium structure, in a statistical sense, of the US steel industry.

Here, we wish to pursue the implications of this sort of analysis further, in an analytical rather than empirical sense. Now let A be an $(r \times r)$ matrix of *actual proportions* of firms moving from one size class to another in a unit period. That is, in place of probabilities Π_{ij} we now have actual proportions a_{ij}. A feature of the Markovian approach developed so far is that the Π_{ij} were constant. More generally, one would expect them to depend on economic variables. Dealing now with proportions, rather than probabilities, we will assume that the a_{ij} are dependent on price p. Thus we write the A matrix as $A(p)$. What we wish to be able to express rigorously is the loose notion that A is in some sense 'increasing' in price. In his *Principles* (p. 343) Marshall did in effect define the appropriate form of change in the transition matrix when he argued that a price greater than normal supply price

would increase the growth of the rising firms, and slacken, though it may not arrest, the decay of the falling firms; with the net result of an increase in the aggregate production. On the other hand, a price lower than this would hasten the decay of falling firms, and slacken the growth of rising firms; and on the whole diminish production; and a rise or fall of price would affect all in like manner though perhaps not in an equal degree those great joint-stock companies which often stagnate, but seldom die.

One way of modelling growth and decay in this Marshallian sense is through putting restrictions on the elements of $A(p)$. Growth is captured by super-diagonal elements of A (i.e. elements like $a_{i,\ i+k}$, $k > 0$), and decline by subdiagonal elements. Now *Marshall's rule*, in the terminology of Newman and Wolfe (1961, p. 56) may be expressed as follows. If $p_1 > p_2$ then the difference matrix $D = A(p_1) - A(p_2)$ has the following appearance in terms of signs of coefficients:

$$
\begin{bmatrix}
\bullet & + & + & + & \cdots\cdots & + \\
- & \bullet & + & + & \cdots\cdots & + \\
- & - & \bullet & + & \cdots\cdots & + \\
\cdot & \cdot & \cdot & \cdot & \cdot & \cdot \\
\cdot & \cdot & \cdot & \cdot & \cdot & \cdot \\
\cdot & \cdot & \cdot & \cdot & \cdot & \cdot \\
- & - & - & - & \cdots\cdots & \bullet
\end{bmatrix}
\tag{5.26}
$$

That is, superdiagonal elements of this difference matrix are positive, and subdiagonal elements are negative. The sign of elements along the principal diagonal is indeterminate. What is desired from this analysis is an equilibrium distribution of output which is greater for the matrix $A(p_1)$ than for $A(p_2)$.

We need first to demonstrate how an equilibrium distribution of output is attached to an equilibrium distribution of firms for a given transition matrix A. Then by making A dependent upon price one introduces the required associa-tion of a long-run equilibrium output with a particular price. If Q is the vector of means for the various class sizes, and M the vector of number of firms in each size class, then industry output is MQ. Further, for a given price p and the associated matrix of transition proportions $A(p_1)$, the corresponding industry equilibrium output is the limit of $MA(p_1)^n Q$ as n tends to infinity. To each possible price there will correspond a distinct equilibrium output for the industry, and this defines a supply curve which will be upward sloping. Note that it is the industry's output which is in equilibrium, not that of the individual firm. Supply price at a given output level for the industry can be identified with the cost of production (including normal profit) of the 'representative firm'.

In order to get such results, Newman and Wolfe (1961) had to assume that the A matrix had positive elements on the principal diagonal and adjacent diagonals, but zero elements elsewhere. It is to be noted that the matrices obtained by Adelman (1958) conform to this pattern. However, this appearance of the A matrix to a considerable degree depends on the level of aggregation chosen in selecting size classes, and the choice is arbitrary. The Newman and Wolfe assumption (which they define as 'continuity') implies that firms grow and die by moving up or down the full range of outputs very rapidly. This seems unrealistic. However, they have only given sufficient conditions for an upward-sloping industry supply curve to exist, and no doubt considerably weaker conditions could lead to the same result.

The application of stochastic process theory and statistical equilibrium theory to an analysis of the growth and decay of firms and of industry equilibrium is part of the Marshallian research agenda in industrial organization. Some limited success has already been achieved since the work of Newman and Wolfe (1961). See, for example, Hart (1962), Prais (1974). In Steindl (1965) an argument is advanced for using stochastic process theory. On an empirical level, he expresses disenchantment with both time series and cross-section data, preferring panel data of the sort that has only recently become available to industrial economists. On a theoretical level he favours the use of birth–death processes. In Näslund (1977, chapter 5) an appeal is made to statistical equilibrium theory. Firms are classified into size classes, and these classes are ordered such that

$$x_i < x_{i+1} \qquad i = 1, 2, \ldots, n$$

where x_i is the size measure (such as assets, sales, labour force, or, as above, output) and i is the ith size class. If there are m_i firms in size class i, then the number of ways of obtaining a certain distribution of firms is given by:

$$P = \left[\sum_{i=1}^{n} (m_i)! \right] \bigg/ \left[\prod_{i=1}^{n} (m_i)! \right] \qquad (5.27)$$

Then Näslund shows that the most likely distribution of firms can be obtained by maximizing (5.27) subject to constraints on industry size and profitability. Logically these approaches are related to more mechanical applications of stochastic process theory to explain the size distribution of firms, without any obvious appeal to economic intuition. More satisfactory approaches are becoming available, of which the simulation work of Nelson and Winter (1976, 1982) exploring the relationship between the effectiveness of technological imitation and industrial concentration, and the econometric work of Davies and Lyons (1982) exploring the relationship between minimum efficient scale and concentration, are worthy of mention.

5.7   CONCLUSION

At one point it appeared that Marshallian methods would be neglected as being too unsophisticated. Indeed, to talk of 'a Marshallian approach' was almost to use a pejorative term. Only now is it becoming clear that the fault lay with expository accounts of Marshall. Loasby (1978, p. 2) has argued that Marshall's theory was too difficult for his successors, who therefore replaced it with 'a plain and simple doctrine'. The purpose of this chapter has been to reintroduce some of the subtleties of Marshallian analysis which are of particular relevance to industrial organization. As we shall see shortly, his emphasis on the evolutionary pattern of industrial development has something in common with the Austrian view, but is more pacific in orientation. 'Natura non facit saltum' (nature abhors a vacuum) were words Marshall wrote on the title page of his *Principles*. This is unlike the 'unquiet' market process emphasized by the Austrians, and very unlike the disruptive effects of innovation characteristic of Schumpeterian analysis; these are issues to which our attention must now be turned.

6

The Austrian revival

6.1 INTRODUCTION

The Austrian School has its roots in the writings of Carl Menger, Friedrich von Wieser, and Eugen von Böhm-Bawerk. All were subjective value theorists who were active and influential in the late nineteenth and early twentieth centuries. Their principal, and long-lived, successors in upholding and advancing the tenets of this school were Ludwig von Mises and Friedrich von Hayek. However, despite the enormous intellectual powers of von Mises and Hayek, and their vast scholarly output in the twentieth century, for most of their lives the Austrian School was in decline.

It has only been from the early 1970s that there can be said to have been an Austrian revival. To some extent this has involved a reaffirmation of the significance of central Austrian ideas (e.g. competition as a process rather than a state), but there have also been significant theoretical extensions of them (e.g. entrepreneurial 'alertness'). More recently, given the disenchantment with which traditional Keynesian policies have been viewed in many advanced industrialized economies, and the willingness of economists influential in policy circles to contemplate objectives at the microeconomic level, the Austrian revival has led to the formulation of a distinctive economic policy agenda. Today, the Austrian approach could be said to have three crucial elements: a methodological position, centred on individualism; a theoretical corpus, which emphasizes ignorance, complexity, and processes; and a public policy stance, which is libertarian in flavour and favours unfettered markets operating within an appropriate ethical, legal, and political framework. Austrian economics is much broader than the study of industries, and extends over all the traditional areas of theoretical enquiry, including business cycle analysis, monetary economics, and international trade. However, central to all these analyses is the market, and for this reason the industrial economist has a vested interest in inquiring into what Austrianism has to say.

A characteristic of the purer strains of Austrianism, especially those deriving from the writings of von Mises, is an opposition to mathematical and econometric methods. Whilst many Austrians from Menger onwards have made important contributions to economic theory, this has been expressed almost entirely in literary terms, with no more than the odd numerical example to drive home a point already established in words. However, there seems no intrinsic reason why any literary statement of a theory should not be expressible in mathematical terms. One of the distinctive aspects of this chapter is that it will use the mathematical mode of reasoning fairly freely. This is no heresy to the author, for he is not writing from the Austrian perspective himself, but rather expounding and criticizing it. But further, it seems likely that certain aspects of Austrianism are particularly amenable to mathematical analysis, and provide rich material for deeper theoretical investigation. Of especial relevance here is the use of game theoretic techniques to analyse market trading games. Building on Menger (1871) before him, Böhm-Bawerk (1888) in his *Positive Theory of Capital* attempted a rigorous analysis of trade. There is a continuous thread running from this work through the technical virtuosity of von Neumann and Morgenstern's (1944) *Theory of Games and Economic Behaviour*, to the more modern treatments contained in Telser (1972) and Shubik (1982, 1984). Of contemporary Austrians, many have been unwilling to accept the connection of this subtle body of theory with certain aspects of Austrianism, with the signal exception of Littlechild (1979). It is recognized by Littlechild that the framework of game theory might impose restrictions on the Austrian perspective, but that this might be a price worth paying in order to enrich its sparse theoretical structure.

6.2   AUSTRIANISM FROM THE VON NEUMANN–MORGENSTERN PERSPECTIVE

Rather than plunge into methodology, and hence the discussion of such vexed terms as 'praxeology', we have chosen in this chapter to start somewhat unusually by taking the *Theory of Games and Economic Behaviour* as the point of departure. Based on an analysis deriving from that developed by Böhm-Bawerk (1888) in considering trading in a horse market, the treatment starts with bilateral monopoly analysis and builds up to a treatment of the general market problem in which there are l sellers and m buyers. Some of the more amorphous aspects of Austrianism will be considered later in the course of this chapter, but it is felt to be more constructive, and perhaps more suggestive of how the Austrian research agenda might develop, if the initial approach is made quite precise in an analytical sense.

Consider first a market with just two traders, a seller and a buyer. This can be thought of as a two-person game. In von Neumann–Morgenstern fashion, utility will be regarded as unrestrictedly transferable, and therefore might as well be described as money. Denote the seller by 1 and the buyer by 2, and suppose that the conditions surrounding a single transaction are to be investigated. Thus a simple form of bilateral monopoly is being considered.

Let the value of possession of a single unit of the good (e.g. a horse, or a house) be u for 1 and v for 2, and the value of non-possession to the buyer be zero on his utility scale. An obvious condition that a transaction must satisfy is

$$u < v \qquad (6.1)$$

If 1 suggests a price of p to 2, the latter may accept or decline. If he accepts, the utilities of 1 and 2 are p and $v - p$ respectively; and if he declines, they are u and 0. A condition that p must satisfy is

$$u \leqslant p \leqslant v \qquad (6.2)$$

Let us now introduce in a heuristic fashion some technical terms from game theory, leaving until later more rigorous statements. Players may act together in coalitions, and for such a set, say S, the *characteristic function* $v(S)$ describes what the coalition S can obtain from their opponents (the complement of S in the full set of players). The division of the proceeds of the coalition amongst its members is known as the *payoff* or *imputation*, and for a k-person coalition may be denoted $(\alpha_1, \alpha_2, \ldots, \alpha_k)$. In the two-person game considered so far, the solution is the set of imputations

$$a = \{(\alpha_1, \alpha_2)\}$$
$$\alpha_1 \geqslant u \qquad \alpha_2 \geqslant 0 \qquad \alpha_1 + \alpha_2 = v \qquad (6.3)$$

For the various coalitions that can be formed, the characteristic functions may be derived as follows. If 1 chooses not to exchange he can guarantee a utility of u. If 2 chooses not to exchange and declines every price offered by 1, again 1 ends up with u. Similarly if 2 is unwilling or unable to exchange with 1, he ends up with a utility of zero. Acting together, the players can obtain either u or v, but by (6.1) v is preferable. Thus the characteristic function for the coalitions $\{1\}$, $\{2\}$, and $\{1,2\}$ is

$$v(\{1\}) = u \qquad v(\{2\}) = 0 \qquad v(\{1,2\}) = v \qquad (6.4)$$

It should be emphasized that the characteristic function is constructed under the assumption that there is a conflict of interest between players in the game, and each player assumes that his rival will attempt to inflict a maximal loss on him. Thus the characteristic function is used to specify the 'security levels' of utility for all possible coalitions in the game, including single-player coalitions and the coalition of all players.

Now let us move on from this rather special case to permit transactions which involve trading one or more units of an indivisible, homogeneous good. Denote the units of the good as $A_1, A_2, \ldots, A_s$. Possession of j units of the good by player 1 (the seller) confers on him a utility of $u_j (j = 0, 1, 2, \ldots, s)$, where it is assumed that having no units to sell confers a zero utility ($u_0 = 0$). Similarly, the value to 2 (the buyer) of j units of the good after the transaction is concluded is denoted $v_j (j = 0, 1, 2, \ldots, s)$, with non-possession conferring a zero utility ($v_0 = 0$). Each player can 'block' all sales: if a seller, by offering a price which is unacceptably high; or if a buyer, by declining every price offered. Further, for a transaction involving the transfer of j units of the commodity, the two players participating in this voluntary exchange will obtain a total utility of $u_{s-j} + v_j$. Thus the characteristic function for this game is defined by

$$v(\{1\}) = u_s \qquad v(\{2\}) = 0 \qquad v(\{1,2\}) = \max_j(u_{s-j} + v_j) \tag{6.5}$$

Suppose the maximum problem in (6.5) is solved for $j = j_0$ units traded. Then, by definition of a maximum we have:

$$u_{s-j_0} + v_{j_0} \geqslant u_{s-j} + v_j \qquad \text{for all } j$$

For convenience, this inequality when $j \neq j_0$ may be expressed in two parts

$$u_{s-j_0} - u_{s-j} \geqslant v_j - v_{j_0} \qquad j > j_0 \tag{6.6}$$

and

$$u_{s-j} - u_{s-j_0} \leqslant v_{j_0} - v_j \qquad j < j_0 \tag{6.7}$$

Now (6.6) holds in particular for $j = j_0 + 1$

$$u_{s-j_0} - u_{s-j_0-1} \geqslant v_{j_0+1} - v_{j_0} \tag{6.8}$$

and (6.7) for $j = j_0 - 1$

$$u_{s-j_0+1} - u_{s-j_0} \leqslant v_{j_0} - v_{j_0-1} \tag{6.9}$$

Note that conditions (6.8) and (6.9) are necessary but (in the absence of further conditions) not sufficient for a maximum. At this point, it is useful to introduce a central tenet of subjectivism, the principle of diminishing marginal utility. Menger (1871, p. 125) in discussing consumption observed that 'further satisfaction has a progressively smaller importance'. When one compares the utility of j units purchased (u_j) with the utility of $j+1$ units purchased (u_{j+1}), the extra or marginal utility is $u_{j+1} - u_j$. By the principle of diminishing marginal utility, the sequences of such marginal utilities in this game obey the inequalities

$$u_1 - u_0 > u_2 - u_1 > \ldots > u_s - u_{s-1} \tag{6.10}$$

$$v_1 - v_0 > v_2 - v_1 > \ldots > v_s - v_{s-1} \tag{6.11}$$

where here strictly diminishing marginal utility is implied. By induction, the conditions under (6.8) and (6.9) are now necessary and sufficient. Conditions (6.8) to (6.11) may be expressed, following von Neumann and Morgenstern (1944, p. 562), as each one of

$$u_{s-j_0} - u_{s-j_0-1}, \quad v_{j_0} - v_{j_0-1}$$

is greater than each of

$$u_{s-j_0-1} - u_{s-j_0}, \quad v_{j_0+1} - v_{j_0},$$

These terms correspond to the 'marginal pairs' defined by Böhm-Bawerk in his *Positive Theory of Capital*. In terms of the notion of imputation introduced under (6.3), we have

$$\alpha_1 = v - \alpha_2 \geqslant u \qquad \alpha_2 \geqslant 0$$

implying

$$0 \leqslant \alpha_2 \leqslant v - u \tag{6.12}$$

where $u = u_s$ and $v = u_{s-j_0} + v_{j_0}$. Now if j_0 units are transferred to 2, the buyer, at price p per unit of A, we have

$$v_{j_0} - j_0 p = \alpha_2$$

Thus (6.12) can be rewritten

$$0 \leqslant v_{j_0} - j_0 p \leqslant u_{s-j_0} + v_{j_0} - u_s$$

or

$$\frac{1}{j_0}(u_s - u_{s-j_0}) \leqslant p \leqslant \frac{1}{j_0} v_{j_0}$$

which in turn can be written

$$\frac{1}{j_0}\sum_{i=1}^{j_0}(u_{s-i+1} - u_{s-i}) \leqslant p \leqslant \frac{1}{j_0}\sum_{k=1}^{j_0}(v_k - v_{k-1}) \tag{6.13}$$

where $v_0 = 0$. A point of some significance is that the limits for price determined in (6.13) are not those first propounded by Böhm-Bawerk. According to him, price should lie between the utilities of the 'marginal pairs' mentioned above. That is to say, he holds that the appropriate inequalities on price should be

$$\max(u_{s-j_0+1} - u_{s-j_0} \cdot v_{j_0+1} - v_{j_0}) \leqslant p \leqslant \min(u_{s-j_0} - u_{s-j_0-1} \cdot v_{j_0} - v_{j_0-1}) \tag{6.14}$$

To compare Böhm-Bawerk's inequality (6.14) with von Neumann–Morgenstern's (6.13), consider the further inequality

$$u_{s-j_0+1} - u_{s-j_0} \leqslant p \leqslant v_{j_0} - v_{j_0-1} \tag{6.15}$$

Now by (6.10) and (6.11), the left-hand side of (6.15) is greater than the left-hand side of (6.13); and the right-hand side of (6.15) is less than the right-hand side of (6.13). Further, (6.15) contains the interval (6.14). Thus (6.14) is contained in (6.13). In short: Böhm-Bawerk's analysis implies a smaller price interval than von Neumann–Morgenstern's, whilst both analyses agree on the number of units that will be traded.

One might well ask why this discrepancy over the price interval arises. The answer lies in the restriction in Böhm-Bawerk's analysis to a unique common price for all transactions that take place. By contrast, in the von Neumann–Morgenstern analysis, premiums and rebates are permitted, and the price p per unit specified in (6.13) is really an average price, and naturally is defined over a wider interval.

It is possible to progressively build up the above argument by considering the consequences of adding one more buyer, and so on. However, for brevity, let us move on to consider the general market case in which there are l sellers and m buyers, making up the totality of $m + l$ traders. Denote the set of sellers by

$$L = (1, 2, \ldots, l)$$

and the set of buyers by

$$M = (1', 2', \ldots, m')$$

where the prime distinguishes a buyer from a seller, and we have clearly stopped short of a more general analysis in which each trader may choose whether he wishes to become a buyer or a seller. In the notation adopted, $1' = l + 1, \ldots, m' = l + m$. The set of all participants is given by

$$I = L \cup M = (1, 2, \ldots, l; 1', 2', \ldots, m')$$

If the ith seller possesses s_i of the good, then

$$\sum_{i=1}^{l} s_i = s_i$$

Suitably modifying the notation used above for just two market participants, write the utilities to sellers and buyers as:

$$u_0^i, u_1^i, \ldots, u_{s_i}^i \quad (i = 1, 2, \ldots, l)$$

$$v_0^j, v_1^j, \ldots, v_s^j \quad (j = 1', 2', \ldots, m')$$

where $u_0^i = 0$, $v_0^j = 0$. The principal analytical task now is to define the characteristic function $v(S)$, where $S \subseteq I = L \cup M$. There are three cases to be considered.

Firstly, $S \subseteq C$, in which case S consists solely of sellers, and they carry out no transactions among themselves. Then

$$v(S) = \sum_{i \in S} u_{s_i}^i$$

Secondly, $S \subseteq M$, in which case S consists solely of buyers, who having no units of the good could not carry out any transactions among themselves. In this case,

$$v(S) = 0$$

Thirdly, and most significantly, the case of neither $S \subseteq L$ nor $S \subseteq M$. In other words S contains sellers as well as buyers, and hence a basis for undertaking transactions is established. Then the characteristic function is defined as

$$v(S) = \max_{\substack{t_i \\ i \in S \cap L}} \left\{ \sum_{i \in S \cap L} u^i_{k_i} + \sum_{j \in S \cap M} v^j_{r_j} \right\} \qquad (6.16)$$

$$t_i = 0, 1, \ldots s_i$$

where

$$\sum_{i \in S \cap L} k_i + \sum_{j \in S \cap M} r_j = \sum_{i \in S \cap L} s_i$$

$S \cap L$ is the set of all sellers in S, and $S \cap M$ is the set of all buyers in S. There are k_i units of the commodity transferred from the ith seller, with r_j units transferred to the buyer j. Note that it is not strictly necessary to specify which seller concludes a transaction with which buyer when defining $v(S)$. Furthermore, all the negotiations that traders might be engaged in (involving such manoeuvres as granting rebates and premiums, and forming coalitions) are automatically accommodated within the theory.

In (6.3) and in the discussion immediately prior to it we introduced the notion of an imputation in a relatively informal manner. Now let us look at this concept rather more rigorously. An imputation has three properties (Shubik, 1982, p. 141; von Neumann and Morgenstern, 1944, pp. 263–4). If I is the set of all players, this vector satisfies *feasibility* (sometimes called *effectiveness*)

$$\sum_{i \in I} \alpha_i \leqslant v(I) \qquad (6.17)$$

and the condition

$$\sum_{i \in I} \alpha_i \geqslant v(I) \qquad (6.18)$$

which together with (6.17) amounts to *Pareto optimality*, and finally *individual rationality*, which may be expressed

$$\alpha_i \geqslant v(\{i\}) \qquad \text{for all } i \in I \qquad (6.19)$$

It is now possible to state the important definition of the *core* in terms of imputations and the characteristic function. The core is the set of imputations such that

$$\sum_{i \in S} \alpha_i \geqslant v(S) \qquad \text{for all } S \subseteq I \qquad (6.20)$$

Intuitively, this set leaves no coalition the possibility of improving all members' payoffs. In games of this type, the core is the solution given by Böhm-Bawerk. Thus it leads to the inequality (6.14), defining the range within which a uniform market price will be established. If buyers and sellers are numerous and if the utilities u_i and v_i are sufficiently varied, then this range diminishes to a point and a single, determinate market price is established along the lines of classical supply and demand analysis.

It is possible to construct a variety of solution concepts based on the characteristic function, and very full treatments may be found in Shubik (1982, 1984). Here the treatment will be brief. Still retaining the assumption of transferable utility, the *strong ε-core* is the set of α such that

$$\sum_{i \in S} \alpha_i \geqslant v(S) - \varepsilon \qquad \text{for all } S \subseteq I \tag{6.21}$$

and the *weak ε-core* is the set of α such that

$$\sum_{i \in S} \alpha_i \geqslant v(S) - n\varepsilon \qquad \text{for all } S \subseteq I \tag{6.22}$$

where n is the number of players in the coalition S. Under the strong definition (6.21) a total excess of ε must be obtained before an outcome can be ruled out, whereas under the weak definition (6.22) a per caput excess of ε is required. The concepts introduce the possibility of modelling the costs of coalition formation, where ε might represent expenses of communication or organization. In this way it is possible to introduce players into the game who perform the function so central to Austrian analysis of the market, namely entrepreneurship.

There are several related solution concepts which emerge once one defines a concept which represents the amount by which the worth of a coalition exceeds its payoff. The *excess* of a coalition is just such a concept, and is defined as

$$e(S, \alpha) = v(S) - \sum_{i \in S} \alpha_i \tag{6.23}$$

For the core, no excess exceeds zero; and for the ε-core no excess is greater than ε. The *near-core* may be defined as the smallest non-empty ε-core, and consists of those imputations for which the maximum excess, as defined by (6.23), is as small as possible. The *nucleolus* is the imputation for which the maximum excess obtained by any coalition is minimized. Intuitively, the nucleolus minimizes dissatisfaction, with priority being accorded to the most dissatisfied coalitions. For illustrative examples, the reader is referred to the expositional *tour de force* of Shubik (1984, chapter 9) in which the original example of Böhm-Bawerk's horse trading market is analysed from the viewpoint of many solution concepts.

6.3 THE ENTREPRENEUR IN A TRADING GAME

We have seen in section 6.2 that the concept of an ε-core enables one to consider the organizational costs of forming coalitions. A firm can be regarded as a type of coalition, with the function of the pure entrepreneur being simply to bring together suitable sets of economic agents. The institutional form of the firm need not yet be specified, though it has been given detailed consideration by Shubik (1984, chapter 17); it consists of the form of the set of imputations and the characteristic function.

So far, the game has been specified objectively, and assumed to be of a form known to all players. However, though this approach can be related to the writings of leading Austrians like Böhm-Bawerk, it nevertheless neglects much that is essential to the Austrian approach. Littlechild (1979) has argued that what is required is to model a market *process* in game theoretic terms, where players are initially ignorant. Then the proper object of analysis is the process by which players come to understand and play the game. What he proffers is a theory of the bargaining process which is developed in the context of an experimental game. The treatment is therefore informal, and less than entirely rigorous, though suggestive of lines which might fruitfully be pursued.

In the experimental approach, human subjects are required to play economic roles. In Littlechild's case, players are told they are to play a game, and each player is given a copy of the characteristic function, this being the institutional equivalent of the game theoretic concept used extensively in the previous section. The characteristic function details the payments which the organizer of the game will make to each coalition of players. The proof of an established coalition is a set of signatures, one from each member. The objective aspect of the game is therefore knowledge of the set of players I and of the characteristic function v. The subjective aspect is the pattern of players' responses, and these are not specified. The set of players may be partitioned into active and passive participants. The former may be described as 'entrepreneurs', for it is they who in organizing gainful coalitions are exhibiting that entrepreneurial characteristic which Kirzner (1973) has described as 'alertness'. The role chosen by passive participants involves simply waiting for offers and accepting what seems reasonable. The choice of role is based on the objective knowledge of the characteristic function, but is otherwise subjective. There is, therefore, the distinct possibility that players can mistake the intentions of other participants.

Given that a player has chosen his role, he must next decide how to further his interest by coalition formation. The passive player is assumed to put a reservation price on his willingness to join a coalition. It is in his interest to do the best he can for himself, but the disincentive to setting the reservation price too high is that he might not achieve it at all, or that he might have to wait longer than otherwise to achieve it. He can at least lower his reservation price in the light of experience, whereas an initially low reservation price, whilst offering the prospect of early settlement, commits him to an agreement on which he cannot renege even if subsequent offers should be more attractive. On the other hand, rejection of offers which at one stage may appear unattractive, opens up the possibility that they will not be made again subsequently when they have become more attractive.

The active participants (entrepreneurs) have to decide which passive participants they can profitably entice into a coalition. As specified, the game leaves open the possibility of participants revising their plans, and even of revising their sales. Formally, this game can be specified as follows.

The game is defined by the pair (I, v), where $I = \{1, 2, \ldots, n\}$ is the set of players (traders) and $v(S)$ is the characteristic function. The set of participants who choose to be active and assume entrepreneurial roles is denoted $M = \{1, 2, \ldots, m\}$, where M is a subset of I. For the purposes of play, it is necessary to define an artificial entrepreneur (index 0) who is always willing to offer the value $v(\{j\})$ to the player j acting alone. This corresponds in the terminology of game theory to the *status quo* or *security level* of a single player. Denote by $S_i(t)$ $(i = 1, 2, \ldots, m)$ the set of players who at time t have committed themselves to the coalition of the ith entrepreneur, and by $A(t)$ the set of players who at that time remain uncommitted. Because a player may put his signature to only one entrepreneur, the sets $S_i(t)$ are disjoint. Finally, as all players are committed to a coalition or not, the union of the $S_i(t)$ and $A(t)$ is the set I.

Let the game be indexed by times $0, 1, 2, \ldots, t, \ldots$, with play commencing at the base time $t = 0$. All entrepreneurs are initially uncommitted, $A(0) = M$ and $S_i(0) = \{i\}$; that is, each entrepreneur has initially only himself in his own coalition. The artificial entrepreneur does not constitute a coalition on his own; thus $S_0(0) = \emptyset$. Play is completed at time T if all players have been signed up by an entrepreneur. Then the set of non-committed players is empty and the sets $S_i(T)$ form a partition of I.

Play proceeds by entrepreneurs actively offering prices to uncommitted players; and by each uncommitted player signing up with that entrepreneur who offers him the best price, provided it exceeds his reservation price. Denote by $p_j^i(t)$ the ith entrepreneur's offer to the jth inactive player, with $j \in A(t)$, and $p_j^0(t) \equiv v(\{j\})$, the latter being the security level that the jth player can be assured of obtaining from the artificial entrepreneur. Denote by $r_j(t)$ for $j \in A(t)$ the jth player's reservation price, for offers below which he cannot be induced to join any coalition – at time t, at least. The set of players whom entrepreneurs manage to persuade to join coalitions is denoted $B_i(t)$, where

$$B_i(t) = \{j \in A(t) \mid p_j^i(t) \geqslant p_j^k(t), \, k \neq i \text{ and } p_j^i(t) \geqslant r_j(t)\} \qquad (6.24)$$

That is, the set of players who become committed to an entrepreneur's coalition at a given time is made up of individuals who have been given at least one bid which exceeds their reservation price, and have accepted the best of such bids.

The sets of committed and uncommitted players are determined by the following recursive relationships:

$$S_i(t + 1) = S_i(t) \cup B_i(t) \tag{6.25}$$

$$A(t + 1) = A(t) - \overset{m}{\underset{i=0}{\cup}} B_i(t) \tag{6.26}$$

By (6.25) we mean that committed players at time $t + 1$ are made up of players who were already committed by time t, and players who become committed at time t. By (6.26) we mean that the set of uncommitted players at time $t + 1$ is made up of the set of uncommitted players at time t, less the totality (i.e. union) of sets of players who became committed to one of the m entrepreneur's coalitions at time t. The sets $S_i(t)$ and $A(t)$ are respectively non-decreasing and non-increasing over time in the sense that

$$t_2 > t_1 \quad \text{implies} \quad \begin{matrix} S_i(t_1) \subseteq S_i(t_2) \\ \text{and} \quad A(t_2) \subseteq A(t_1) \end{matrix} \tag{6.27}$$

Each entrepreneur in the set M clearly has an optimization problem. Let $\hat{p}_j^i(t)$ denote the price which the ith entrepreneur believes he must offer the jth trader in order to get him to join his coalition, with $\hat{p}_j^0(t) \equiv v(\{j\})$. The entrepreneur will control his set of additional signatures, $D_i(t)$, to his own end. His optimization problem is

$$\max_{D_i(t)} v[S_i(t) \cup D_i(t)] - \sum_{j \in D_i(t)} \hat{p}_j^i(t) \tag{6.28}$$

subject to $D_i(t) \subseteq A(t) \quad (i = 1, 2, \ldots, m)$

Then price is set according to the rule

$$p_j^i(t) = \begin{cases} \hat{p}_j^i(t) & \text{for } j \in D_i(t) \\ 0 & \text{for } j \in [A(t) - D_i(t)] \end{cases} \tag{6.29}$$

Littlechild (1979, pp. 156–7) points out that a sufficient condition for this game to be concluded in a finite number of plays is that each uncommitted player, after a certain play, will reduce his reservation price by at least a fixed minimum amount each play. This seems a reasonable condition to impose.

The outcome of this game is to partition the set of players into disjoint coalitions once all players are committed, i.e. once $A(T) = \emptyset$ for some finite T. For each coalition $S_i = S_i(T)$ at the conclusion of play there is a payoff or imputation such that

$$\sum_{j \in S_i} \alpha_j = v(S_i) \quad (i = 1, 2, \ldots, m) \tag{6.30}$$

The passive players get what they were promised on joining the coalition, and the entrepreneur's payoff is the balance:

$$\alpha_i = v(S_i) - \sum_{\substack{j \in S_i \\ j \neq i}} \alpha_j \quad (i = 1, 2, \ldots, m) \tag{6.31}$$

The relationship of (6.31) to the strong ε-core definition embodied in (6.21) is obvious. It is conjectured by Littlechild (1979, p. 161) that under repeated plays, if the core is non-empty, the payoff vector will tend to lie in the core and, further, near to the nucleolus.

The market as viewed in section 6.2 gave no insight into how bargaining took place between buyers and sellers. Like a clock, one could observe the hands move, but the mechanism remained concealed. The entrepreneurial game of this section provides the wherewithal for looking at mechanisms in an empirical sense, but we still lack data. Of course, in the absence of data, one can make conjectures. Thus a player seems more likely to behave passively if he is less experienced, less alert, less impatient, less extrovert, more risk-averse, and so on. It does seem helpful, however, to explore at least some of these possibilities formally; so let us focus on risk aversion.

In an important paper modelling entrepreneurial activity, Kihlstrom and Laffont (1979) take the work of Frank Knight (1921) as their source of inspiration. It is assumed, as in the market game above, that each agent in the economy can become an entrepreneur. Whether he does so or not depends on his attitude to risk. All agents have costless access to a production technology characterized by the following production function:

$$y = y(L, x) \tag{6.32}$$

where y is output, L is labour, and x is a random variable bounded away from zero. All agents have the same belief about the distribution of x. Agents can become entrepreneurs and receive an uncertain profit income, or they can become workers and have the certainty of receiving the competitive wage w. If an agent decides to become an entrepreneur, and to hire the amount L of labour at the wage rate w, his net income will be

$$y(L, x) - wL \tag{6.33}$$

where the output price has been normalized to unity. It is assumed that all agents start with equal endowments of A units of income. Each agent is identified with a point β on the unit interval, and for an income Y has a von Neumann–Morgenstern utility function $u(Y, \beta)$ with $\partial u/\partial Y > 0$ and $\partial^2 u/\partial Y^2 \leqslant 0$. Thus agents may be risk-neutral or risk-averse, but risk-loving conduct is ruled out.

Let us turn now to the decision which an agent makes on whether to become an entrepreneur or a worker. The agent indexed by β in the interval $(0, 1)$ considers his random profit function

$$\Pi(w, \beta) = y[L(w, \beta), x] - wL(w, \beta)$$

He will choose to be an entrepreneur if

$$E\{u[A + \Pi(w, \beta)], \beta\} > u(A + w, \beta)$$

that is, if the expected utility of the risky alternative (becoming an entrepreneur), bringing the prospect of income $A + \Pi(w, \beta)$, is greater than the utility of the sure prospect (becoming a worker), with a certain income of $A + w$. This treatment is an advance on our previous discussion in that the choice of role of a player is made endogenous, and a form of production technology is introduced, rather than confining attention to the case of pure exchange.

6.4 THE MARKET PROCESS

A general feature of the Austrian method is its emphasis on the market process, as distinct from market situations. In chapter 2, on structure, conduct, and performance, attention was focused on equilibrium market *situations*, which were characterized by certain features such as concentration, and the extent of deviation of price from marginal cost. To Austrian economists such an approach is misleading, for they emphasize the 'unquiet' nature of markets – the continual adaption of markets to new tastes and technologies.

In terms of the market models developed in section 6.2 we need to consider the possibility that the subjective valuations which lead to the utilities u and v are not constants, but rather shift with the information at the disposal of economic agents. The upshot of the discussion in section 6.3 is that some agents adapt more rapidly in the light of new information. They are more alert to the new possibilities which arise as a result of it, and less timid about acting on their evaluations, as compared with more passive agents. In 1921 Taussig published a classical paper entitled 'Is market price determinate?', in which he pointed out the importance of expectations in determining supply and demand. We have previously indicated the circumstances under which the u and v imply supply and demand functions of classical form. Taussig argued that though price may assume a long-run equilibrium 'on the average', it nevertheless fluctuates within what he calls a *penumbra*, because of uncertainty. A simple example which illustrates the content of Taussig's argument is the case of fixed supply so beloved of the Austrians. Let supply be fixed, but fixed at a value which is uncertain. Thus Taussig (1921, p. 399) argues that 'crop reports may prove inaccurate, unexpected deficiencies or surpluses may be discovered'. To model this situation, suppose that supply S is given by the random variable

$$S = S^\star + \mu \tag{6.34}$$

where $S^\star$ is mean supply. For simplicity, μ has a uniform distribution; that is, it has the density function

$$f(\mu) = 1/a \qquad \text{for } -a/2 \leqslant \mu \leqslant a/2 < S^\star \qquad (6.35)$$

with parameter a. Again for simplicity, let demand be described by the rectangular hyperbola $D = k/p$ with k a positive constant. Then it is easily shown that price has the probability density function

$$g(p) = \frac{k}{ap^2} \qquad \text{with } \frac{k}{S^\star + a/2} \leqslant p \leqslant \frac{k}{S^\star - a/2} \qquad (6.36)$$

where the range of variation of price given in (6.36) may be identified with Taussig's 'penumbra' of price.

The Austrian view is that typically there will be a distribution of prices in the market for a good, at a given time, even if the good is homogeneous. Note this is not the same as the argument that there will exist a distribution of prices in the market for a differentiated good, for even if traders had the time and resources to become fully informed, an irreducible spread of prices would remain, reflecting the distribution of tastes over traders. Under the Austrian interpretation, the market process involves a diminution in the 'spread' of prices over time, leading to a unique equilibrium price in the case of a homogeneous good, or a stable equilibrium price distribution in the case of a heterogeneous good. In terms of the density given in (6.36), the effect of the market process over time would be to cause the distribution to 'collapse' around a fixed value.

In order to develop this argument further, the market terminology used has to be precisely expressed. We loosely talk of there being a market for gold on the New York Stock Exchange, or a market for Deutschmarks on the London Stock Exchange. Equally, we are frequently quite happy to talk of the world market for gold and the world market for Deutschmarks. The truth is, our terminology 'the market' is a convenience, and its meaning depends on the context of our discussion. At a general level, it would be sensible to regard the New York Stock Exchange and the London Stock Exchange as being submarkets of a world market. In the formal discussion that follows, we will consider a homogeneous good which is traded on various submarkets. These submarkets are linked, either directly or indirectly, and hence the collection of such submarkets represents 'the market', in the large, for the good. Entrepreneurs play the role of linking the submarkets. As Kirzner (1973) has emphasized, entrepreneurs facilitate the passage to equilibrium. There is a distribution of efficiency or alertness across entrepreneurs, and this will be reflected both in variations in knowledge of submarkets and in the zeal with which trade is promoted between submarkets to take advantage of price differentials. Following Littlechild and Owen (1980), let $y_{ik}^j(t)$ denote the amount of good y that is bought in market i and sold in market k by entrepreneur j in time t. Using a dot to denote rate of change with respect to time, assume that each entrepreneur takes price as given, and that the rate at which the good y is transferred from one submarket to another is directly proportional to the price discrepancy between the submarkets. Formally

$$\dot{y}_{ik}^j(t) = \sigma_j(p_i - p_k) \tag{6.37}$$

where σ_j is a 'speed of adjustment' coefficient. Two submarkets may be linked either directly or indirectly: directly, if some entrepreneur is aware of them both; or indirectly, if there is a chain of directly linked submarkets, with the two submarkets in question being at either end of the chain. Then it can be shown that the dispersion of prices between submarkets will tend to vanish over time, ultimately establishing a uniform price across all submarkets. To complicate this picture further, suppose that an entrepreneur, who does not know of the existence of a market at time t, has a probability of discovering it which is proportional to its 'attractiveness'; the latter term is defined by the potential gain which can accrue to the entrepreneur by exploiting the highest and lowest price known to him in the submarkets in which he is currently trading. Then it can be shown that whatever the initial distribution of knowledge amongst entrepreneurs, prices will 'almost certainly' (i.e. with limiting probability of unity) converge to a uniform price.

Here the action of the entrepreneur promotes greater market co-ordination, an interpretation favoured by Kirzner (1973). However, the formalization is somewhat too narrow, for it ignores considerations of the profitability of transfers between submarkets, and makes entrepreneurs price-takers rather than price-makers. The process is certainly efficient in the sense of Kirzner (1973, p. 235), for 'each step in the process improves the co-ordination of existing information and eliminates some of the discordant decisions made earlier'. If this process continues in all markets, the economy established is, in the terminology of Rothbard (1962), 'evenly rotating'. A rather similar concept appears in Schumpeter (1934) as the 'circular flow' economy. But whereas Austrians like Kirzner emphasize the equilibrating consequences of entrepreneurial action, others like Schumpeter (1942) see their action as being essentially disruptive. This contrast in approach is developed in further detail by Jacobsen (1986). For Kirzner, the essence of the entrepreneur is to be alert to new opportunities, and to capitalize on them for gain, and in so doing to move the economy towards equilibrium. For Schumpeter, the very approach to a 'circular flow' provides a stimulus for the entrepreneur to disrupt existing patterns of production. He engages in 'creative destruction', driving out old methods in favour of the new, and confronting consumers with novel consumption opportunities. This view leads to an attitude towards monopoly which is very different from that adopted by economists coming from the structure–conduct–performance tradition.

6.5   MONOPOLY: GOOD OR BAD?

Ever since Adam Smith (1776, p. 163) wrote that 'monopoly is a great enemy to good management', there has been a presumption by economists that monopoly is necessarily bad. Smith (1776, pp. 78–9) expressed the argument against monopoly as follows:

> The monopolists, by keeping the market constantly understocked, by never fully supplying the effectual demand, sell their commodities much above the natural price, and raise their emoluments, whether they consist in wages or profit, greatly above their natural rate. The price of monopoly is upon every occasion the highest which can be got. The natural price, or the price of free competition, on the contrary, is the lowest which can be taken.

Though most Austrians continue to draw much inspiration from Adam Smith, it is doubtful whether many would accept his condemnation of monopoly. Indeed, as Kirzner (1979) has documented in a detailed way, Smith lacked a theory of entrepreneurship, and this would militate against his expressing any sympathy for monopoly, be it even temporary in nature.

In fact, Smith's analysis is remarkably close to the partial equilibrium argument against monopoly advanced by writers like Marshall. This argument revolves around the 'deadweight' loss of consumers' and producers' surplus which exists in the monopoly situation. A special case of this argument was used by Harberger (1954) in a classical empirical study of the magnitude of monopoly welfare loss in US manufacturing for the period 1924–28. If price is raised above long-run average cost ('the price of free competition') by Δp and output curtailed from the competitive level ('keeping the market constantly understocked') by an amount Δx, then Harberger's measure of welfare loss is $\Delta p \Delta x/2$. For the case of linear schedules this is illustrated in figure 6.1. In this diagram, DD' is the demand function; p_1 the monopoly (profit maximizing) price; C is long-run unit cost, assumed constant and incorporating the cost of capital; S is consumers' surplus; Π is profit; and L is the welfare loss of monopoly given by the triangle EFG. The welfare loss triangle may then be approximated as follows:

$$L = \tfrac{1}{2}(p_1 - C)^2 \frac{\mathrm{d}x}{\mathrm{d}p} = \frac{\Pi}{2}\eta\,\frac{p_1 - C}{p_1} \tag{6.38}$$

where η is the absolute value of the price elasticity of demand. In Harberger's analysis it was assumed that $\eta = 1$, and on this basis his finding was that the welfare loss due to monopoly was less than 1 per cent of national income. This was confirmed by a subsequent study of Schwartzman (1960). However, using

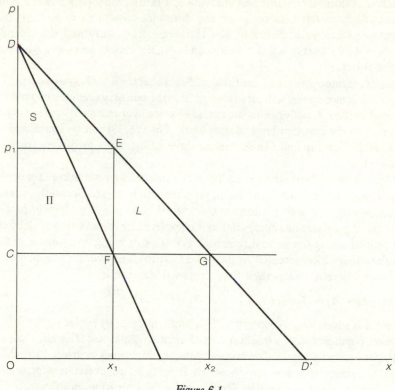

Figure 6.1

a revised methodology, Kamerschen (1966) came to the conclusion that dead-weight loss could be as high as 8 per cent of national income. Two specific features of Kamerschen's methodology probably explain this. Firstly, he obtained direct estimates of industry elasticities of demand. Secondly, he did not regard a number of selling costs, for example advertising, as a part of monopoly profit, and excluded them from his cost curves. In the same spirit is the more recent study by Cowling and Mueller (1978) which suggests monopoly welfare losses as high as 13 per cent of gross corporate profit. This study provides a suitable vehicle for illustrating the practical consequences of taking a structure–conduct–performance approach to monopoly, as distinct from an Austrian.

Littlechild (1981), writing from an Austrian standpoint, has challenged the study of Cowling and Mueller (1978) on four grounds. Firstly, he suggests they overestimate welfare loss even within their own chosen frame of reference. Secondly, the emphasis on long-run equilibrium which is characteristic of the Harberger methodology is argued to be inappropriate, as it ignores profits which arise from uncertainty and innovation. Thirdly, monopoly power has its nature misinterpreted, as to its extent, duration, costs, and origins, in the Harberger framework. Fourthly, the Harberger framework and the amendments to it by writers such as Cowling and Mueller cannot serve as a basis for public policy.

Let us examine this argument further. From chapter 2 we know that a profit maximizing monopolist will set price such that the industry elasticity of demand is equal to the ratio of price to the excess of price over marginal cost (equal in this case to the constant level of unit cost). Thus (6.38) can be simplified to $L \cong \Pi/2$. Cowling and Mueller make three adjustments to this measure of welfare loss.

Arguing that advertising expenditure is a device for promoting monopoly power, such expenditure is included with monopoly profit. Secondly, advertising expenditure is then added to this extended notion of monopoly profit. Thirdly, the welfare loss computation is completed by the addition of all after-tax profits, net of the normal return on capital, this being an estimate of the expenditures which potential rivals would have to incur in order to gain access to monopoly rents. Thus their final proposed measure is

$$\tfrac{1}{2}(\Pi + A) + A + (\Pi - T) \quad \text{or} \quad \tfrac{3}{2}(\Pi + A) - T \tag{6.39}$$

where A is advertising expenditure, Π is profit adjusted by replacing the firm's interest payments with a (higher) cost of capital figure, and T is tax.

Provisionally taking the Cowling and Mueller framework as given, Littlechild (1981) suggests four respects in which it leads to an overstatement of the welfare losses due to monopoly. Firstly, price discrimination, multipart tariffs, and discounts are ignored, the existence of which tends to reduce welfare loss. Further, for companies such as Shell and BP which were a very significant source of welfare losses for UK firms, at least part of the welfare loss would not be borne by the UK economy as such. Secondly, Cowling and Mueller entirely ignore the informational aspect of advertising. Thirdly, Littlechild argues that post-tax profits overstate the socially wasteful costs of acquiring a monopoly position, as initial resource owners will receive at least some monopoly rents. Fourthly, the adjustment upwards of profit rates to take account of patents and goodwill is regarded as inappropriate. Advertising expenditure, as well as R & D expenditures, whilst in an accounting sense regarded as expenses in the year in which they are incurred, should be regarded as intangible assets. These expenditures generate incomes over a sequence of years and should therefore be capitalized and then depreciated against subsequent incomes. In this way Brozen (1977), for example, was able to demonstrate that corrected rates of return in the US pharmaceuticals industry were 5.4 percentage points lower than accounting rates of return.

More fundamental than these criticisms, which take the Harberger framework as appropriate and criticize, as it were, 'from within', are those which reject the framework as inappropriate. Littlechild accepts the Austrian emphasis on competition as a process, and therefore rejects the use of a neoclassical long-run equilibrium framework for analysing monopoly welfare loss. He points to substantial variations of rates of return within industries as evidence of disequilibrium.

Littlechild argues that the weakness of Harberger's framework is that all profits are regarded as indicative of a welfare loss in a long-run equilibrium framework. In addition to this monopoly rent, profits might arise from windfall gains and losses and from differences in entrepreneurial ability between firms. If there is a distribution of gainers and losers, it is faulty methodology to select only the gainers and to assume that their above-average returns imply a welfare loss. Firms operating in relatively risky environments will have both to pay a risk premium to attract capital, and to generate relatively higher rates of return to make possible the payment of higher dividends. Perhaps more important is Littlechild's emphasis on the Austrian concept of entrepreneurship. Referring back to figure 6.1, consider an entrepreneur, who by dint of superior creativity or foresight achieves the position of sole seller and is able to set a price of p_1. Then, as the relevant alternative to his producing is that no production takes place at all, the entrepreneurial action generates a social gain of profit Π plus consumers' surplus S. This gain will not exist in the long run, however, but only as long as it takes for the market to respond to, and attempt to benefit from, the opportunities opened up by this first entrepreneur in the field. As entry causes price to be competed down from p_1 to C, entrepreneurial profit becomes converted into consumers' surplus. In addition, Littlechild argues, entrepreneurial alertness has enabled the market to bring to consumers the surplus on output $x_1 x_2$ *earlier* than under alternative institutional arrangements.

To stylize the differences between the Cowling–Mueller approach and the alternative Austrian approach proposed by Littlechild, we may proceed as follows. Cowling and Mueller work in a long-run equilibrium framework which is in the SCP tradition developed in chapter 2. Profit is regarded as caused by monopoly, and this is wasteful both in itself and in the sense that it imposes waste on competitors. The monopoly profit of the incumbent is in a sense the cost set on competing. Littlechild rejects the long-run equilibrium framework, and identifies most profit as arising from windfall gains, or as the short-term rewards for entrepreneurial alertness. The former approach suggests a public policy directed towards eliminating monopoly profit; the latter suggests a public policy directed towards eliminating barriers to entry.

6.6 CONCLUSION

The Austrian approach to economics is often identified with a painstaking literary mode of analysis which takes care to establish any proposition proffered in meticulous detail. In this chapter, by contrast, we have chosen at the outset not to avoid more concise mathematical methods of exposition. This has permitted us to emphasize the contribution that game theory can make to the Austrian research programme. It is a mournful experience to read recent books by eminent Austrian economists which are no more than elegant restatements of arguments developed in earlier works. This leaves one with a distinct sense of degeneracy in the Austrian research programme. By contrast, if one accepts the insights offered by game theorists into classical models of Austrianism, like Böhm-Bawerk's horse trading market, whole new vistas of research possibilities appear. To mention but two: the comparative analysis of solution concepts for given market situations; and experimental gaming with human subjects. Both offer the potential for intellectual excitement. The starting points are as with the older Austrianism – individualism, subjectivism, uncertainty, and market processes – but modern analytical methods now offer the possibility of genuine theoretical advance, as distinct from barren restatement of established propositions.

7

Workable competition

Although US antitrust policy as represented by the Sherman Act of 1890 can be regarded as the earliest embodiment of the doctrine of workable competition, the seminal scholarly contribution was made by Clark (1940). He made the simple yet powerful point that even if the ideal of competition as epitomized by the model of perfect competition cannot be attained, there is still a role for public policy in influencing the nature of competition, with a view to making it 'workable' if not 'perfect'. In this chapter, Clark's basic insight will be regarded as a precursor of the theory of the second best. Clark was concerned with laying bare the character of competition by reference to factors like product heterogeneity, concentration, price conduct, and the pattern of costs, but made no specific listing of criteria for workability. His characterization of competition was very close to the Marshallian concept of 'free competition' introduced in chapter 5. It is apparent that Clark himself would have particularly emphasized technical progressiveness and the proliferation of substitutes with relatively price-insensitive quality differentials when appraising the workability of competition in any particular industry. Since he wrote that classical article the devising of lists of criteria for workability has become something of a black art, and Sosnick (1958) in his influential critique of concepts of workable competition codifies 18 such lists. The unifying theme for Sosnick's codification is the structure–conduct–performance framework which was expounded in chapter 2. The difficulty with his approach lies in its sheer eclecticism. The criteria developed seem frequently arbitrary and vague, and occasionally inconsistent. We argue that the structure–conduct–performance version of workability may usefully be viewed in a social welfare function framework which certainly removes inconsistency, and hopefully diminishes arbitrariness and vagueness.

Opposed to the view that a fixed list of criteria for workable competition can be developed is the stance of Markham (1950). He argues that each industry should be looked at as a case in its own right, and the question that should be asked is whether there are policy changes which could be implemented that would lead unambiguously to a welfare improvement. This leaves open the question of the welfare sense in which an improvement could be said to have been attained. In much judicial interpretation it is clear that welfare improvement in a Paretian sense is not being considered, for judgements are usually based on a partially qualitative balancing of benefits against costs, and the application of what has been described as an economist's 'rule of reason'. Thus economic changes – some of which compensate the losers, and some of which might even involve the theoretical opportunity for losers to bribe gainers into not making the move but offer no practical mechanism for doing so – are sanctioned by judicial decisions in a way which welfare economists often find unsatisfactory.

If, following Markham (1950) a case by case approach has to be adopted, the question of the legitimacy of the piecemeal approach to welfare analysis is raised. Williamson (1968) proposed a welfare trade-off analysis in which the undesirable effect of monopolization, entailing elevated price–cost margins, is balanced against the desirable effect of economies of scale. This is just one of the many ways in which costs and benefits may be weighed against one another in a piecemeal approach. The issue is of considerable practical importance, for the UK approach to antitrust is in essentials a piecemeal one. The famous 'tail piece' of restrictive practices legislation in the UK requires that the benefits must outweigh the detriments for an agreement to be acceptable in the eyes of the court.

The final approach to workability to be considered in this chapter is the 'contestable markets' analysis of Baumol et al. (1982). They recognize the problems that arise from vagueness in the criteria laid down for workability but applaud the attempt to work with a competitive norm other than that of perfect competition. What they attempt to produce is an analysis which is both precise and consistent, as well as being concerned with a feasible workably competitive norm. However, it is not free of weaknesses, the most significant of which is its dependence on an assumption of ultra-free entry. The search for rigour and policy relevance is however commendable, and indicative of an attitude which may lead to a new and potentially fruitful approach to the doctrine of workable competition.

7.2   WORKABILITY AND THE THEORY OF THE SECOND BEST

In the original exposition of workable competition by Clark (1940), there are a number of remarkable insights quite apart from his argument for developing a new competitive norm. The most significant is a precise statement by Clark of 'the theory of the second best' made familiar to economists in a rigorous analytical form by Lipsey and Lancaster (1956). Clark (1940, p. 242) states the proto-theory of the second best as follows:

If there are, for example, five conditions, all of which are essential to perfect competition, and the first is lacking in a given case, then it no longer follows that we are necessarily better off for the presence of any of the other four. In the absence of the first, it is *a priori* quite possible that the second and third may depend on achieving some degree of 'imperfection' in these other two factors.

In his earliest exposition Clark is apparently talking of an 'amended' competitive norm, which like the perfectly competitive is static in character. Later, Clark (1955, 1961) was to develop his ideas further and to favour a dynamic conception of competition which has a lot in common with the Austrianism discussed in chapter 6. Let us for the moment confine ourselves to static arguments, and follow the approach of Lipsey and Lancaster in explaining the nature of a second-best solution.

Consider an economy in which some industries are subject to government control and others are monopolized in a way which defies immediate remedy. Now a piecemeal approach would suggest that the government-controlled industries be required to engage in marginal cost pricing. A second-best approach would recognize that limited application of Paretian rules might well lower the productive efficiency of the economy and reduce the welfare of economic agents. To simplify, consider a three-sector economy, producing goods in amounts x_1, x_2, and x_3. Suppose that the first sector (industry 1) is irrevocably monopolized and is setting price above marginal cost, and restricting output. If resources are fully employed then it will be producing less of the monopolized good x_1 than is required for a Pareto optimum, and correspondingly the non-monopolized sectors (industries 2 and 3) will be producing more than the optimum amounts of x_2 and x_3. If one of the non-monopolized industries were to be brought under government control and required to behave competitively, it would overproduce compared with the requirement of Pareto optimality. If it behaved in some measure imperfectly competitively, this would limit its own relative overproduction compared with the monopolized sector, but exacerbate the tendency of the remaining sector to overproduce in relation to itself and to the totally monopolized sector. Clark (1940, p. 249) observed, using the figurative language of an earlier generation, that we require a theory in which 'one kind of imperfection requires another to take part of the curse off it'. He perceived that we need a guide to the appropriate degree of imperfection for a second-best world. Let us seek such an appropriate set of rules in the context of our simple model.

Suppose labour is available in a fixed amount L, and all labour is fully employed, by amounts l_1, l_2, and l_3 in the three industries or sectors. Then

$$l_1 + l_2 + l_3 = L \tag{7.1}$$

Let output in each industry be characterized by the simple proportional one-factor production functions

$$x_1 = l_1/a_1 \qquad x_2 = l_2/a_2 \qquad x_3 = l_3/a_3 \tag{7.2}$$

where the a_i are given parameters. If the competitive wage rate is w, then marginal costs in each of the three sectors are

$$MC_1 = wa_1 \qquad MC_2 = wa_2 \qquad MC_3 = wa_3 \tag{7.3}$$

Consider a community preference function which has the same form as that of the identical economic agents who, we will assume, make up the society. Let it be of the form

$$U = x_1^{\alpha_1} x_2^{\alpha_2} x_3^{\alpha_3} \qquad \alpha_1, \alpha_2, \alpha_3 > 0 \tag{7.4}$$

For the production technology specified by (7.1) and (7.2) the transformation function is given by

$$a_1 x_1 + a_2 x_2 + a_3 x_3 = L \tag{7.5}$$

If there were no constraints on the economy other than (7.5), the first-best or Pareto optimal situation would be characterized by the solution to the optimizing problem

$$\max U \qquad \text{subject to } a_1 x_1 + a_2 x_2 + a_3 x_3 = L \tag{7.6}$$

which yields the following familiar equivalences of ratios of marginal utilities (or prices) to marginal costs:

with

$$\left.\begin{array}{cc} \dfrac{U_1}{U_3} = \dfrac{a_1}{a_3} & \dfrac{U_2}{U_3} = \dfrac{a_2}{a_3} \\[4mm] \dfrac{U_1}{U_3} = \dfrac{p_1}{p_3} & \dfrac{U_2}{U_3} = \dfrac{p_2}{p_3} \end{array}\right\} \tag{7.7}$$

where p_1, p_2, and p_3 are the competitive prices of x_1, x_2, and x_3 respectively. By (7.3) and (7.7) we have the conditions

and similarly

$$\left.\begin{array}{c} \dfrac{U_1}{U_3} = \dfrac{a_1}{a_3} = \dfrac{wa_1}{wa_3} = \dfrac{MC_1}{MC_3} = \dfrac{p_1}{p_3} \\[4mm] \dfrac{U_2}{U_3} = \dfrac{MC_2}{MC_3} = \dfrac{p_2}{p_3} \end{array}\right\} \tag{7.8}$$

Now if each industry were to follow a $p_i = MC_i$ pricing rule, these conditions would be satisfied. However, we are assuming that industry 1 is irrevocably monopolized, in which case

$$\frac{p_1}{p_3} > \frac{MC_1}{MC_3} \tag{7.9}$$

Now for the preference function (7.4) $U_1/U_3 = \alpha_1 x_3/\alpha_3 x_1$, which equals p_1/p_3 assuming utility maximization and price-taking behaviour. Thus (7.9) can be manipulated, using (7.3), to yield

$$\frac{\alpha_1 x_3}{\alpha_3 x_1} > \frac{a_1}{a_3}$$

which implies that

$$\alpha_1 a_3 x_3 > a_1 \alpha_3 x_1$$

or

$$\alpha_1 a_3 x_3 = k a_1 \alpha_3 x_1 \qquad k > 1 \tag{7.10}$$

To obtain the second-best optimum, consider the modified optimization problem

$$\max U \quad \text{subject to} \quad \alpha_1 a_3 x_3 = k a_1 \alpha_3 x_1$$
$$\text{and} \quad a_1 x_1 + a_2 x_2 + a_3 x_3 = L \tag{7.11}$$

where (7.10) is now introduced as an additional constraint. It can then be shown by routine manipulation that for the second-best solution obtained by solving the optimizing problem (7.11) we have

$$\frac{p_2}{p_3} = h \frac{MC_2}{MC_3} \tag{7.12}$$

where

$$h = 1 \bigg/ \left(1 - \frac{k-1}{k} \frac{\alpha_1}{\alpha_1 + \alpha_3}\right) > 1$$

If we regard industry 2 as subject to regulatory control, what (7.12) does is to confirm Clark's intuition that 'one kind of imperfection requires another', for it indicates that for industry 2 a positive degree of monopoly in relation to industry 3 is required in a second-best world. It can be shown further that the ratio of price in the regulated industry to price in the monopolized industry is

$$\frac{p_2}{p_1} = \frac{a_2}{a_1} \left(\frac{\alpha_1 + \alpha_3}{\alpha_1 + k\alpha_3} \right) = \frac{MC_2}{MC_1} g \tag{7.13}$$

where g, denoting the bracketed term, is less than unity. That is, the price–cost margin in the regulated industry is lower than in the monopolized industry. These specific results have been obtained by using particular and highly specialized functional forms, as embodied in (7.2) and (7.4). They are intuitively appealing, for they imply deliberately imposing a measure of market imperfection in one sector to compensate for a market imperfection elsewhere by employing a cure which is less damaging than the disease; that is, by imposing a lesser degree of monopoly. In a more general framework, neat and intuitively appealing results like this are not available and there can be no *a priori* expectations about the nature of the second-best solution. Suppose there is a policy objective function $F(x_1, \ldots, x_n)$ to be maximized subject to a feasibility constraint $G(x_1, \ldots, x_n) = 0$ and a second-best constraint

$$F_1/F_n = rG_1/G_n \tag{7.14}$$

where subscripts denote partial derivatives, and r is a constant different from unity. The first-order conditions for this optimization problem can be written

$$F_i/F_n = r_i G_i/G_n \qquad r_1 = r, r_n = 1 \tag{7.15}$$
$$(i = 1, 2, \ldots, n)$$

where in general the $r_2, \ldots, r_{n-1}$ are distinct and different from r and from unity. Thus the Pareto conditions $F_i/F_n = G_i/G_n$ are in general not satisfied in this second-best world. The r_i involve second-order partial derivatives of the objective function and the feasibility constraint and generally are too complex to afford guidance on the nature of the second-best solution. All this is to suggest that the prospect of applying a piecemeal policy in a regulatory framework in a fashion which avoids logical contradiction is rather bleak. Boadway and Harris (1977) have shown that a sufficient condition for the application of piecemeal policy prescriptions is that the cross-price elasticities of uncompensated demand and supply between the distorted sector and any undistorted sector should be zero. These conditions seem stringent, but suggest that under a variety of separability assumptions piecemeal rules may legitimately be applied.

An alternative approach to the second-best difficulty might seem to be to equalize the degree of monopoly across industries. In the first industry we had a situation in which $p_1 = \lambda MC_1 (\lambda > 1)$. Now if the regulatory authorities required that prices be set in the second and third industries so that

$$p_2 = \lambda MC_2 \quad \text{and} \quad p_3 = \lambda MC_3 \tag{7.16}$$

the first-best conditions as embodied in (7.8) would be attained. This proposition was first favoured by Kahn (1935) and subsequently quoted with approval by McManus (1959). However, it is misleading. The consequence of regulatory action would be to raise the prices in the non-monopolized industries and thus lower the relative price in the monopolized industry. This would stimulate demand in the monopolized industry and, provided costs were not too rapidly decreasing, would provide an incentive for an increase in nominal price in this sector. In brief, if rule (7.16) is imposed by regulation, a higher λ would be set in the monopolized industry, which by assumption is not subject to remedial action. Thus the intent of regulatory action is thwarted.

We have stated that Clark's argument for an alternative welfare norm to perfect competition was in effect an argument for the second-best solution. Following the tighter analytical reasoning of Lipsey and Lancaster (1956) we saw that it was no easy task to characterize the second-best solution. In retrospect, it is not surprising therefore that Clark himself was unable to actually say what workable competition would look like. He specified instead a set of ten conditions which would determine the character of competition:

1   Extent of standardization of the product
2   Degree of seller concentration
3   Method of setting price
4   Extent of market intermediation (e.g. by brokers, salesmen)
5   Extent, type, and quality of market information
6   Spatial distribution of consumers and producers
7   Responsiveness of actual supply to production
8   Pattern of long-run costs
9   Pattern of short-run costs
10 Flexibility of capacity variation

However, Clark did no more than hint at the qualitative or quantitative nature of these conditions. Under workable competition, how much product differentiation should be expected and how might it be measured? Similarly, what is an appropriate level of concentration for workability, and what index should be used to gauge its extent? As Clark's argument advances we obtain a better idea of what workable competition might look like, but the picture is never complete. We have already observed that perhaps the simplest way of viewing the matter is to say that for Clark (1940, p. 243) competition had a Marshallian flavour, it being defined as follows:

> Competition is rivalry in selling goods, in which each selling unit normally seeks maximum net revenue, under conditions such that the price or prices each seller can charge are effectively limited by the free option of the buyer to buy from a rival seller or sellers of what we think of as 'the same product', necessitating an effort by each seller to equal or exceed the attractiveness of the others' offerings to a sufficient number of sellers to accomplish the end in view.

Clark immediately admits, however, that 'this is not a complete definition', although it does 'bring out certain features crucial to . . . the argument'. Under workable competition it is clear that individual demand curves will not generally be horizontal. As in the very simple algebraic example above, there will generally be a positive degree of monopoly in most industries. Individual firms will set price sufficiently above marginal cost that average cost will be covered in the face of cyclical variations in demand. Firms will typically operate with some measure of reserve capacity. Quality is one of the variables under the control of the firm and price differentials within a product group are related to quality variation. It is clear that all these attributes could be embodied in a static version of workable competition. We have seen that a useful way of looking at this concept of workable competition is as a second-best solution. In the 1960s when the theory of the second best was being rigorously analysed for the first time, it seemed to have damning implications for the piecemeal approach. As much regulatory activity proceeds on an industry by industry, or even firm by firm, basis this would seem to minimize the significance of workable competition as a kind of second-best optimum. However, in the past twenty years, piecemeal policy has continued to be regarded favourably. Typical of current opinion is the view of Brown and Jackson (1986, p. 20) that

> We may still allow some scope for 'piecemeal welfare economics' since the second-best argument seems to have greatest practical relevance to cases in which the sectors (industries) under consideration are significantly interdependent. As with externalities, in such cases we should consider the interdependent sectors together, as a whole; and we may then be justified in neglecting the second-order effects arising from their relations with other sectors.

Davis and Whinston (1965) were the first to show how separability arguments of the sort suggested by Brown and Jackson might soften the gloomy implications of the theory of the second best, and concluded (p. 12) that 'when the additional constraint(s) contain only variables subject to the choice of the deviant, then, except for the deviant, all Pareto conditions and behavioural rules are of the same form as those for the second-best problem'. Santoni and Church (1972) furthered this line of argument and demonstrated that if production and utility functions have a Cobb-Douglas form then second-best conditions are equivalent to Pareto conditions for all inputs and outputs other than those giving rise to the initial distortion. Dusansky and Walsh (1976) developed more general arguments on separability and were able to show that the class of functions which reinstates the usual optimality conditions for the non-deviant commodities is less destructive, more general, and considerably larger than had been hitherto suggested. In the definitive analysis of this issue, Boadway and Harris (1977) developed sufficient conditions for piecemeal policy, as noted above, and their work provides a caution to the school who were too optimistic about the implications of separability. The inability of economists to provide a cast-iron theoretical case for piecemeal policy was confirmed in a highly technical paper by Guesnerie (1980), who noted, however, that many potential difficulties which theorists can readily identify may not be significant in specific contexts. It remains for theorists to weaken the perhaps overly sufficient conditions which have been established for legitimate piecemeal policy. A move in this direction has been made by Jewitt (1981) who provides much weaker conditions for validly employing piecemeal policy. Specifically, he shows that necessary and sufficient conditions for a second-best optimum in his model are that consumer preferences be 'pseudo-separable'. If preferences are pseudo-separable, the marginal rate of substitution between commodities in a group depends only on the quantity of goods consumed within that group and on the level of utility.

It seems, therefore, that there does remain scope for piecemeal policy, though the consequences of the theory of the second best add a cautionary caveat to its application. In the remainder of this chapter we shall make some appeal to piecemeal welfare arguments without at every point mentioning these caveats. This is not, however, to minimize their significance.

7.3 WORKABLE COMPETITION IN A STRUCTURE–CONDUCT–PERFORMANCE FRAMEWORK

In chapter 2, on structure, conduct, and performance, only the performance dimension was viewed in a welfare framework. In a narrow Paretian frame-work, positive price–cost margins were regarded as symptomatic of inadequate performance. Given the discussion of section 7.3, inadequate performance might also be viewed as departure from a second-best optimum, it being displayed in the form of the incorrect degree of market imperfection. But both of these approaches do confine welfare considerations to the performance dimension.

However, since the treatments of workable competition by Sosnick (1958) and Liebhafsky (1971) it has been perceived that components of structure, conduct, and performance should – all three – contribute to a welfare evalua-tion. Whilst the performance dimension remains the one of ultimate signifi-cance, it may not be the best direct target for regulatory activity. Firstly, although the extremes of good and bad performance are usually easy to detect, finer discrimination is harder to achieve given variations in product mix, accounting practices, depreciation, obsolescence, and so on. Secondly, it is not always easy to directly manipulate performance by public policy. Safety at work, adulteration of products, and dishonesty are susceptible to direct monitoring and control by regulatory authorities, but cost minimization and technical progressiveness cannot so obviously be moved in beneficial direc-tions by direct regulation. Some action on structure and conduct would be advantageous in the latter cases. Action on structure has the advantage that precise tests can be formulated which lend themselves to administrative procedures and judicial application. Action on conduct has the advantage that it seems to some economists to get at the core of the problem, which is to ensure 'a fair field and no favours', letting consequences take care of them-selves. However, there is likewise no particular virtue in confining attention to structure or conduct. The structure–performance relationships referred to in chapter 2 are not statistically robust, and it would be rash to conclude that an inevitable consequence of regulating structure would be to control performance, as predicted by a regression equation. Concerning the direct regulation of conduct, considerable difficulties arise in determining how one ensures a 'fair field'. In section 2 of the US Sherman Act, it is stated that 'to monopolize, or attempt to monopolize or combine or conspire' constitutes a misdemeanour. However, to show such actions have been attempted it is necessary to prove intent, which can often be a troublesome and plastic concept.

It is clear that a general analysis involves considering all dimensions of structure, conduct, and performance. We will defer for the moment consideration of the possibility that not all dimensions may be available to the policy-maker in a specific context. Clark (1940) provided a representation of workable competition in terms of sets of characteristics, but little guidance on appropriate norms. Sosnick (1958), basing his analysis on a wide array of writings on workability, went further and provided an exhaustive set of dimension norms for workability under structure, conduct, and performance headings. These norms are listed in figure 7.1. Merely by stating them one has not solved many problems, though some progress has been made. In almost every instance, problems of measurement arise, and judgements of some delicacy must be made concerning matters of degree over dimensions like 'some uncertainty', 'reasonable availability', 'unreasonable discrimination', 'excessive expenses', and 'appropriate exploitation'. There is some redundancy in the norms suggested. For example parts of 2 and 3 under conduct norms which are concerned with shielding or coercive tactics are implied by 1 on independent rivalry; and under performance norms, 6 which is concerned with quality may be subsumed under 9 which is concerned with satisfying buyers' needs. Particularly under performance norms, some of the requirements seem over-ambitious, or outwith the normal sphere of action – most notably 11 and 12 on national security and excessive political and/or economic power, respectively.

Economists might well differ to some degree on how they would draw up lists comparable with those in figure 7.1, but few would protest that no such lists could be devised. For any given lists, there would no doubt be further disagreement on where norms should be set, but again few would maintain that the concept of a norm is thereby invalid. Denote a set of structure, conduct, and performance characteristics by the vectors

$$\boldsymbol{S} = (S_1, \ldots, S_l)$$
$$\boldsymbol{C} = (C_1, \ldots, C_m) \tag{7.17}$$
$$\boldsymbol{P} = (P_1, \ldots, P_n)$$

The corresponding structure, conduct, and performance norms will be written

$$\boldsymbol{S}^\star = (S_1^\star, \ldots, S_l^\star)$$
$$\boldsymbol{C}^\star = (C_1^\star, \ldots, C_m^\star) \tag{7.18}$$
$$\boldsymbol{P}^\star = (P_1^\star, \ldots, P_n^\star)$$

Structure norms

1 No dominance, and traders as large as economies of scale will permit
2 Quality differentials which are moderate and sensitive to prices
3 No impediments to mobility
4 Reasonable availability of market information
5 Some uncertainty about response to price cutting
6 Freedom from legal restraint
7 Development of new markets and trade contacts

Conduct norms

1 Independent rivalry, in pursuit of profit
2 No shielding of inefficient rivals, suppliers, or customers
3 No unfair, exclusionary, predatory, or coercive tactics
4 No unreasonable discrimination
5 No misleading sales promotion
6 Rapid response by buyers to differentials in attributes of products

Performance norms

1 Efficient production and distribution
2 No excessive promotional expenses
3 Profits sufficient to reward investment, efficiency, and innovation
4 Output consistent with efficient resource allocation
5 Prices that do not intensify cyclical problems
6 Quality consistent with consumers' interest
7 Appropriate exploitation of improved products and techniques
8 Conservation requirements respected
9 Sellers responsive to buyers' needs
10 Entry as free as the industry sensibly permits
11 Regard for national security requirements
12 Avoidance of excessive political and economic power in few hands
13 Regard for employees' welfare

Figure 7.1

Thus (7.18) is no more than a symbolic formulation of the lists given in figure 7.1. Sosnick (1958) gave no formal interpretation to his framework. However, it is clear that his framework can be interpreted in terms of a social welfare function. Consider his statement (p. 399) that 'if the concept of workable competition is to provide a reliable criterion for judging whether a market situation is socially satisfactory, it must ignore no dimensions of normative significance and appraise simultaneously those which are interdependent'. It makes two points: firstly, that social states can be judged in terms of consequences of structure, conduct, and performance dimensions; and secondly, that there are interdependencies between these dimensions. A natural way of interpreting this is in terms of the social welfare function

$$W = W(\boldsymbol{S}, \boldsymbol{C}, \boldsymbol{P}) \tag{7.19}$$

where S, C, and P are interdependent in a fashion which may be captured by the side relationship

$$\phi(S, C, P) = 0 \tag{7.20}$$

Now such an approach has been adopted by Ferguson (1964) in his attempt to develop a theory of the workably competitive economy. The key definition of Ferguson (1964, p. 80) is: 'An economic system is workably competitive if there is no feasible change in industrial and union structure that would make attainment more likely, given the probability limits imposed upon our knowledge by its origin in empirical research.' Ferguson is therefore concerned with applying the social welfare function approach at the aggregate level, as indeed the title of his book, *A Macroeconomic Theory of Workable Competition*, suggests. His welfare function has as arguments national product, employment, and the price level. It is these which provide the basis for setting policy targets. These three variables are in turn regarded as dependent on microeconomic variables, such as industrial concentration, firm size and output, unionization, and a time trend. By contrast, the interpretation put forward here uses a microeconomic social welfare function, relevant to a particular industry rather than the macroeconomy, and makes welfare dependent on all the dimensions of structure, conduct, and performance rather than simply national product and the price level. If Ferguson's welfare function is 'solved out' to give an 'indirect' welfare function, the arguments of this function then do become dependent on microeconomic variables, but only a limited subset of the set of industrial structure dimensions.

In welfare economics deriving from the work of Bergson (1938), social welfare functions have been given a variety of interpretations. In view of the important discovery by Arrow (1951) that it is hard to construct consistent social rankings based on reasonable democratic voting procedures, it is preferable at this point to adopt the so-called 'dictatorial' interpretation of W. This too is the conclusion reached by Ferguson (1964, p. 67) who writes: 'One may regard the function as dictated by the legislature. Thus while the function itself is dictated, it is dictated by a democratically selected group. It may not be possible for a representative democracy to approach pure democracy more closely than this.' Here, our function W represents the preferences of regulatory authorities over structure, conduct, and performance dimensions. The information on which they construct such a function is of two kinds. Firstly, there is the body of law relating to the regulation of industrial organization, including antitrust law, the law of business taxation, labour law, consumer protection legislation, environmental protection legislation, restrictive practices legislation, and ethical advertising legislation. Secondly, there is the body of case studies and legislative enactments developed by the various regulatory authorities.

The arguments of the function W, namely S, C, and P also require further discussion. The components of S and P are fairly familiar. Thus structural attributes like concentration and the extent of product differentiation can be given scalar measures like the Herfindahl index and the cross-elasticity of demand, respectively. Performance attributes like the degree of monopoly and inventiveness can be given measures like the price–cost margin and expenditure on research and development, respectively. It is reasonable to assume that W is a continuous function of variables such as those in the sets of S and P. By contrast, conduct attributes might seem more difficult to measure at all, and even when they can be quantified might seem to be more obviously categorical or dichotomous variables, rather than continuous variables. Concerning the latter point, one might ask whether there *is* (value unity) or *is not* (value zero) price discrimination. Or one might ask whether there is or is not misleading advertising. However, this might not be a fruitful way of proceeding. Some degree of price discrimination is present in virtually every industry; and almost all advertising, if only by the appropriate selection of information to be presented, is in some measure misleading. In each case the question is really *how much* price discrimination, and *how misleading* is advertising. This sort of question can be answered by a variety of objective and subjective means. An objective measure of price discrimination might be an index appropriately weighted by proportions of customers paying different prices for the same good or service. A subjective measure of price discrimination could be constructed by polling customers, or experts on the industry, with a view to soliciting their opinions on the significance of price discrimination (e.g. on a scale of one to ten, in order of increasing significance). Traditionally, economists have been reluctant to handle such variables, although Reid (1981) has argued in favour of such subjective evidence. Such variables are used extensively in attitude measurement in subject areas like market research, psychology, and sociology. They introduce problems of 'scaling', but the methodology for handling these difficulties is highly developed, and economists have probably been unnecessarily wary of using such variables. The upshot of this discussion is that it is possible to characterize any market situation by a vector of structure, conduct, and performance attributes.

7.4   IMPROVABLE WELFARE AND MALLEABLE POLICY DIMENSIONS

Given that a social welfare function of the form $W(S, C, P)$ can be defined, one must next consider how this device can be deployed to achieve workable competition. A primary consideration is whether all the elements of the vectors S, C, and P are, in the terminology of Sosnick (1958), 'malleable'. A better expression might be 'manipulable', for we are concerned here with those dimensions of structure, conduct, and performance which the regulatory authorities can manipulate. Typically it will not be considerations of logic that dictate which dimensions of structure, conduct, and performance are manipulable, but political expediency, institutional rigidity, historical accident, social convention, the legal code, and no doubt many other factors besides. The fixity of some dimensions of S, C, and P in any particular policy context might be regarded as determining some of the constraints under which the welfare objective is pursued.

The exact nature of the welfare objective is the next issue to consider. Welfare maximization is the objective that immediately springs to mind. In a piecemeal context, where a particular firm or industry is being examined, with all the features of other sectors being regarded as given, welfare will typically be conceived of in terms of the sum of Marshallian consumers' and producers' surplus. However, other concepts of welfare are possible. Whatever the nature of the function W, this approach implies the maximization problem

$$\begin{aligned}
\text{maximize} \quad & W(S_1, \ldots, S_l; C_1, \ldots, C_m; P_1, \ldots, P_n) \\
\text{subject to} \quad & S_i = \bar{S}_i && i = 1, 2, \ldots, j \leqslant l \\
& C_k = \bar{C}_k && k = 1, 2, \ldots, h \leqslant m \\
& P_r = \bar{P}_r && r = 1, 2, \ldots, g \leqslant n \\
& \phi(S_1, \ldots, S_l; C_1, \ldots, C_m; P_1, \ldots, P_n) = 0
\end{aligned} \tag{7.21}$$

where, without loss of generality, the leading elements of the vectors S, C, and P, numbering j, h, and g respectively, are regarded as non-malleable in this particular context and are denoted by barred variables in (7.21). However, in terms of much of the workable competition literature, the welfare problem is not viewed in this light. It is helpful to distinguish between *maximizing*, *improving*, and *target attaining* policies. The general maximizing problem has already been stated in (7.21). Given initial structure, conduct, and performance dimensions (S_1, C_1, P_1) and the dimensions attained by regulatory control (S_2, C_2, P_2), policy is *improving* if

$$W(S_2, C_2, P_2) > W(S_1, C_1, P_1) \tag{7.22}$$

Finally, given dimension norms of $(S^\star, C^\star, P^\star)$, targets are attained when welfare is

$$W = W(S^\star, C^\star, P^\star) \tag{7.23}$$

In comparing (7.23) and (7.22) Sosnick (1958, p. 406) has remarked that 'unimprovability rather than specific attainment must usually be the keynote'. In fact the argument seems to be overstated, if not confused. An obvious problem with targeting is that typically targets are not met; put alternatively, the regulatory authorities find it difficult to bring all malleable dimensions of structure, conduct, and performance into line with workably competitive norms. One then has to introduce auxiliary conditions like penalty functions which describe the costs of deviating from the various norms, and the hypothesis of penalty minimization, which starts to bring back the optimization of welfare argument by the back door. Now a situation is improvable if an inequality like (7.22) obtains. The policy of 'unimprovability' favoured by Sosnick would exhaust all such improving changes, and one would in fact have attained a maximum on W. Indeed, were the optimal $(S^\circ, C^\circ, P^\circ)$ specified as targets in the first place, then the outcomes of maximizing, exhausting improvements, and targeting would all be the same:

$$W_{max} = W(S^\circ, C^\circ, P^\circ) \tag{7.24}$$

It is clear then, as Ferguson (1964) observed in his treatment of the corresponding macroeconomic problem, that it is very difficult to get away from maximizing policy rules. Possibly a more fruitful distinction is between policy optimization and the policy process. Optimization can rarely be achieved. It takes time, is costly, and has large informational requirements. However, at any stage of the policy process, a legitimate goal might be simply to improve the situation. Improvement might be sought through the attainment of specific targets. In principle, of course, improvement could lead to optimality, as specified in (7.24). It would be naïve to expect that a sequence of improving steps would ultimately lead to an optimum by analogy with 'hill-climbing' algorithms of numerical analysis. The argument is logically impeccable, but practically unrealistic. The functions W and ϕ are not likely to be stable between successive stages in the policy process, and hence 'improvability' rather than 'unimprovability' might be the most pragmatic policy requirement. A consideration which may be of practical significance, given a 'one-shot' regulatory intervention, is how much improvement is aimed for and attained. The changes in welfare depend on changes in S, C, and P, which will be denoted ΔS, ΔC, and ΔP. But these welfare changes should be regarded as 'gross' rather than as 'net', in the absence of any consideration of the costs of moving from one set of dimensions to another. The welfare loss or cost can be captured by

$$G = G(\Delta S, \Delta C, \Delta P) \tag{7.25}$$

where the ΔS, ΔC, and ΔP are related by the implicit function

$$\psi(\Delta S, \Delta C, \Delta P) = 0 \tag{7.26}$$

However, this is to complicate the picture, and in the two examples that follow we shall for the sake of simplicity ignore the welfare costs that may arise in moving from one set of S, C, P dimensions to another. It should be borne in mind, however, that there may be cases in which costs associated with changes of certain magnitudes may have significant effects on the welfare analysis.

Our two examples are taken from piecemeal welfare analysis. In the first, a monopoly example, the regulatory authorities are presented as having structure as the malleable dimension; and in the second, a duopoly example, it is conduct that is malleable.

Example 1   Monopoly

Suppose a monopolist produces according to the total cost schedule $C(x)$ with the inverse market demand schedule being $p = f(x)$, where x is output and p is price. Then profit is $px - C(x)$, which is maximized for that price–output pair $(\bar{p}, \bar{x})$ at which the following equality holds:

$$\bar{p} + \bar{x} f'(\bar{x}) = C'(\bar{x}) \tag{7.27}$$

which is the familiar marginal revenue (MR) equals marginal cost (MC) condition. In terms of the sort of structure, conduct, and performance taxonomy developed as in figure 2.3, we can characterize this example as follows.

Structure

Sole seller (monopoly)
Industry demand (reflected in industry elasticity of demand $(dx/x)/(dp/p)$)

Conduct

Profit maximization $(MC = MR$ with $MR' < MC')$

Performance

Monopoly deadweight loss (represented by sum of lost producers' and consumers' surpluses, as compared with perfectly competitive situation)

In chapter 2, where no detailed consideration of welfare issues was undertaken, the performance yardstick was expressed in terms of the deviation of price from marginal cost. In fact, this is no more than convenience. Adopting the Marshallian framework of chapter 5, one could say that the price–cost margin is being used to gauge the extent of deadweight loss. This is, of course, indicated by the sum of consumers' and producers' surplus lost as compared with the competitive situation. Denote the welfare maximizing price–output pair by $(p^\star, x^\star)$, from which we get

$$p^\star = C'(x^\star) \tag{7.28}$$

that is, price equals marginal cost, with a zero price–cost margin. The sum of consumers' and producers' surplus is maximized and is given by

$$\int_0^{x^\star} [f(x) - C'(x)] \, dx \tag{7.29}$$

In terms of the workable competition framework we have been developing, expression (7.29) corresponds to the W_{max} of (7.24) with the S, C, and P dimensions being embodied in the functional form of (7.29) (e.g. the elasticity of $f(x)$) and in the profit maximization assumption. We have seen that in terms of many norms of workable competition, W_{max} may not be achieved. Under some second-best situations it would be optimal to set price equal to marginal cost, even if there were distortions in other sectors which could not be remedied, provided certain separability conditions were satisfied. Under other second-best situations it would be optimal to have a certain specific degree of monopoly, given distortions in other sectors, in which case W_{max} would not be achieved. Again for simplicity, let us consider the case in which separability makes the pursuit of W_{max} desirable. The question that arises is how best the regulatory authorities can attain this level of welfare. We have already indicated that an important consideration is which dimensions of S, C, and P are malleable. In this example, we shall take conduct (namely profit maximization) as given, with policy choices being between structure and performance dimensions. Of the structure dimensions we shall assume that in the relevant policy time frame only industry demand is malleable (via the elasticity of demand), with entry by other firms not being immediately feasible. With regard to performance, we shall assume that the regulatory authorities can assign price or output at a desired level, which (given the technology) amounts to saying that they set the price–cost margin.

It is apparent now that there are several ways in which the regulatory authorities can proceed to improve welfare over the monopoly situation characterized by (7.27). In a familiar way we have $\bar{p} > p^\star$ and $\bar{x} < x^\star$, indicating a raised price and a restricted output under monopoly. For a monotonically decreasing average revenue (i.e. inverse demand) schedule and a monotonically increasing marginal cost schedule, choices of output x' in the interval $(\bar{x} \leqslant x' \leqslant x^\star)$ cause welfare to be increasing in x'. Further, the price–cost margin is decreasing in x'. Thus decreasing the price–cost margin by increasing output and lowering price away from the monopoly level results in a monotonically increasing welfare. By an appropriate choice of this margin the authorities can fix performance at a desired level. A common view in the world of regulatory activity is that it is not necessarily desirable, effective, or practical to affect performance directly. A significant misgiving, as noted by Liebhafsky (1971, p. 243) is that the instituting of direct performance controls, bypassing structure and conduct, would ultimately pave the way for a rigidly controlled, non-market economy. Further it is frequently felt that the measurement, administration, and judicial sanctioning of structure dimensions is easier than for performance dimensions, particularly in more complex situations where the latter include amorphous elements like 'dynamism' and 'progressiveness'. That being the case, control of the price–cost margin might not be viewed as a malleable dimension of the S, C, P triple. Supposing this to be the case with our monopoly example, the authorities could work on structure instead. The malleable dimension of structure available to them is demand, or average revenue. Suppose the monopolist's revenue is augmented by a subsidy per unit produced of s. Then the monopolist's profit function is $px - C(x) + sx$, and the subsidy can be used to induce the monopolist to expand production to a desired level. If that level corresponds to the output x^* defined by (7.28) then the relevant equilibrium condition, given profit maximizing conduct by the firm, is

$$p^* + x^* f'(x^*) + s = C'(x^*) \tag{7.30}$$

which defines the appropriate norm for the structure dimension s by solving (7.30), given the requirement (7.28). Thus

$$s = s^* = -x^* f'(x^*) = p^* - MR^* \tag{7.31}$$

a well-known condition in public finance, which we are interpreting here in a workability framework. In general, the subsidy is greater than the profit reduction. If the good has a zero income elasticity for all consumers and lump-sum taxes are collected from them leaving them at their initial utility levels, and if a lump-sum tax is collected from the monopolist leaving it at its initial profit level, then it can be shown that the net tax proceeds are positive. These proceeds are known as the 'social dividend' and are equal to the familiar dead-weight loss triangle of monopoly misallocation theory. Using this sort of welfare framework where producers' and consumers' surplus are added together without regard to distribution is tantamount to employing the Hicks–Kaldor compensation criterion.

Example 2 Duopoly

As a second example, consider the case of homogeneous duopoly. Let us refer back to the duopoly diagram of figure 2.2, introduced to illustrate equilibrium using reaction functions. It was possible there to contrast two game theoretic solutions, the one co-operative (von Neumann–Morgenstern) and the other non-co-operative (Cournot–Nash). A similar figure is reproduced here as figure 7.2.

Suppose now that conduct is regarded as the malleable dimension, and that the performance norm is the non-co-operative outcome. The von Neumann–Morgenstern solution set lies along NM, and an acceptable output pair would be at D, the point (x_1', x_2'). Here $x_1' + x_2' = X = OM$, and the relevant maximization problem is

$$\max_{x_1} \Pi(x_1, X - x_1) \tag{7.32}$$

where X is total output and $\Pi(\cdot)$ the profit function. The Cournot–Nash

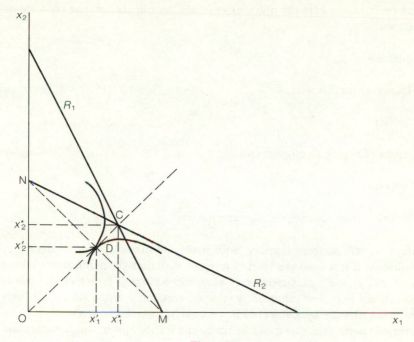

Figure 7.2

solution is at C, with outputs (x_1^*, x_2^*), where the relevant maximization problem is

$$\max_{x_i} \Pi(x_1, x_2) \qquad (i = 1, 2) \tag{7.33}$$

Between D and C there is a smooth passage from collusion (monopoly) to non-co-operation (Cournot–Nash). Clarke and Davies (1982) develop a model in which a single parameter α is used to indicate the degree of apparent collusion in an industry, and provide one way of representing algebraically the spectrum from collusion to non-co-operation illustrated in figure 7.2. Recall formula (2.13), where the gross-profits/sales ratio is represented by

$$\frac{\alpha + (1 - \alpha)H}{\eta} \tag{7.34}$$

with η the industry elasticity of demand and H the Herfindahl index. When $\alpha = 1$ we have complete collusion (monopoly), and when $\alpha = 0$ complete non-co-operation (Cournot–Nash). Again using the taxonomy of structure, conduct, and performance as in the previous example, we can characterize this case as follows:

Structure

Homogeneous duopoly

Conduct

Degree of apparent collusion (α)

Performance

Deviation from Cournot–Nash outcome

Here we will suppose that the only malleable dimension is the degree of collusion. If it is fixed at a level of $\alpha = \alpha^* = 0$, then the performance norms $x_1 = x_1^*$, $x_2 = x_2^*$ characteristic of Cournot–Nash will be achieved. This is completely to outlaw collusion, a view on regulatory action which has been favoured strongly by Kahn (1953). Of course, in terms of workability a less stringent norm than this could be used, and a choice of α^* made within the interval $0 \leqslant \alpha^* \leqslant 1$ in order to attain it.

7.5　WORKABILITY AND THEORETICAL DEVELOPMENTS

Most of the ideas on workability have been expounded in this chapter in the familiar static equilibrium framework. One important direction in which theory can be developed is to embrace dynamics. Clark (1955, 1961) made a start in this direction, and today one can find rigorous theoretical discussions of dynamics in a regulatory framework as developed by writers such as Spence (1986). An alternative approach which has also found favour is to set out to consciously develop a coherent, rigorous static theory of competition which has desirable welfare properties, but is more pragmatic in its view of the modern capitalist industry than is the theory of perfect competition. A new static norm for competition known as 'contestability' has been developed by Baumol et al. (1982). Contestability theory analyses market structure by seeking solutions to two questions, the one normative and the other behavioural. The first question is whether the industry's output vector can be produced most cheaply by a small number of firms; and the second is whether that specific number of firms will tend to be established in the industry by market forces.

Let us turn first to dynamics. Subsequently to developing his idea of workable competition in what we would now call static second-best terms, Clark started to rethink his ideas. Clark (1955) began to favour a dynamic view of workability, with the key features of competition that led to social benefit being the capacity to initiate and sustain innovation. Abandoning the terminology of workable competition, he laid down the following dynamic criteria for 'effective competition':

Elements required for progress

1   Leadership in introducing economical methods of production (for example, aggressive price leadership)
2   Ample product differentiation (for this encourages producers to explore and influence consumers' tastes)
3   Development of new products

Diffusion of benefits of progress

1   Lowering prices for consumers; raising wages for labour
2   Maintaining incentives for innovation (which requires a constant renewal of the system of profit differentials in the face of renewed innovation)
3   Creating the possibility of new products becoming available for unexploited massed markets
4   Creating markets in which search is minimized

Desirability of freedom

1   Limiting discretionary power (firms should not obstruct the progress of the productive arts)
2   Limiting restrictions which prevent the benefits of technical progress from accruing to customers

Rather than profit maximization, Clark (1955, p. 457) favoured the view that 'the decisive motive' of the business enterprise was to be found in 'a preference for eroded profit on a larger volume of business'. In a positive rather than normative framework, Reid (1979) has more recently favoured an analysis of this sort, with an emphasis on the role of the aggressive price leader.

Although second-best theory has usually been developed in a static framework, there is no reason why it should not be applied in dynamic contexts. In a sense, therefore, Clark was mistaken in his view that in moving from statics to dynamics one was really going on to address an entirely new class of theoretical problem. Furthermore, his clear feeling that dynamic analysis must inevitably lead to indeterminacy in theoretical conclusions was perhaps more a reflection of the literary mode of analysis than of the true nature of economic dynamics as applied to the industry.

An example – no more – of what modern economic theory has to say about the dynamics of competition in a regulatory framework is contained in the article by Spence (1986). He develops a dynamic model of competition and industry performance which enables one to investigate the consequences for performance of regulatory intervention. In a market system a firm promotes technical progressiveness of the sort that keeps it ahead of the pack by undertaking R & D (research and development) expenditures. It is profitability that ultimately determines the level of R & D, and Clark's emphasis on volume rather than profitability is misplaced, save if it appropriately proxies long-run profitability. A special feature of R & D is that it almost inevitably leads to externalities. Of course externalities can be a problem in the static case, but they are not inevitable. By contrast, they are really an essential feature of the dynamic case. Externalities arise because the results of R & D are not necessarily appropriable. The restoration of appropriability, perhaps by deliberately fostering some measure of monopoly power, has been regarded by some economists as a second-best solution for an innovative industry. Unfortunately that argument may be attacked on the grounds that it is also possible to undertake excessive levels of R & D, and in a sense to obtain cost reduction at too high a cost. In the model of Spence (1986), unit costs fall as firms' accumulated investments increase, and firms are assumed to maximize the present value of profits net of R & D expenditures. It is shown that each firm goes immediately, or as fast as possible, to equilibrium and that an increase in spill-over (that is lack of appropriability) reduces the incentive to undertake R & D and cost reduction, and reduces the amount of cost reduction in market equilibrium. However, with policy intervention, the situation can be improved. Spence (1986) shows that incentives can be restored through subsidies. Without subsidies, loss of potential surplus can be high (as high as 35 per cent in his parameterization). The effectiveness of subsidies depends on the magnitude of the spill-over effect. Define the 'performance ratio' as the ratio of the surplus actually achieved in a market to the first-best optimal surplus, expressed in percentage terms. When spill-over effects are zero, subsidies have little effect on performance. When spill-over effects are significant, subsidies can improve performance by as much as 90 per cent. For a given market structure (including numbers of firms) the subsidies chosen are optimal, in the sense of being surplus maximizing. Thus what Spence is comparing is a second-best world with a first-best world. For his parameterization, at least, the former is almost as attractive as the latter. The conclusion depends, however, on what dimension(s) of structure, conduct, and performance are malleable – a viewpoint we had already reached in the static cases discussed earlier. For example, Spence shows that it is counter-productive to regulate margins for a single firm without also subsidizing R & D. If not, investment in R & D will fall as margins fall, and dynamic technical efficiency will be reduced. However, regulating price *will* work. If a single firm is assigned a price that emerges from the second-best calculation, it will invest the second-best optimal amount of R & D. This begs the question, of course, of how the regulators determine the appropriate second-best price.

Looking again at static developments of the theory, much attention has recently turned to contestability theory. A perfectly contestable market is defined as one in which the industry configuration is in equilibrium when it is 'sustainable', in the sense that it offers no opportunity for profitable entry, taking prices of incumbent firms as fixed. An important test of whether industry behaviour is consistent with contestability is whether there is industry-wide cost minimization. The regulatory implications of contestability lean somewhat in the 'hands-off' direction, a view not far distant from that first held by Clark (1940). The reduction of artificial impediments to entry and exit is favoured, including those which have been imposed by public policy. By logical extension, the promotion of contestability would imply removing impediments to international trade. Alongside enhanced ease of entry should be suitable reductions in restrictions on price-setting. Without the latter requirement, it would be possible for enhanced entry to provide a safe haven for inefficient entrants, their inefficiency being fostered by the protection conferred on them by the regulatory authorities. An important aspect of contestability theory is that it puts forward a benchmark or norm that does not suggest a *prima facie* case for regulation when the number of firms in an industry is small. Provided there is scope for 'hit and run' entry, it is argued, such market structures may still be socially efficient. In multifirm contestable markets it is argued that the $p = MC$ condition for first-best Pareto optimality must be satisfied in equilibrium. For a natural monopoly, the rule that $MC \leqslant p = AC$ is argued to be the necessary condition for equilibrium in a perfectly contestable market, where this rule satisfies the 'Ramsey pricing' second-best optimality requirement. The theory has a number of special features, however, which make it of lesser generality and power than one might suspect. For example, the requirement of free entry is very strong, and really implies ultra-free entry in which a new entrant can supply *all* of the market at a price which slightly undercuts that set by the incumbent firms. This, and further issues, will be examined in greater detail in the next chapter.

7.6 CONCLUSION

Practical people, and economists who are also practitioners, have never been powerfully persuaded by perfect competition as an ideal, and have adopted an instrumental or pragmatic approach to policy problems in industrial organization. The purpose of this chapter has been to suggest that this pragmatism can also be allied to serious analytical reasoning, even when the perfectly competitive ideal has been abandoned.

Part IV
New Departures

8

Contestability and natural monopoly analysis

8.1 INTRODUCTION

We have seen in chapter 7 that from a public policy point of view, it is important to have a welfare norm in order to judge the efficiency of an industry. In the structure–conduct–performance framework developed in chapter 2, the familiar Paretian criteria for the optimality of perfect competition were used as welfare norms. In chapter 7, various alternative norms were examined under the heading of workable competition, the purpose there being to discuss criteria which in practice, as well as in principle, could be satisfied by any actual industry. The first approach is precise, involving an exact mathematical statement of the conditions required for welfare optimality. However, it is perhaps *too* precise, for we know from the theory of the second best that, in a world where in practice some firms do not follow a marginal cost pricing rule, the extension of it to those firms does not necessarily increase welfare and could even reduce it. Thus the precision of this approach is allied to impracticality. In the second workable competition approach, we found a list of plausible criteria for competition in concentrated industries as in Sosnick (1958), but it is a list that appears *ad hoc* and imprecise, and includes some criteria that look mutually inconsistent. This approach is almost the exact converse of the first, in that it is practical but imprecise.

In this chapter we wish to explore the theory of contestable markets, which hopes to bring to the analysis of industrial organization a set of welfare criteria for judging efficiency which are at the same time precise and practical. In the course of this chapter, a precise characterization of contestable markets will be undertaken, but it may prove useful initially to provide a less exact statement of the purpose and content of the theory. We shall conclude by considering related issues in natural monopoly analysis.

The first requirement for a contestable market has already been met in chapter 5, where the Marshallian concept of competition was explored. It is that potential entrants should be able to sell to the same customers as the incumbent firms without hindrance, using the same techniques of production. Stigler (1968) defined an entry barrier as a cost imposed on a potential entrant which exceeded that borne by present incumbent firms in entering the industry. This sort of entry barrier is ruled out by the first requirement of contestability. The second requirement is that potential entrants to any industry should use the prices charged by incumbent firms *before* entry takes place as a basis for evaluating the profitability of entry. This second requirement allows for 'hit and run' tactics on the part of a potential rival, provided capital is mobile between markets. Here again there is a similarity to Marshallian competition, where it is assumed that firms within submarkets can be subject to competition from other submarkets, because of the flexibility of potential rivals to vary their product range. The possibility of incumbents eventually lowering price would not deter potential entrants who saw profitable opportunities in the contestability framework, for it is assumed that exit is costless.

The notion of contestability was specifically designed to have perfect competition embraced within it. A perfectly competitive market is necessarily contestable, but many markets which are not perfectly competitive, even including monopoly, may be contestable. In both perfectly competitive and contestable markets there is free entry and exit. However, perfectly competitive markets are necessarily atomistic, involving large numbers of sellers; and each seller assumes that his output decisions cannot influence the going market price. By contrast, in a contestable market each firm, both existent and potential, expects that the route to increasing sales is by undercutting rivals. This too is consistent with Marshall's notion of the firm's individual demand curve being less than infinitely price elastic, providing therefore an opportunity for price-setting as distinct from the passive quantity-setting of perfect competition.

An important concept in the contestability literature is that of *sustainability*. It provides a way of examining the controlling effect that the free-entry condition imposes on firms operating in a contestable market. There are three requirements for sustainability. Firstly, aggregate output of incumbent firms must satisfy the market demand of the prices set. Secondly, those prices must imply non-negative net revenues for incumbents. Thirdly, to potential entrants who take the prices set by incumbent firms as given, there must be no opportunity for profitable entry. Only those contestable markets that are sustainable can be consistent with equilibrium. Perfect competition can be shown to be the only sustainable contestable market as the size of producers becomes increasingly small in relation to the market as a whole. However, a monopoly can likewise be a sustainable contestable market. Put informally, a natural monopoly is a single firm that can produce at lower cost than any collection of two or more firms. In the case of natural monopoly, the only sustainable market form is that of a single seller, provided the conditions for contestability hold. Such a firm would operate efficiently, in the sense of setting so-called Ramsey-optimal prices, these being prices that maximize consumer welfare subject to the constraint that the enterprise balances its budget. Of course such prices fall short of the Paretian ideal which is achieved when prices are set to marginal cost. However, they do constitute second-best prices in that they generate sufficient revenue to balance the firm's budget with minimum loss of aggregate net benefit to consumers.

All these issues, which we have merely introduced here, will be explored in greater detail later. However, it should be said that notwithstanding the technical merits of the theorizing underlying the contestability literature, one must be cautious of being blinded by technique. An important, and strong, theoretical requirement for contestability is that exit should be costless. It is for this very reason that 'hit and run' tactics can prove profitable. An example which writers in this field have emphasized is the case of small, naturally monopolistic airline markets. In Baumol et al. (1982) the case considered is of the market for air travel between two towns where the demand generated is only sufficient to warrant one flight per day. An airline company flying this route has a natural monopoly, and furthermore can exit from this market in a costless manner. If it should discover another profitable market it need do no more than transfer to this route (presumably not *quite* costlessly) and compete by undercutting the fare of the incumbent company. Even if the incumbent should retaliate by cost cutting, the new entrant would have a number of options open to it, including moving to another profitable route, returning its rented aircraft if it had not been owned, or selling its aircraft in what is an active second-hand market. Bailey (1981), Bailey and Panzar (1981), and Bailey et al. (1983) in their empirical studies of airlines claimed that a contestable pattern of behaviour is empirically observable in this instance. However, the airline industry is clearly a rather special case. One can imagine many important examples in which exit is not at all costless, as in the case where the plant used is very durable, and sufficiently specialized that no active second-hand market for it exists.

In its policy aspect, the contestability literature offers some fairly simple guidelines. The presumption is in favour of an extension of unregulated competition. A two-part test of the desirability of intervention, along the lines of the work of Joskow and Klevorick (1979), is favoured. The first part involves establishing whether the market is contestable. A nine-point check list for this is proffered by Baumol et al. (1982, pp. 470–1), and if this part of the test is satisfied there are no grounds for regulatory intervention. The second part of the test, which only arises if some items in the check list are not satisfied, proposes that regulation should only be approved on the basis of a balancing of costs and benefits. After the considerable technical virtuosity which has been displayed in the contestability literature, it is rather disquieting to discover that what is offered to policy-makers, as in the traditional workable competition approach examined in chapter 7, is a long list of criteria, followed by the bland advice to weigh costs against benefits if the application of these criteria should prove inconclusive. However, this is to anticipate an argument which will be more fully developed later in this chapter. Our immediate task is to develop in greater detail some of the purely technical aspects of the theory of contestable markets.

8.2 STRUCTURE AND PERFORMANCE IN SINGLE-PRODUCT CONTESTABLE MARKETS

Most of the theory of contestable markets was developed for the multiproduct case, but following Baumol et al. (1982) it is a useful expository device to start by considering the single-product case. Amongst other things, this makes geometrical illustration of many of the ideas of contestability much simpler.

A contestable market may be regarded as a generalization of the perfectly competitive market in two senses. Firstly, in the case of many rivals, the same implications as the perfectly competitive model can be developed using fewer assumptions. Secondly, the theory of the contestable market is also applicable to other market structures in which there exists some degree of monopoly.

In order to develop the theory in further detail, some concepts of costs need to be precisely defined. We have already met in chapter 5 the Marshallian view that rationalization of production can lead to efficiency gains. The reasoning put forward was that any given output could be produced more cheaply by one firm than could that same output, in aggregate, by a collection of firms. This led Marshall to a fairly sympathetic treatment of monopoly, but one which differs from more recent writings in that Baumol et al. (1982) see a lesser case for regulation than did Marshall, mainly because they are more impressed by the strength of the influence of potential competition. In modern terminology, what Marshall was asserting was that costs are subadditive, and that this provided the basis for natural monopoly. A cost function $C(x)$ is said to be *subadditive* at x if, for all outputs $x_1, x_2, \ldots, x_n$ which sum to x, we have

$$C(x) < \sum_{i=1}^{n} C(x_i)$$

Here we are contrasting the case in which the output x is produced by a population of n firms, the ith firm contributing x_i towards industry output x, with the case in which a single firm produces x. For subadditivity to hold we require that the above inequality should hold for any outputs of each member of the population of firms less than x. The concept of subadditivity is therefore a global rather than a point concept, and has rather considerable informational requirements. If the subadditivity condition is satisfied, the industry is said to be a natural monopoly. Marshall, of course, talked of natural monopoly in terms of a falling expenses of production curve (i.e. falling supply curve). It is worth noting that a falling average cost curve implies subadditivity. For distinct outputs x and x', falling average costs imply an inequality relationship of the form

$$\frac{C(x)}{x} < \frac{C(x')}{x'} \quad \text{for } x > x' \tag{8.1}$$

Suppose that outputs of n firms are $x_1, x_2, \ldots, x_n$, with

$$x_1 + x_2 + \ldots + x_n = x$$

Then

$$\frac{C(x)}{x} < \frac{C(x_i)}{x_i} \quad (i = 1, 2, \ldots, n)$$

and so

$$\frac{x_i}{x} C(x) < C(x_i)$$

$$\Sigma \frac{x_i}{x} C(x) < \Sigma C(x_i)$$

$$C(x) \Sigma \frac{x_i}{x} = C(x) < \Sigma C(x_i)$$

which is the condition for subadditivity.

Economies of scale are conveniently defined in terms of cost curves, rather than the production function. Returns to scale will be described as increasing, constant, or decreasing according to whether the cost elasticity of output is greater than, equal to, or less than unity. The relevant elasticity is

$$\delta = \frac{dx}{dC} \frac{C(x)}{x} = \frac{C(x)/x}{dC/dx} = \frac{AC}{MC} \tag{8.2}$$

Another way of categorizing returns to scale is to say that they are increasing, decreasing, or constant according to whether $d[AC(x)/dx]$ is less than, greater than, or equal to zero. Summarizing, the alternative ways of expressing returns to scale in terms of cost curves are

	$\dfrac{dx}{dC} \dfrac{C(x)}{x}$	$\dfrac{d[AC(x)]}{dx}$
Increasing returns	> 1	< 0
Constant returns	$= 1$	$= 0$
Decreasing returns	< 1	> 0

$$(8.3)$$

An important attribute of the contestability literature is that it enables one to determine endogenously the sizes and numbers of firms in an industry, given the cost curves and industry demand curve. This of course has always been true of the models of perfect competition and monopolistic competition, but typically in oligopoly theory one takes the number of firms as given. To see the way in which this argument is developed, a definition of industry equilibrium is necessary. A set of outputs $x_1, \ldots, x_n$ is regarded as being feasible if the sum of outputs at price p equals industry demand, and if each firm earns non-negative profits at this price, for its chosen level of output.

If an industry has a feasible configuration of firms, then in the terminology of Baumol et al. (1982) it is said to be *sustainable* if the following conditions are met. Firstly, entrants operate under the assumption that incumbent firms will not change their prices in the face of entry, and thus base their expected profit calculations on the prevailing price p^*. Secondly, a feasible plan for a potential entrant involves setting a price p^e which does not exceed that currently prevailing, and choosing an output x^e which does not exceed the amount which would be demanded by the market, $D(p^e)$, at the chosen price p^e. Thirdly, it should not be possible for any potential entrant to make a non-negative profit for such a feasible price–output pair (p^e, x^e). A refinement of the last condition is to require that no potential entrant can find a feasible price–output pair such that the implied profit exceeds the cost of entry $E(x^e)$. To summarize this condition of sustainability in a succinct fashion, the requirements are

$$p^e x^e - C(x^e) \leqslant 0 \tag{8.4}$$

or, in the case of entry costs,

$$p^e x^e - C(x^e) - E(x^e) \leqslant 0 \tag{8.5}$$

$$\text{for } p^e \leqslant p^* \quad \text{and} \quad x^e \leqslant D(p^e)$$

where (p^e, x^e) is the potential entrant's feasible price–output pair, and p^* is the prevailing price set by incumbent firms.

The most significant result of the contestability literature can now be stated. It is that when *several* firms are in a sustainable industry configuration, in the sense made precise above, each firm will earn zero profit, and set price equal to marginal cost. Consider first the marginal cost pricing result. We prove first that price cannot be less than marginal cost. Suppose to the contrary that a firm earns non-negative profit at a price less than marginal cost. Then an entrant could make a positive profit by operating as this incumbent firm does, but with an output shaded below the incumbent's. But this possibility of profitable entry violates sustainability; hence price cannot be less than marginal cost. Now let us prove that price cannot be greater than marginal cost if there are several firms. If a firm in a sustainable market produces an output at which price exceeds marginal cost, this would guarantee that an entrant could make a positive profit at the same price (or at a price shaded below that of the incumbent) by producing an output a shade above that of the incumbent. The existence of at least one other firm in the industry is necessary for this reasoning to be valid, for it ensures that the output shading strategem of the entrant does not substantially lower market price; the entrant's shaded output increase will be strictly less than the outputs of the one or more additional firms. We have thus established that $p \leqslant MC$ and previously that $p \geqslant MC$, from which we get $p = MC$, the first half of the theorem. Turning to the second half, note that a firm which produced an output x_i at the prevailing price p^* such that $p^* x_i < C(x_i)$ would violate the condition of feasibility. Further, if we had, rather, the inequality $p^* x_i > C(x_i)$ an entrant could set a price p^e a shade below p^* such that $p^e x_i > C(x_i)$, providing a positive profit at the same output level. Thus each and every incumbent will earn a zero profit, $p^* x_i = C(x_i)$, which completes the theorem.

The last important analytical point to be considered in this section is the existence of sustainable prices. It turns out to be true that when there are few rivals, each characterized by U-shaped cost curves, then a sustainable price will generally not exist. This is a rather devastating limitation of the theory. Sustainability will only be a general property of the sorts of models being considered if average cost curves are horizontal, or at least are flat bottomed for a range of outputs. Figure 8.1 illustrates unsustainability. Suppose the curve AC is relevant to an incumbent monopolist for whom costs are subadditive up to x_3. Assuming output cannot be rationed, a price $p_u < p_2$ could not be set by the monopolist without making a loss. If a price $p_u \geqslant p_2$ were charged, at an output somewhat less than x_2, a potential entrant could sell, for example, an amount x_1 at a price less than p_u but above p_1 at a positive profit. Thus price p_u is not sustainable. If, however, we adopt the assumption that average costs are constant over a range of outputs, then the existence of a sustainable price is likely. Consider figure 8.2, where the average cost curve for one of several incumbent firms in the industry is given by AC_i, with average cost being constant from output level x_i to $2x_i$. Even if there are not large numbers of firms in the industry (industry output is denoted x_I, with subscript I referring to the industry), the industry supply curve $AC_I(x_I)$ will be defined for outputs greater than x_i, at an average cost which is constant and equal to that attained over the horizontal section of the AC_i curve. Suppose the industry demand curve $D(p)$ cuts a horizontal line extended through the flat section of the $AC_i(x_i)$ curve at a non-integral multiple of x_i. In figure 8.2 this occurs between outputs $4x_i$ and $5x_i$. More generally, we are looking at the case in which industry output is lying in the interval

$$(nx_i, (n + 1)x_i) \tag{8.6}$$

where n is an integer. In the diagram, clearly four firms producing x_i, and one

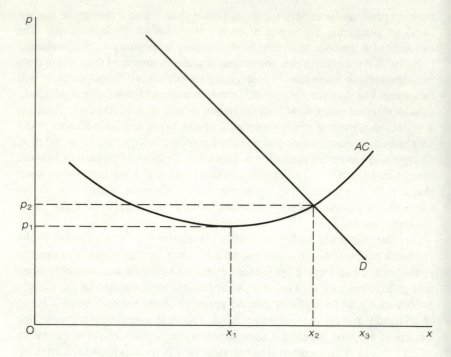

Figure 8.1

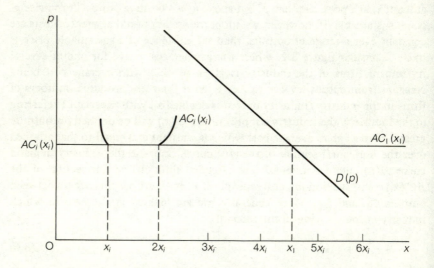

Figure 8.2

firm producing the remaining $(x_1 - 4x_i)$, will in aggregate produce an amount which satisfies industry demand in the sense that $x_1 = D(AC_i)$. Provided industry output exceeds $2x_i$, price will always be set equal to this constant average (and marginal) cost. Such a price is Ramsey optimal in the sense that the condition for a social optimum is satisfied (price equals marginal cost) *and* profit is equal to zero (or more generally some predetermined level), which in this case amounts to the equality of average revenue and average cost. For the case of many firms with flat-bottomed average cost curves, we have established that a price is sustainable if and only if it is Ramsey optimal. This fundamental result − the sustainability of Ramsey prices − can be generalized to the case of the multiproduct firm, though the analysis required to establish the proposition is very much more complex.

Let us conclude this section by contrasting the contestability approach with more traditional methods of analysis. It is to be noticed that the so-called Sylos postulate, that incumbents will maintain their output levels in the face of entry, is abandoned. This is necessary because the contestability model requires free entry and exit whereas the Sylos postulate only makes sense if there are barriers to entry and exit. If there were not, hit and run tactics by entrants would be possible. An alternative to assuming outputs of incumbents are held constant in the face of entry is to assume, as in Chamberlin's model of monopolistic competition, that entrants will enjoy the same market shares as incumbents, though of course these market shares will diminish as entry proceeds up to that point at which profits are zero. The price p_u set in such a market is unsustainable because it would be profitable for an additional entrant to produce an output at which average cost was minimized, but at a price below p_u yet above minimum average cost.

8.3 MULTIPRODUCT CONSIDERATIONS

In the previous section, contestability theory was deliberately introduced in the context of single-product firms for the sake of simplicity. However, this is to neglect some very important issues that arise in the multiproduct case. To give two examples: the average cost function is not well defined in the multiproduct case; and it can be shown that increasing returns are neither necessary nor sufficient for natural monopoly in the multiproduct case. For a detailed exposition the reader is referred to Bailey and Friedlander (1982). Here we shall concentrate on the central issues.

The essence of multiproduct considerations can be captured by confining attention to the case of production involving two outputs x_1 and x_2. Then total cost may be expressed as $C(x_1, x_2) = C(x)$. In the single-output case, average cost is defined by $C(x)/x$, but here this concept is not well defined as we have the choices $C(x_1, x_2)/x_1$ and $C(x_1, x_2)/x_2$. What Baumol et al. (1982) suggests is that we consider how total costs vary as outputs vary in fixed proportions (i.e. along a 'ray' in output space). For such a ray, *ray average cost* (RAC) is the ratio

$$C(x_1, x_2)/(x_1 + x_2) \tag{8.7}$$

where by an appropriate choice of units $x_1 + x_2 = 1$. This concept is illustrated in figure 8.3. The ray of output proportions is given by R. By an appropriate choice of units of measurement, unit amounts of one and two are defined. Total cost varies according to the curve OCA and ray average cost is measured by the slope of the straight line OA. In the particular case illustrated, ray average cost is declining.

Incremental cost is defined in the following way. Compare the costs of producing the output vector (x_1, x_2) with those of the output vectors $(x_1, 0)$ and $(0, x_2)$. Then incremental cost for the ith product (IC_i) is

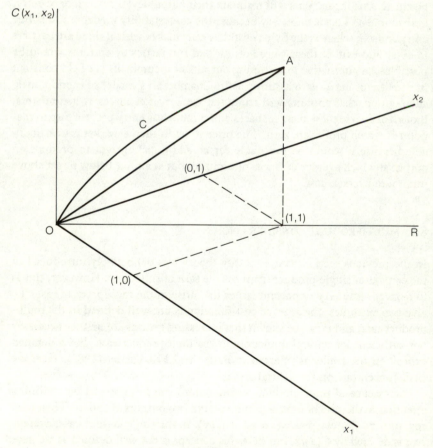

Figure 8.3

$$IC_1(x_1, x_2) = C(x_1, x_2) - C(0, x_2)$$
$$IC_2(x_1, x_2) = C(x_1, x_2) - C(x_1, 0)$$

(8.8)

The definition of average incremented cost then follows naturally as

$$AIC_1(x_1, x_2) = IC_1(x_1, x_2)/x_1$$
$$AIC_2(x_1, x_2) = IC_2(x_1, x_2)/x_2$$

(8.9)

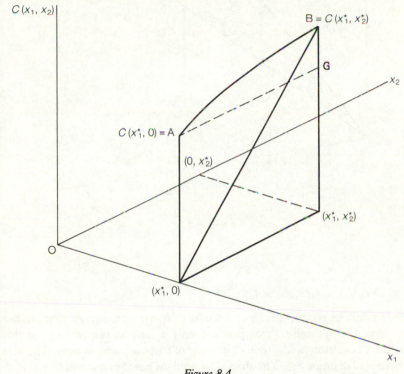

Figure 8.4

These concepts are illustrated in figure 8.4. In this diagram a cross-section is taken through the total cost surface for an assigned level of x_1^*, and amounts of x_2 varying from zero to x_2^*. In the absence of a fixed cost which must be incurred simply to commence production of x_2, the extra cost incurred in moving from $(x_1^*, 0)$ to (x_1^*, x_2^*) is given by $C(x_1^*, x_2^*) - C(x_1^*, 0)$, which is the incremented cost of output 2, IC_2, it being measured by GB in figure 8.4.

Let us now turn to *economies of scope*. It is a familiar notion that economies may derive from the scale of operation of a firm, but less well appreciated that economies may arise from simultaneously producing several outputs in one firm, rather than in a range of single-output specialized firms. If

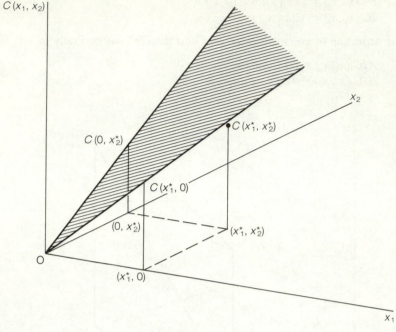

Figure 8.5

$$C(x_1, x_2) < C(x_1, 0) + C(0, x_2)$$

then it would be more profitable to produce (x_1, x_2) with a single firm, rather than have two specialist firms produce only x_1 and x_2 respectively. If this inequality condition holds, then economies of scope are said to exist. The idea is illustrated in figure 8.5. The shaded hyperplane has the equation $C = k_1 x_1 + k_2 x_2$ for constants k_1 and k_2. Thus $C(x_1^*, 0) = k_1 x_1^*$ and $C(0, x_2^*) = k_2 x_2^*$ define these constants. For economies of scope, we require that the hyperplane passes *above* $C(x_1^*, x_2^*)$, which is indeed the case in the diagram. It will become apparent that economies of scope are as important as economies of scale in establishing whether an industry is a natural monopoly. If a firm experiences declining ray average costs, but no economies of scope, it will pay to break up production into the hands of several specialized firms.

A further attribute of the cost surface can be investigated using the notion of the *trans-ray convexity*. It is concerned with the costs of firms producing a weighted average of the outputs of specialized firms, compared with the costs of specialized firms. The concept is illustrated in figure 8.6. Along AB,

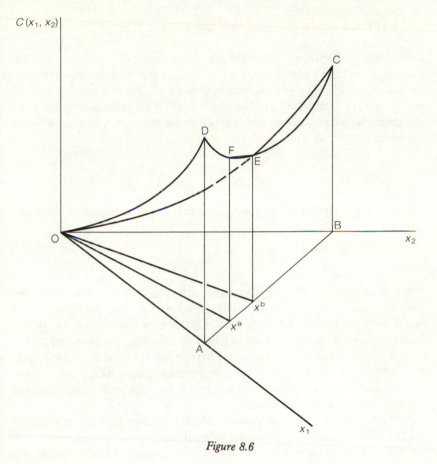

Figure 8.6

combinations of x_1 and x_2 are produced according to the convex linear combination

$$k\boldsymbol{x}^a + (1 - k)\boldsymbol{x}^b \qquad 0 < k < 1$$

when $\boldsymbol{x}^a$ and $\boldsymbol{x}^b$ are arbitrary vectors on AB. Then trans-ray convexity requires that

$$C[k\boldsymbol{x}^a + (1 - k)\boldsymbol{x}^b] \leqslant kC(\boldsymbol{x}^a) + (1 - k)C(\boldsymbol{x}^b) \qquad (8.10)$$

Geometrically, we require that the line segment FE be produced everywhere above the segment FE of the curve DFEC. In the discussion of natural monopoly in section 8.5, the crucial condition is cost subadditivity. An important result is that, given declining ray average cost (DRAC), trans-ray convexity is sufficient for subadditivity.

8.4   NATURAL MONOPOLY ANALYSIS AND RAMSEY PRICING

Let us return now to some important theoretical concepts introduced in earlier sections. Consider a vector of outputs $(x_1, \ldots, x_n) = x$ produced in a particular market. Represent by $C(x)$ the total cost of producing x. Consider now the choice between centralized production of x all taking place within one firm, and decentralized production with a set of output vectors $x^1, x^2, \ldots, x^n$ being produced by each of n firms, where

$$\sum_{i=1}^{n} x^i = x$$

Centralized production will be more efficient than decentralized production if

$$C(x) < \sum_{i=1}^{n} C(x^i) \tag{8.11}$$

where it is assumed that all firms have identical cost functions C. If this inequality holds for any possible disaggregation of x, then the function C is said to be subadditive at x and the market is said to be a *natural monopoly* at x. This idea involves a simple generalization of subadditivity, as introduced in section 8.2 in a single-output context. There, it was shown that falling average cost implied subadditivity. In turn, scale economies imply falling average cost, so the traditional association of natural monopoly with increasing returns or falling average cost is vindicated.

However, we have seen in section 8.3 that average cost is not uniquely defined in the multiproduct case. Even worse, in this case economies of scale are neither necessary nor sufficient for natural monopoly. Thus, whilst we will initially direct our attention at single-product natural monopoly, it would be misleading to think that the results obtained may be generalized in an obvious fashion. The analysis of multiproduct natural monopoly is complex but, put crudely, some form of 'cost complementarity' combined with economies of scale is sufficient to ensure subadditivity for multiple-output cost functions, and thus natural monopoly.

Turning first to the single-product case, a market is a natural monopoly if

$$C(x) < \sum_{i=1}^{n} C(x_i) \quad \text{for } \sum_{i=1}^{n} x_i = x \tag{8.12}$$

The next task is to present a precise definition of sustainability for natural monopoly. Let $D(p)$ denote the market demand curve. Then the natural monopoly is *sustainable* if the following three conditions are satisfied:

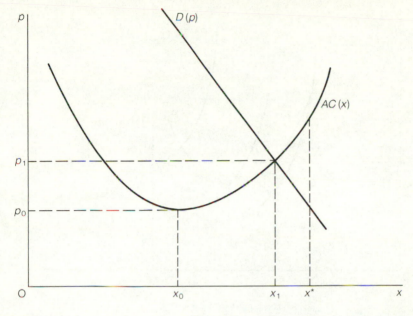

Figure 8.7

$$x = D(p)$$
$$px - C(x) = 0$$
$$p^e x^e - C(x^e) < 0 \qquad\qquad (8.13)$$
$$\text{for} \quad p^e \leqslant p \quad \text{and} \quad x^e \leqslant D(p^e)$$

In setting up these conditions it is assumed that the monopolist would maintain its price in the face of entry and would take up any residual demand at that price. Price and quantity (p^e, x^e) are choices that can be made by a firm contemplating entry; the third condition of (8.13) says that sustainability prevails if such choices provide no inducement for entry.

An important result now follows: 'A natural monopoly need not be sustainable.' (Sharkey, 1982, p. 88) This proposition is demonstrable using figure 8.7. This result has been anticipated by the reasoning attached to figure 8.1. Output x^* represents the greatest output that is consistent with natural monopoly, which here is beyond the market clearing quantity x_1. Now at (p_1, x_1) the first two conditions of sustainability are satisfied. But what of the third? Suppose a price less than p_1 were set $(p < p_1)$; then the monopolist could only meet the full market demand at a loss. Suppose instead that price is set above p_1 $(p > p_1)$; then a potential entrant could enter with the price–quantity combination (p_1, x_1). Indeed, if the monopolist chose price p_1, the potential entrant

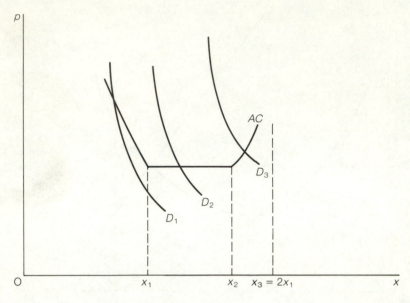

Figure 8.8

could profitably set a lower price between p_1 and p_0 producing a quantity less than x_1. For example, it could set a price $p_3 = p_1 - \varepsilon$ for ε small and sell x_0, thus guaranteeing itself positive profit.

It is clear that for a single-product natural monopoly, sustainability holds if and only if $AC(x_1) \leqslant AC(x_2)$ for all $x_1 > x_2$, where $AC(x) = C(x)/x$ (Sharkey, 1982, p. 88). The question that naturally comes to mind is: how likely is a single-product natural monopoly to be sustainable? There is no simple answer to this as subadditive cost functions can take many forms. In addition, the demand function is relevant. Consider a single-product firm having the average cost curve given in figure 8.8. The stage of scale economies, when AC is falling and demand is D_1, and the stage when AC is constant with demand at D_2, characterize a sustainable natural monopoly. However, once AC starts to rise the situation is less clear, for when output reaches $x_3 = 2x_1$ the industry is no longer a natural monopoly, as two firms could produce at the same average cost as one. Sharkey (1982, p. 89) suggests that the ratio $(x_3 - x_2)/x_3$ is an indicator of the probability that the natural monopoly is unsustainable.

Having explored the properties of single-product natural monopoly, it is important to extend the analysis to the multiproduct firm as many new complications arise in this, the more realistic case. The idea of a *supportable* cost function is implied in the single-product result above that a natural monopoly with price p and output $x = D(p)$ is sustainable if

$$p = \frac{C(x)}{x} \leqslant \frac{C(x')}{x'} \qquad \text{for all } x' \leqslant x \tag{8.14}$$

which may be expressed equivalently as

$$px' \leqslant C(x') \qquad \text{for all } x' \leqslant x \tag{8.15}$$

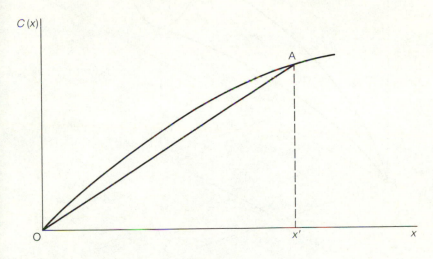

Figure 8.9

This is illustrated in figure 8.9. Average cost is measured by the slope of the ray OA. This ray lies below the total cost curve for all outputs x' less than or equal to any x. The cost function is said to be *supportable* at x. This idea may be generalized to the multiproduct case as follows. Now let x denote a vector of outputs and p the corresponding price vector. Then $C(x)$ is supportable at x if there exists a price vector p such that

$$px = \Sigma p_i x_i = C(x)$$
$$\text{and} \quad px' \leqslant C(x') \qquad \text{for all } x' \leqslant x \tag{8.16}$$

Geometrically, this says that a plane going through the origin and intersecting the cost function at x lies everywhere below the cost function over the rectangle defined by $0 \leqslant x' \leqslant x$. This concept is illustrated in figure 8.10 with the rectangle in the output space drawn below the cost surface. It should be noted that the cost function displayed also has the property of trans-ray convexity previously illustrated in figure 8.6 and defined by inequality (8.10). In the case of a multiproduct natural monopoly, the sustainability definition relevant to the single-product case, as exemplified by (8.13), should be generalized as

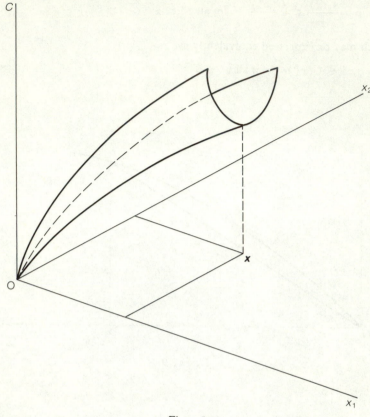

Figure 8.10

follows. A natural monopoly with cost function $C(x)$ and vector demand function $D(p)$ is sustainable if there is a price vector p and an output vector x such that

$$x_i = D_i(p) \quad \text{for all } i$$
$$px = \Sigma p_i x_i = C(x)$$
$$p'x' < C(x') \qquad (8.17)$$
$$\text{for all } p', x' \quad \text{with } p' \leqslant p \text{ and } x' \leqslant D(p')$$

As before, the prices p announced by the natural monopolist are sustainable if the monopolist is financially viable at these prices and no potential entrant can find a profitable marketing plan. It is clear from the definition of supportability in (8.16) and sustainability of a natural monopoly in (8.17) that supportability is a necessary condition for sustainability.

The concept of sustainability finds its principal importance in the theory of optimal pricing. A view that can be traced back to Ramsey (1927) is that a public utility or enterprise should aim to balance its budget. When there are several outputs, the assumption of 'Ramsey pricing' theory is that optimal prices should be chosen to maximize the aggregate net benefit to customers from consuming the outputs x, subject to the proviso that the firm should break even. Thus Ramsey prices can be regarded as second-best prices which enable the monopolist to raise enough revenue to cover the total cost, with the least possible sacrifice of consumer welfare. Ramsey pricing rules are particularly easy to derive in the case of independent demands, so we shall briefly consider this case. Under the independence assumption let $p_i(x_i)$ denote the inverse demand function in the ith market, and $R(x_1, \ldots, x_n) = \Sigma p_i(x_i)x_i$ the total revenue from sales in the n markets for which the firm produces. Let $C(x)$ be the cost function. Then the firm should choose outputs $(x_1, \ldots, x_n)$ so as to maximize the surplus

$$\sum_{i=1}^{n} \int_{0}^{x_i} p_i(s)\mathrm{d}s - C(x) \tag{8.18}$$

subject to the constraint that $R(x) = C(x)$ (i.e. a balanced, or break-even, budget). First-order conditions for the maximization problem (8.18) are

$$p_i - \frac{\partial C}{\partial x_i} = -\lambda\left[\frac{\partial R}{\partial x_i} - \frac{\partial C}{\partial x_i}\right] \quad (i = 1, 2, \ldots, n) \tag{8.19}$$

where λ is a Lagrange multiplier. Setting $MC_i = \partial C/\partial x_i$ to denote marginal cost and defining $k = \lambda/(1 + \lambda)$, expression (8.19) can be written

$$\frac{p_i - MC_i}{p_i} = -\frac{k}{\eta_i} \quad (i = 1, 2, \ldots, n) \tag{8.20}$$

where η_i is the price elasticity of demand for output x_i. This is often expressed as the Baumol and Bradford (1970) 'inverse elasticity rule'

$$\left(\frac{p_i - MC_i}{p_i}\right)\eta_i = \left(\frac{p_j - MC_j}{p_j}\right)\eta_j \tag{8.21}$$

The rules embodied in (8.20) and (8.21) are relevant to firms subject to scale economies which would suffer losses if marginal cost pricing rules were followed. That is they are applicable to natural monopolies of the sort that we have been discussing, where the assumption in formulating these rules is that the firm is subject to a regulatory authority which requires it to adopt a second-best optimality rule. If all decreasing cost firms were subject to second-best rules like (8.20), with k chosen to achieve budgetary balance, the question of how prices should be set in other sectors of the economy would still remain unanswered. We saw in chapter 7 that this raised a tricky problem in second-best theory, but one that could be solved, particularly if certain separability conditions held.

The most general formulation of the Ramsey pricing problem sets up the constraint such that profit Π is equal to the maximal economic profit E permitted by barriers to entry, rather than equal to zero. Then the Ramsey conditions are:

$$p_i - MC_i = -\lambda(MR_i - MC_i) \qquad (i = 1, 2, \ldots, n) \tag{8.22}$$

where λ is a Lagrange multiplier and $\Pi = E$. When we substitute $MR_i = p_i(1 - 1/\eta_i)$, under the assumption of independence of demands, (8.22) may be expressed in the simpler form of either (8.20) or (8.21).

Suppose that the cost function of a natural monopolist exhibits trans-ray convexity and declining ray average cost, as in figure 8.10. If outputs are weak gross substitutes (implying that a rise in all prices but the ith will not lower the demand for the ith output) and certain further technical conditions are satisfied, then the following holds:

Weak invisible hand theorem

Ramsey prices, as defined by (8.22), are sustainable.

This result has been much emphasized in the contestability literature, for it leads to the surprising conclusion that second-best pricing will deter entry of competing firms. The detailed proof of the weak invisible hand theorem is intricate and is contained in Baumol et al. (1982, pp. 231–9). Here we shall present a less general, heuristic proof. In the case of a monopolist selling the output vector $(x_1, x_2) = x$, consider first the total revenue surface defined by $R(x) = \Sigma x_i p_i(x)$ where $p_i(x)$ is the inverse demand function for the ith output. Consider now the augmented cost function $\tilde{C} = C(x) + E(x)$, where C denotes operating costs and E denotes entry costs. It is assumed that $\tilde{C}$ exhibits trans-ray convexity and declining ray average cost. The intersection of the total cost surface and the total revenue surface defines a closed curve B for which $C(x) + E(x) = R(x)$. That is, B is the hypercurve $\Pi(x) = E(x)$, where Π denotes profit. Suppose the monopolist announces a profitable set of fixed prices (p_1, p_2) for his outputs. It is assumed that customers may buy as much as they wish of the outputs at these fixed prices. As a potential entrant must price at, or below, the monopolist's prices in order to be able to sell any of the same goods, the revenue which the entrant can expect to get must obey the inequality

$$R^e \leqslant \Sigma p_i x_i^e \tag{8.23}$$

where the 'e' superscript is used to denote expected revenue and expected sales volume, respectively. As the hyperplane H given by $\Sigma p_i x_i^e$ does not in general represent market revenue, being defined for a fixed set of prices only, it is

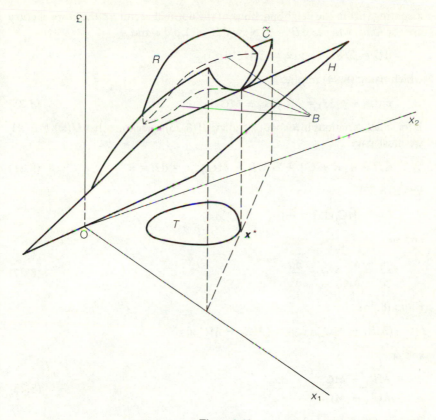

Figure 8.11

referred to as the pseudo-revenue hyperplane. The surfaces R, $\tilde{C}$, and H are represented in figure 8.11 together with the hypercurve B. The projection of B on to the output space defines the boundary of the set of outputs T for which the monopolist makes a profit which is no less than entry costs. It is assumed that T is convex, and that it contains every output vector which a potential entrant could hope to produce profitably. It is clear that tangency between H and $\tilde{C}$ is sufficient for sustainability. Over the relevant set T, H lies everywhere below the cost surface, except for the output vector $x^\star$. For the prices defining H the pseudo-revenue and the market revenue coincide for the output vector $x^\star$, and as B lies in $\tilde{C}$, tangency of H with $\tilde{C}$ implies tangency of H with B. The tangency between H and $\tilde{C}$ at output $x^\star$ with $\Pi(x^\star) = E(x^\star)$ requires $dH = d\tilde{C}$, from which

$$dH = dC + dE$$
$$= dC \tag{8.24}$$

assuming that in the neighbourhood of the optimal vector x^* the costs of entry are constant, whence $dE = 0$. Now $dH \equiv \Sigma p_i dx_i$ and

$$dC = \Sigma(\partial C/\partial x_i)dx_i = \Sigma MC_i dx_i$$

which using (8.24) implies

$$p_1 dx_1 + p_2 dx_2 = MC_1 dx_1 + MC_2 dx_2 \tag{8.25}$$

If for small variations in x about x^* along B (8.25) we require that $\Pi(x) = E(x)$, we must have

$$d\Pi = d\{R - C\} = \Sigma(MR_i - MC_i)dx_i = dE = 0 \tag{8.26}$$

From (8.25)

$$(p_1 - MC_1)dx_1 = -(p_2 - MC_2)dx_2$$

and so

$$\frac{p_1 - MC_1}{p_2 - MC_2} = -\frac{dx_2}{dx_1} \tag{8.27}$$

From (8.26)

$$(MR_1 - MC_1)dx_1 = -(MR_2 - MC_2)dx_2$$

and so

$$\frac{MR_1 - MC_1}{MR_2 - MC_2} = -\frac{dx_2}{dx_1} \tag{8.28}$$

Equating (8.27) and (8.28)

$$\frac{p_1 - MC_1}{p_2 - MC_2} = \frac{MR_1 - MC_1}{MR_2 - MC_2} \tag{8.29}$$

where (8.29) is exactly the set of Ramsey optimality conditions which emerge from solving out the Lagrange multiplier in the first pair of Ramsey conditions in (8.22).

Although the weak invisible hand theorem suggests that under certain circumstances Adam Smith's 'invisible hand' may extend its benefits to monopoly markets, it does not guarantee the optimality of natural monopoly pricing with free entry. Firstly, we observe that strict conditions on the form of the cost schedule were imposed to obtain the weak invisible hand theorem. Sharkey (1982) considers the case in which fixed costs are associated with individual outputs, rather than being common to all outputs. Under Ramsey pricing, an output for which demand was highly inelastic would bear a dispro-portionate share of fixed costs, through aiming to maximize welfare. Potential entrants who ignore aggregate welfare would therefore find entry for these outputs to be attractive. Secondly, Ramsey pricing is sufficient, but not necessary, for sustainability. There is no strict reason why other sustainable prices might not be chosen, should they exist. Such choices would have no desirable welfare properties. It should be remarked, however, that under Ramsey pricing sustainability has lower informational requirements than under non-Ramsey pricing. Provided costs obey the qualitative properties assumed, of which declining ray average cost is the most significant, only local information on costs and demands is required. With non-Ramsey pricing, global information on costs and demands is required. Thirdly, the results developed above assume a linear price schedule − a restriction which rules out of consideration welfare improving devices like non-linear or multipart tariff schedules.

To conclude this section on natural monopoly, it should be observed that an alternative approach to the one used by Baumol et al. (1982) is to analyse natural monopoly using game theoretic tools. The basic ideas of co-operative game theory were developed in chapter 6, and it is these which constitute the relevant tools. Sharkey (1982, chapter 6) develops a co-operative game analysis in which the term 'market' refers to a collection of buyers and a set of outputs. A market is said to be stable if the core of the associated game is non-empty. If it is non-empty, the market is said to be characterized by destructive competition. For a co-operative game with no side payments in which buyer's utility functions are quasi-concave and there are declining ray average costs, it can be shown that the core is non-empty. There is clearly a close relationship between this result and the weak invisible hand theorem, and equally clearly both are driven by virtually the same condition on costs.

We started this section by observing that a natural monopoly, defined by the condition of subadditivity, need not be sustainable. Conditions for sustainability were then explored, by investigating certain restrictions on costs. In this way we were led to the optimistic conclusion of the weak invisible hand theorem. Earlier in section 8.2, which was concerned with contestability, price was shown to be sustainable if and only if it was Ramsey optimal. Over a broad range of market structures there does therefore seem to be a presumption in favour of sustainability. However, this is to confine analysis to the static context. Further difficulties emerge when one engages in dynamic analysis. It is to this issue that we now turn.

8.5 DYNAMIC CONSIDERATIONS: UNSUSTAINABILITY

An issue which Baumol (1982) particularly emphasized in his presidential address was the so-called 'intertemporal unsustainability' result. Having pressed home firmly the view that the invisible hand had an important role to play in a static context, he produced the paradoxical result that it lost its efficacy in a dynamic context. However, the circumstances under which this would occur are somewhat limited. Let us look first at the simple result, and then see how it is affected once one considers a less limited case. It is assumed that demand is growing over time, that there are dynamic increasing returns in the sense that average construction costs fall over time, and that there is a certain finite time horizon beyond which it would certainly be uneconomic to take account of further growth in sales volume in making current choices about capacity. All costs are, for simplicity, assumed to be production costs. The producer is a natural monopolist in the sense made clear in section 8.4.

Denote by y_i the proposed capacity output in the ith period (i = 1, 2), by $K(y_i)$ the capital cost, and by p_i the price. Then if y_1 must be produced in the first period, and y_2 in the second (with $y_2 > y_1$), a requirement for equilibrium prices p_1 and p_2 must be

$$p_1 y_1 + p_2 y_2 \geqslant K(y_1) + K(y_2 - y_1) \tag{8.30}$$

where the left-hand side denotes the total revenue from selling outputs y_1 and y_2 in periods 1 and 2 at prices p_1 and p_2. Note that here prices are expressed in discounted present values, as are capital costs. On the right-hand side of this inequality are the capital costs of producing y_1 in the first period and then of purchasing further plant to produce an additional $y_2 - y_1$ in the second period.

Entry will not be profitable if

$$p_1 y_1 + p_2 y_1 \leqslant K(y_1) \tag{8.31}$$

that is, if the total revenue from selling y_1 in each period does not exceed the construction cost of plant able to produce y_1 per unit period. If conditions (8.30) and (8.31) are satisfied, p_1 and p_2 should be equilibrium prices. Subtracting (8.31) from (8.30) gives

$$p_2(y_2 - y_1) \geqslant K(y_2 - y_1)$$

from which

$$p_2 \geqslant \frac{K(y_2 - y_1)}{y_2 - y_1} \tag{8.32}$$

The dynamic increasing returns assumption can be expressed as

$$\frac{K(y_2 - y_1)}{y_2 - y_1} > \frac{K(y_2)}{y_2} \tag{8.33}$$

which is to say that capacity costs per unit of output fall, an assumption adopted elsewehere by Reid (1979). Then inequalities (8.32) and (8.33) can be combined, giving

$$p_2 > \frac{K(y_2)}{y_2}$$

from which

$$p_2 y_2 > K(y_2) \qquad (8.34)$$

Thus in setting an equilibrium vector (p_1, p_2) the natural monopolist invites profitable entry in the second period. Note that this occurs despite the fact that the natural monopolist should on efficiency grounds continue to produce, and that replication of the incumbent's plant by the entrant would be wasteful. This is the 'intertemporal unsustainability' result.

The conclusion is, perhaps, too devastating; indeed it seems almost implausible, given the common finding that there are first-mover advantages in industries subject to technical change. What is most obviously missing from the simple account above is any analysis of the way in which cost-reducing technical progress is achieved. An approach actually adopted by Baumol et al. (1982) themselves, following work of Rosen (1972), assumes a learning-by-doing effect. In the absence of learning it is assumed that constant returns would prevail, as in the static case. What learning does is to raise productivity in the second period according to the marginal cost function

$$MC_2 = c_2(y_1) \qquad \text{with } c_2'(y_1) < 0 \qquad (8.35)$$

where marginal cost in the second period is assumed to be decreasing in the production of the first period. Then the producer's cost function can be written

$$C(y_1, y_2) = c_1 y_1 + c_2(y_1) y_2 \qquad (8.36)$$

If there are diminishing returns to learning ($c_2'' > 0$) – an assumption that one might well consider reasonable to adopt – then Baumol et al. (1982, pp. 430–2) show that this intertemporal monopoly is sustainable. This conclusion is much more satisfying in an intuitive sense, for it suggests that there is a tangible first-mover advantage which is based on experience. Of course, since Worcester (1957) it has been claimed that dominant firms decline. Originally the argument was that the very success of dominant firms was to lead to their downfall, for these excess profits encouraged entry. However, the tendency to corporate concentration suggests that decline is by no means inevitable. In Reid (1979) firms do not have access to the same technology, but rather there is a distribution of efficiency, with the same aggressive price leader operating the most recent (and efficient) vintage of plant, and followers operating later vintages. The first-mover advantage of the aggressive price leader is never lost, because the leader has a larger mark-up on costs to divert to research and development. The consequences of this process are somewhat similar to Baumol's learning-by-doing variant discussed above. Least plausible is the intertemporal unsustainability result, but perhaps also too rigid is the notion that first movers have an advantage into the indefinite future. Nelson and Winter (1982), in their simulation analysis of Schumpeterian competition, have a more desirable variant, which operates on the assumption that firms have merely a probability of discovering a cost-reducing technical innovation. In this 'chance game of discovery' there will merely be a *tendency* for successful firms to retain leadership; it will not be inevitable.

8.6   EMPIRICAL EVIDENCE ON CONTESTABILITY AND NATURAL MONOPOLY

In a recent survey of contestability, Bailey et al. (1982, p. 104) argue that 'empirical research is required to reveal how widespread such conditions may be and how closely they may be approached in a variety of industries'. Though many studies of an empirical nature do have a bearing on the concept of contestability, few have been specifically directed at it. Here we wish to consider a variety of types of study of contestability, each of which goes about its empirical analysis in a different way. That the approaches are diverse is no doubt a reflection of the unsettled nature of the field. As the slow rise to ascendancy of the statistical approach to structure, conduct, and performance indicates, it was decades before the 'invisible college' of industrial economists started naturally to think in terms of a new paradigm.

Let us turn first to the qualitative analysis by Davies and Davies (1984) of the extent to which contemporary British banking has moved towards the contestability ideal as a result of the policy set out in Competition and Credit Control (1971). They argue that the basic requirements for contestability have been approximated to in recent years by UK banks and building societies. Entry has been unfettered because of a virtual absence of legal prohibition and also a liberal attitude by the Bank of England and the Treasury, particularly towards foreign banks. Banking institutions which are contemplating a move into a new market typically incur low sunk costs, because financial expertise is readily transferred between markets. Entry into, and exit from, such markets is therefore relatively unimpeded. Thus the clearing banks have been able to contest strongly the business of building societies, as they can readily vary the scale of such operations, or indeed exit, with little in the way of irrecoverable costs. Mortgages granted by the banks increased from £600 million in 1979 to almost £5000 million in 1982. Likewise the building societies have started to contest traditional banking areas. Part of the reason for this has been that the sustained boom in house purchasing over the last two decades has led to a substantial increase in retail branches of building societies. Such branches, with their attendant personnel, can readily be adapted to business more traditionally associated with the clearing banks. Even the need to establish retail branches has become less of a barrier to entry, given recent advances in computing and telecommunications technology. For example, the Nottingham Building Society circumvented the barrier of lack of retail outlets by reaching an agreement with British Telecom for the installation of home video units, with the TSB for cheque cashing and other facilities, and with Thomas Cook for travel facilities. In this way, their business was extended without incurring the huge entry costs involved in setting up new high-street branches, and retaining the option of relatively costless exit.

Since the advent of Competition and Credit Control in 1971, the near cartel-like powers of the dominant clearing banks have been removed. Their business has been increasingly contested by foreign banks, to the extent that the six clearing banks are now competing with 650 other banks of which 350 are foreign. Currently foreign banks account for one-third of the value of loans extended to manufacturing enterprises. It is to be noted that foreign firms have been relatively less successful in branch banking, where two significant barriers to entry have curtailed contestability. Firstly, there has been the high cost of investing in the setting up of many branches in a physical sense. This was not a cost which had to be borne by the building societies, who already had extensive branch networks and from this base were able to diversify into banking services. Secondly, and less important, new entrants had to gain access to the London Clearing House. This has now been achieved by Citibank and Standard Chartered, though they have yet to become members of the Clearing Banks Committee.

A quite different way of looking at contestability is in terms of experimental methods. In this approach, which is particularly associated with the pioneering work of Vernon Smith, human subjects play the roles of the firms, based on specific information regarding costs and demands. Coursey et al. (1984) investigate contestability experimentally, undertaking six experiments each with two potential sellers (i.e. the duopoly case) under conditions of zero entry costs. Firms had identical decreasing marginal costs up to capacity, with each firm having sufficient capacity to satisfy the entire market demand. In the pricing procedure adopted, a multiperiod offer system was operated, which entailed sellers quoting offers publicly and buyers making private selections of sellers from whom desired purchases were to be made. In the 'strong version' of the contestable markets hypothesis it is assumed that duopoly prices and quantities converge over time to their competitive values, whereas in the 'weak version' it is assumed that price will be less than the mean of the competitive and monopoly prices, and quantity greater than the mean of the competitive and monopoly quantities. If this weak hypothesis were to be rejected it would imply that firms were closer to the monopoly than to the competitive outcome. Coursey et al. (1984) found very strong evidence in favour of the weak version of the contestability hypothesis, and reasonable confirmation of the strong version. Harrison and McKee (1985) used experimental methods in a decreasing cost environment to compare contestability with a regulatory mechanism developed by Loeb and Magat (1979). The latter proposed an incentive-compatible regulatory mechanism which required only that market demand (but not market costs) be known. Their method requires the regulatory agency to subsidize the monopoly by the amount of the consumers' surplus generated at the uniform price charged by the seller. This leads to a price–output pair identical to the one that emerges in marginal cost pricing. Harrison and McKee found that the regulatory method was more effective than contestability in restraining monopoly power. However, compared with contestability the regulatory method required more information. The choice between the two is therefore not clear cut, and on the policy level a more effective method of promoting social efficiency with high informational requirements would have to be weighed against a less effective method with lower informational requirements.

A common criticism of the contestability and natural monopoly analyses of Baumol et al. (1982) is that the theory is not robust under minor violation of its assumptions. Vickers and Yarrow (1985) have argued that the existence of even small sunk costs is enough to remove the discipline of entry, and this point has also been made by Shepherd (1984). Baumol et al. (1982, 1986) rest most of their case on an unpublished Ph.D. thesis of Kessides (1982) and argue that a market's performance depends continuously on the degree to which it exhibits imperfect contestability. Kessides's basic equation related rate of entry to the height of exit barriers including, besides sunk costs, growth, scale of entry, and initial-year profitability. The model was estimated using data from 266 four-digit industries for 1972 and 1977; it was found that high sunk costs limited entry, and that the effect was continuous and monotonic. However, Shepherd (1984) has argued that to examine the robustness of the theory, tests would have to be confined to free-entry markets, and then focused on the consequences of small deviations from ultra-free entry. Alas, this is almost to say that the robustness of the theory cannot be tested, for rarely are these circumstances encountered.

Clearly subadditivity is crucial to a test of natural monopoly. Baumol et al. (1982) derived necessary conditions, and also sufficient conditions, for subadditivity, but could discover no jointly necessary and sufficient conditions. It is known that economies of scope are a necessary condition. Further, economies of scope allied to declining average incremented cost constitute a sufficient condition. Baumol et al. (1982) recommended testing the necessary and sufficient conditions separately. Then if the necessary conditions were rejected, subadditivity should be rejected; and if sufficiency were accepted, subadditivity should be accepted. They felt, however, that such tests required more information – typically *global* information on costs – than is usually available. However, as Evans and Heckman (1984) point out, if subadditivity is rejected in one region of output, global subadditivity is rejected. They applied this analysis to the Bell telephone system for the period 1947–77, disaggregating outputs into local and long-distance telephone services. They discovered that the evidence refuted the hypothesis that the Bell system's cost function was subadditive. From this, Evans and Heckman concluded that the Bell system was not optimally decentralized and was therefore inefficient. These economists were directly involved in formulating the studies which led to the breaking up of the Bell monopoly.

Finally, let us look at the work of Bailey et al. (1983) on the contestability of airline markets in the USA. It is argued that contestability in this market, until the 1978 Airline Regulation Act, had been precluded because of barriers to entry sanctioned by the Civil Aeronautics Board (CAB). The activities of CAB in themselves generated the need to regulate rates. The formal implications of the Act were to promote freedom of entry to air routes and flexible pricing. Freedom of entry was rapidly established, and many new services were put into operation, running cheap flights at frequent intervals with no frills. It took somewhat longer for price-setting freedom to arrive, but by the end of 1980 substantial price flexibility had been attained. Bailey et al. (1983) looked at measures of concentration before and after regulation. The Herfindahl index indicated an average concentration in 1980 which was 93.3 per cent of what it was in 1978 for the top 100 markets. They argued that such rapid deconcentration would encourage incumbent firms to view potential entry as a real threat. It was found that the more active the market, on a given route length, the lower the fare. Fares in these markets tended to fall below recommended guidelines after deregulation, though this tendency was reversed in thin markets.

8.7 CONCLUSION

When Baumol (1982) introduced his ideas on contestability and natural monopoly to a wider audience through his presidential address to the American Economic Association he emphasized that earlier writings on workable competition, whilst less formal, had the same aim of characterizing efficiency in a market with a small number of firms. Spence (1983) in a detailed review of contestability concluded that indeed its major contribution was 'in providing a welfare standard that is more relevant and useful than the perfect competition paradigm in industries characterized by returns to scale and scope of a variety of kinds'. Brock (1983) too, whilst noting problems of determinacy and robustness, generally found the theory an important development. However, balanced against this are vociferous critics, including Weitzman (1983), Schwartz and Reynolds (1983), Shepherd (1984), Holler (1985), and Vickers and Yarrow (1985). Weitzman has emphasized the difficulty of applying contestability theory to other than constant returns to scale technology. We saw in section 8.2 that sustainability will only be a feature of contestable markets if average cost curves are horizontal. This is true, but the restriction is not as strong as Weitzman suggests. Firstly, we know from empirical investigations that average cost curves are typically not strictly convex, but usually are flat bottomed, being horizontal for a range of outputs. This being so, Baumol et al. (1982) show that even if the flat-bottomed segment of the firm's average cost curve is short, it flattens the industry's average cost curve over a larger region, and there is an output level beyond which the industry's demand curve is horizontal. Specifically, if the flat-bottomed segment for the firm extends from output x' to $x'(1 + 1/n)$, where n is an integer, then there will be n regions in which the industry cost function will be linearly homogeneous (implying horizontal average cost), and further it will be strictly linearly homogeneous for any output $x \geqslant nx'$. Schwartz and Reynolds (1983) argue that there are two implausible conditions attached to perfect contestability. Firstly, it is assumed that when entry is profitable it can occur instantaneously and at any scale. Secondly, it is assumed that the entrant can undercut the incumbent's price, make a quick profit, and exit without a loss of fixed costs. This implies that the exit lag is shorter than the incumbent's price adjustment lag. This point has also been made by Spence (1983). Baumol et al. (1983) reply to this by arguing that Schwartz and Reynolds have introduced sufficient but not necessary conditions, by introducing their own dynamic story. Feasibility, sustainability, and contestability as defined in section 8.2 are entirely static equilibrium concepts. They provide a characterization of a particular type of equilibrium, but no guidance on the dynamics of adjustment to equilibrium. In particular, no assumption is made about relative lags and the rapidity with which industry demand could be fully met by entrants. On the other hand, arbitrary though any descriptions of dynamic adjustment may seem, those proposed by Spence and by Schwartz and Reynolds are not implausible, and do provide insight into the robustness of contestability theory. Shepherd (1984) has argued that what he calls 'ultra-free entry' is a contradictory assumption. If entry is on a trivial scale it has no force, but if entry is ultra-free the assumption of no response by incumbents is not tenable. It can be countered, however, that entrants can offer long-term contracts to supply the full market before physical entry actually occurs. Such a contract could in principle become a tradeable piece of financial paper, with a value equal to the rental to be diverted from incumbents.

It would be unwise to conclude that disputes surrounding contestability theory have been resolved on either an analytical or an empirical level. It remains an active research area. Thus Appelbaum and Lim (1985) have recently developed a model of what they describe as '*ex post* contestability'. The idea is that once a product has been introduced and demand conditions are known, entrants may start competing with incumbents using the same *ex post* techniques and information. They show that in a market where uncertainty and pre-commitment play a role, the latter strategy can be used to take advantage of more efficient production techniques and also to affect the 'degree of contestability' of the market. On an empirical level, the experimental work of Harrison and McKee (1985), and the econometric work on subadditivity by Evans and Heckman (1984), have been alluded to earlier. There does therefore seem a basis for the optimistic conclusion of Baumol et al. (1986) that what is on offer is not only a new normative benchmark, in the workable competition tradition, but also 'grist for the mill of positive economics'.

9

The organizational view of the firm

9.1 INTRODUCTION

So far, little attempt has been made to look inside the 'black box' which micro-economic theorists call 'the firm'. In traditional neoclassical analysis the firm has been assumed to be unitary in form, with shareholders and managers being unanimous in their desire to maximize profits. Of course, there are a variety of ways in which the profit function as a maximand can be represented. In its simplest form it is written $\Pi(x)$, where Π is profit and x is output per unit time, and a formulation such as this has been used to generate a full taxonomy of market structures from perfect competition through monopolistic competition, oligopoly, and duopoly to monopoly, including its multiple-plant and price discriminating variants. However, one is not here generating distinct theories of the firm, but rather different theories of market structure, based on what is essentially the *same* theory of the firm. As well as being unitary in form, and controlled and run by unanimous economic agents, this firm operates in an environment free from uncertainty, with agents being fully informed about costs and demands. If the form of the profit function is extended as in equation (2.1) to embrace other action variables apart from output, such as advertising expenditures, or as in equation (4.1) to embrace intertemporal profit flows and inventory adjustment costs, one is not actually moving a long way from the simplest profit maximization hypothesis in terms of taking account of the institutional form of the firm. The essence of the organizational approach to the firm, which is the concern of this chapter, is to take the significant step of inquiring into the firm as a social organization made up of individuals who often have different objectives, motivations, information sets, and contractual obligations.

We take as our starting point a variety of hypotheses which follow on naturally from the theories of industrial organization discussed so far. Both Adam Smith and Alfred Marshall appreciated the force and economy of the simple profit maximization hypothesis. But they were keenly aware – often markedly more so than their contemporaries, and certainly more so than most of their disciples – that the firm was made up of distinct types of economic agents. The simplest way to incorporate such considerations into a theory of the firm is to move away from a maximand which is profit, to some form of utility function. This idea was given general expression in equation (4.18), where an anticipated utility functional was defined having as its arguments anticipated profit and different types of assets. At a stroke, this theory introduces considerations of both uncertainty and extended utility maximization. More commonly these approaches have been tackled separately, given the analytical difficulties involved. Thus an expected profit function $E(\Pi)$ might be defined, given that demand and/or costs might be subject to stochastic errors; or a deterministic utility function such as $U = U(S, \Pi')$ might be specified, where S is selling expenses and Π' is discretionary profit, the latter being defined as gross profit less taxes and a desired minimum profit. There is nothing to prevent one from incorporating both ideas in the form of an expected utility function $E(U)$, where U is assumed to be a random variable obeying the density function $\phi(U)$; nothing, that is, barring the additional technical difficulties involved in handling this generalization.

However, the maximization hypothesis might itself appear unsatisfactory, no matter how one defines the general maximand. One can criticize any maximizing theory of the firm on the grounds that it involves an implausible form of 'super-optimization', in which all relevant costs and benefits are precisely known, global comparisons of all alternatives are made, and actions are taken which move one immediately to an equilibrium position. This approach ignores the limitations to human cognition that Herbert Simon has particularly emphasized. Not all facts about one's environment can be immediately assimilated: experience of it is typically acquired by local rather than global exploration. Such facts about the environment as one does acquire must be put into a logical relationship with one another, and the mind is limited in its capacity to formulate models of the world – both by imagination and by the logical complexity of comparing one possible model with the other. Finally, making operational one's model of the world requires using computational faculties which are severely limited. Put briefly, in the words of Simon, economizing man displays 'bounded rationality' rather than global rationality, for he is neither omniscient nor possessed of an infinite computational ability. He is likely to use provisional 'satisficing' rules which may be revised as he acquires more knowledge and understanding of his environment, rather than one-shot maximizing rules.

In the previous paragraph, the environment in which economic man makes his decisions has been regarded as complex, but inert. A new range of considerations is opened up once one admits the realistic possibility that the environment is endogenous. Economic man interacts with his environment, be it within the family or the firm, or outside in the market place. An important part of this interaction is with other economic agents. The utility maximizing framework above certainly captures aspects of the interaction between an economic agent and the inert part of his environment (e.g. the market, the legal form of his enterprise), but deals only partially and imperfectly with interactions that involve other economic agents. Institutional aspects of the firm, such as the separation of ownership and control in a corporation, seem to have certain consequences, such as a preference for perquisites by managers. However, the roles of economic agents (e.g. managers, workers, stockholders) and the consequences of their differences are not in themselves an object of enquiry. One moves a step further towards a full understanding of the firm and the industry within which it functions once organizational structure itself becomes the object of enquiry.

In moving on to this sort of inquiry, one is building on rather than abandoning many of the earlier insights of Simon. The industrial economist Oliver Williamson has been pre-eminent in developing this research agenda, and below we shall describe it as being concerned with 'markets and hierarchies', this being the title of one of his most influential works. In the markets and hierarchies approach man is, as Simon (1961, p. xxiv) put it, 'intendedly rational, but only *limitedly* so'. Not only does this imply difficulties with the maximization hypothesis, the point emphasized so far; it also makes allowance for the fact that man in an organizational framework will often behave opportunistically. In simple theories of maximizing behaviour it is assumed that men will reliably fulfil their promises. In the theory of bounded rationality as applied to the markets and hierarchies framework it is assumed that men may make self-disbelieved promises, and that parties to a contract cannot be relied upon to reveal fully and honestly all the facts required to make an informed agreement. As a consequence, men may seek to make self-enforcing agreements in an attempt to ensure *ex post* joint profit maximization for the contracting parties. It has been argued by Williamson (1986) that, looked at in this way, opportunism embraces the narrower concept of 'moral hazard' which has received so much attention in principal–agent analysis. The latter concept was developed from the insurance literature where it was observed that because the insurer cannot directly observe the degree of care exercised by the insured, a fully insured consumer is not motivated to be as careful after taking out insurance as he was before becoming insured. Clearly a consumer who uses this asymmetry of information to his advantage is behaving opportunistically. But opportunism is a broader term used to describe any contracting difficulties that may be associated with transactional activity. It will be noticed that the transaction is central to the markets and hierarchies view. Williamson follows Commons (1934) in regarding it as the basic unit of analysis. Transactions can take place out in the market, or within the firm. Coase (1937) provided the classical explanation for the existence of firms: they economize on transactions costs. This basic insight is retained in the markets and hierarchies approach.

However, it goes further. Coase contrasted allocation by the market with allocation by authority. Because using markets is costly, an authority (which he identified with the entrepreneur) may choose to direct the allocation of resources within the firm. We are still really left with a black box theory of the firm, though as Kay (1982, p. 39) has observed, we do now at least know why the black box exists in the first place. Rather than simply accepting that allocation takes place within the firm through authority, the markets and hierarchies approach substitutes the notion of a *structure* of authority for the simpler notion of the sole authority, or entrepreneur. The structure of authority may take various forms, but typically it involves some kind of hierarchy. A hierarchy is a pyramid of control levels in a firm, with employees at the higher levels of the hierarchy exercising control over employees at the lower level, and earning higher salaries. Typically only a fraction of the intentions of a superior are effected by a subordinate, and hence loss of control across hierarchical levels is cumulative. The degree to which subordinates contribute to the objectives of superiors is known as 'compliance', and this attribute can be affected by incentives and penalties, given that some form of monitoring of subordinates takes place. The extent of monitoring and the appropriate levels of incentives and penalties are as much the stuff of economic analysis in the markets and hierarchies approach as is the determination of the wage or salary in the black box approach to the firm.

Once one recognizes the different functions which economic agents may have within a firm, the simple hierarchy model may itself be modified. Because of loss of control through hierarchical levels, opportunism is likely to flourish, resulting in inconsistencies in the goals pursued at different levels. A variety of modified institutional forms (e.g. the multidivisional) attempt to reduce these effects. The different units that emerge in these various forms (e.g. general office, divisional office, in the multidivisional case) suggest that, borrowing from bargaining game theory, we may view the firm as a coalition of shareholders, employees, and business partners. This is an approach that has been particularly favoured by Aoki (1983). Another (closely related) approach which has been enormously influential in the literature on industrial organization is to view the firm as a set of contracts. According to Jensen and Meckling (1976) the theory of the firm is a special case of the theory of agency relationships, a type of analysis first developed rigorously by Mirrlees (1971). An agency relationship can be viewed as a contract in which a 'principal' employs an 'agent'. In a corporate framework, for example, the stockholders would be treated as principals and the managers as agents. The principal engages the agent to perform some task, and this usually involves delegating responsibility to the agent. However, agents will not necessarily work in the interests of the principal and costs will be incurred to bring about outcomes which are optimal from the standpoint of the principal. The principal will incur *monitoring costs* designed to limit the extent to which agents act against their interests. These might include auditing, formal control systems, budget restrictions, and incentive compatible schemes. In turn it may pay the agent to incur *bonding costs* to provide a form of guarantee that he will not attempt to harm the interests of the principal. These might include contractual guarantees to have accounts audited, explicit bonding against malfeasance, and contractual limitations on the manager's (i.e. agent's) decision-making power. The distinguishing feature of this approach has been captured by Jensen and Meckling (1976, p. 311) in the telling phrase 'the firm is not an individual'.

In early chapters it was apparent that the emphasis in industrial organization has been on interfirm competition. Elaborate theories have been developed using optimization and game theoretic techniques, and the normative properties of these models have been explored. In the terminology of chapter 2, this has been to emphasize the categories of structure and performance and their interrelations. Coase (1937) directed the attention of economists to the way in which the theory of choice could be extended to whether one used the market or firm for allocation, but stopped short of enquiring into the structure of authority within the firm. Managerial theories, such as those of Penrose (1959), Baumol (1959), and Marris (1964), started to look at the way in which the internal structure of the firm would affect conduct, and opened up the possibility that conduct not only would influence performance, but might be deliberately directed at changing structure. In many ways, however, these theories did not depart radically from extended forms of the neoclassical construction. Williamson's work in its earliest form, as in *The Economics of Discretionary Behaviour* (1964), was somewhat in this revisionist mode. However, with the advent of the market and hierarchies approach, drawing together ideas on cognitive function, the nature of contract, and administrative structure, the emphasis turned very much to intrafirm, rather than interfirm, competition. Approaching the firm from the property rights perspective, Alchian and Demsetz (1972) would regard the firm as a privately owned market, with the same potential for efficiency. Others, such as Francis (1983), and Marglin (1975, 1984) would emphasize the exercise of domination within the firm, and draw less optimistic welfare conclusions. What the approaches have in common is a willingness to contemplate different institutional forms. The research agenda has therefore shifted from one which ignored intrafirm competition and emphasized interfirm competition to one which emphasizes the way in which different forms of contracts and alternative terms of control and authority affect allocation within the firm. This makes the form of the firm itself a control variable rather than a datum. What emerges is a type of comparative institutional analysis which asks questions about the relative merits of different organizational forms of the firm, such as the owner-managed firm, the partnership, the non-profit organization, the joint stock company, the cooperative, and the trade union. At the moment the emphasis has been largely theoretical, but there is much in common between the markets and hierarchies view which has no presumption about the best form of a firm, and the case study methodology of chapter 3 which makes no initial presumption about what constitutes the appropriate theory before going out into the field. Clearly there is much important empirical work that requires to be undertaken using field work methods to explore recent ideas concerning intrafirm competition. Of course the final task remains of combining a well-articulated theory of intrafirm competition, which has been subjected to close empirical examination, with the more familiar theories of interfirm competition, which have until quite recently been the preoccupation of industrial economists.

9.2 MANAGERIALISM AND SATISFICING

Managerialism as an approach to the firm and the industry is derived from the pioneering work of Berle and Means (1932) and its development by later writers such as Burnham (1941) and Gordon (1945), who amplified the significance of the separation of ownership and control. At the same time, the significance of this functional separation for managerial conduct was noted by Barnard (1938), Drucker (1946), and others, who discussed managerial motives like empire building and the seeking of perquisites. These insights from business history, business management, business administration, and organizational analysis laid the foundations for theoretical work by economists in the 1950s on the managerial theory of the firm. The literature flourished in the 1960s and has continued apace since then, though becoming increasingly cross-fertilized with other theoretical developments including choice under uncertainty, behaviouralism, and principal–agent analysis.

Parallel to these developments, and often inspired by similar motives, was the emergence of theories of the firm and other organizational forms which emphasized psychological features of economic agents, including the limitations in their cognitive function and the interactions between their aspiration levels and achievements. Of outstanding significance in the development of these ideas have been the writings of Simon, Cyert, and March. As something of a convenience, which by no means does full justice to the fruitfulness and originality of this school, we attach to it the label 'satisficing'.

Expressed simply, the contrast between the managerial and satisficing view is that the former is concerned with the consequences of pursuing and attaining certain goals within a given framework, whereas the latter is concerned with the process of goal formulation and the adaptation of behaviour in the light of an incomplete correspondence between an outcome and a goal. We shall have a lot more to say later about the specific goals considered in the managerial and satisficing approaches, but for the moment will express the matter in more general terms.

A *managerial rule* is of the form:

$$\max_{x} G(x) \quad \text{subject to} \quad h(x) = 0 \qquad (9.1)$$
$$x \geqslant x'$$

where x is a vector (in a known set), each element of which relates to a variable under managerial control. These variables are arguments of a function $G(\cdot)$ describing managerial tastes, and also appear in the side relations specified in (9.1). These are of two types. The first, the function $h(\cdot)$, specifies human and institutional restrictions on the ways in which various magnitudes of the variables under managerial control are continuously related. The second is a set of inequalities which specifies boundary conditions on the variables under managerial control. These are determined by human, physical and institutional circumstances.

A *satisficing rule* (for specific examples, see Baumol and Quandt, 1964 and Cyert and Kamien, 1967) is of the form:

$$\text{if} \quad H(x_{t+r}) > H_0(t) \quad \text{for } r = 0, 1, \ldots, \tau \quad \text{then} \quad H_0(t + \tau + 1) > H_0(t)$$

and
$$(9.2)$$

$$\text{if} \quad H(x_{t+s}) \leqslant H_0(t) \quad \text{for } s = 0, 1, \ldots, \tau'$$
$$\text{then} \quad H_0(t + \tau' + 1) < H_0(t)$$

In (9.2) H_0 is the aspiration level or goal, and H is the achievement level. $H(x_t)$ is the satisfaction derived from taking courses of action described by the vector x; x is embedded in a set of higher dimensionality, which in general is not fully known to the economic agent. Thinking of this rule as being applied over a sequence of trials or time periods, $\tau + 1$ periods of exceeding a goal leads to an upward revision of the aspiration level, and $\tau' + 1$ periods of failing to better a goal leads to a downward revision of the aspiration level.

The rules specified under (9.1) and (9.2), though expressed in fairly general terms, fall far short of the level of generality one might aspire to in a more detailed treatment. In Shubik (1961) more general forms than (9.1) are considered involving intertemporal choice, uncertainty, and the possibility of bankruptcy. In Simon (1957, chapter 14) information gathering and multiple aspiration levels are some of the considerations which take us beyond the formulation in (9.2). However, for comparative purposes the rules described in (9.1) and (9.2) are adequate.

The important differences between the rules are as follows. Firstly, the managerial rule is concerned with maximization, whereas the satisficing rule is concerned with achieving a certain aspiration level. Secondly, the full set of possible instruments or controls is known in the managerial case, whereas in the satisficing case a limited set of controls is used out of (possibly irremediable) ignorance. Thirdly, the constraints are effectively fixed in the managerial case, whereas in the satisficing case, rather than aspiration levels being constraints, they are modified in the light of experience. Another way of contrasting the two approaches is to say that managerial rules tell you how to go about what you have decided to do, whereas satisficing rules tell you how to decide what you want to do. Machlup (1967), in a justifiably famous methodological essay on marginalist, behavioural, and managerial theories of the firm, made the important point that theories of the sort developed by Baumol (1958) and Williamson (1963) are a form of 'managerial marginalism'. Despite new symbols and a borrowed jargon from the organizational literature, the methodology is very familiar. The same is not true of the satisficing approach, but it has led to few new pure theories (though work like that of Cyert and Kamien, 1967 is significant) and has perhaps been more influential in the design of simulation models of the firm or the industry. The latter are not in a strict sense theoretical developments.

But is even the claim that satisficing introduces something substantially novel a well-founded one? It is clear that in a stable environment with well-informed economic agents, maximizing and satisficing conduct have the same equilibrium outcome. Take the simple case of maximizing a managerial utility function $U(x)$ with x a single managerial control. Maximizing requires finding the root $x^\star$ of $U'(x) = 0$. Then max $U = U(x^\star)$. If U is known, if x is controllable, and if the manager has computational ability, this maximum will be directly attained. Suppose, however, that history is significant and in some initial situation the variable x is at a level x_0, with utility below its maximum. Is there a rule for getting from x_0 to $x^\star$? There may be many such rules, but one in particular is obvious. Write $U'(x) = 0$ as

$$x = \phi(x) \tag{9.3}$$

and we have an appropriate rule. If new levels of the variable x are determined according to

$$x_{n+1} = \phi(x_n) \tag{9.4}$$

given an initial value of x_0, then provided certain restrictions on ϕ hold

$$\lim_{n \to \infty} x_n \to x^\star$$

where $x^\star = \phi(x^\star)$ is a fixed point. The expression (9.4) is a kind of satisficing rule. It does not take us immediately to the optimum, but it does move us steadily towards the optimum. A suitable condition to ensure convergence on the optimum would be $0 < \phi' < 1$. For this satisficing rule, the economic agent is generating a sequence of utilities $U(x_0)$, $U(x_1)$, $\ldots$ which has as its limit the maximum utility max $U = U(x^\star)$. The agent can be thought of as continuously raising his aspiration level to attain this when initially $x_0 < x^\star$, and continuously lowering it when $x_0 > x^\star$. By the elementary theory of first-order difference equations applied to (9.4), cyclical alterations between aspiration levels which are too high and then too low are also possible (this being the case in which $-1 < \phi' < 0$).

Supporters of the behavioural standpoint would, however, strongly dispute this interpretation that the application of satisficing rules will in the long run amount to maximizing rules. The above naïve illustration would be held to be misleading on at least three counts. Firstly, economic agents have not there been regarded as having problems with perceiving which factors can affect their wellbeing (i.e. their utility U). Both use the same instrument or control variable. The reaction of a behaviourist might be to enquire immediately whether there were other variables which could be controlled by the economic agent to enhance welfare. Secondly, the behavioural rule is unmodified in the light of experience. Successive applications of the rule actually reveal information about the environment, and raise the possibility of accelerating the passage to enhanced wellbeing by appropriately modifying the rule. It may seem that this favours the argument of 'managerial marginalists', but in fact it does not, even though the achievement of the maximum is apparently facilitated by adaptive rules – precisely because the theory is about the process of adaptation, and not about the equilibrium. Thirdly, the environment is itself changing, according to the behavioural school which favours satisficing rules. Processes never have enough time fully to work themselves out, before new environmental changes make further demands on the adaptive capabilities of the economic agent. In this emphasis on the process of adaptation, and the requirement that economic agents be alert to the possibilities of a changing environment, those who favour the satisficing approach have a lot in common with the Austrians. However, unlike the Austrians they have been willing to go beyond philosophical speculation and have used scientific, empirical observation on human subjects to inform their theories. Simon, for example, was much influenced by the literature in psychology on aspiration levels and has himself made important contributions to artificial intelligence (see Simon, 1982).

So far, the distinctions that have been made are rather neat. When one moves from the general level of discussion to the specific, distinctions become blurred. Let us now consider as a group three very widely applauded managerial theories of the firm: the sales revenue maximizing model of Baumol (1958); the growth maximizing model of Marris (1964; and Marris and Wood, 1971); and the managerial discretion model of Williamson (1963). In a slightly different category is the theory of Penrose (1959), which we would wish to regard as a variant of the profit maximization view, with Marshallian features. Furthermore, it was not a theory that could be readily expressible in the formal language of Baumol, Marris, and Williamson. Though none the less persuasive or significant for that, we exclude further discussion of Penrose, and focus on formal theory.

The maximization problems of Baumol (B), Marris (M), and Williamson (W) may be expressed as

$$\max_{x,\,S} R = R(x, S) \qquad \text{subject to} \quad \Pi \geqslant \Pi_0 \qquad \text{(B)}$$
$$x, S \geqslant 0$$
$$\max_{g,\,v} U = U(g, v) \qquad \text{subject to} \quad v = v(g) \qquad \text{(M)} \quad (9.5)$$
$$v, g \geqslant 0$$
$$\max U = U(S, M, \Pi_D) \qquad \text{subject to} \quad S, M, \Pi_D \geqslant 0 \qquad \text{(W)}$$

where R is revenue; x is output; S is expenditure on staff, sales promotion, and advertising; g is the growth rate of real assets; v is the 'valuation ratio', defined as the ratio of market value to assets; M refers to managerial emoluments (perquisites); and Π_D is discretionary profit, defined roughly as the minimum profit demanded. More precisely, if Π_0 is the minimum (after-tax) profit demanded, T is taxes, Π is actual profit, and $\Pi_R = \Pi - M$ is reported profit, then discretionary profit is $\Pi_R - \Pi_0 - T$. The inequality constraint $\Pi_D \geqslant 0$ under (9.5)(W) is frequently expressed $\Pi_R \geqslant \Pi_0 + T$. It will be observed that all three theoretical formulations (B), (M), and (W) in (9.5) are of the type considered under the general managerial rule expressed by (9.1).

Let us first consider the rationale for each specification and then turn to theoretical implications. Baumol (1958) candidly refers to 'his own rather spotty observation of the behaviour of a number of American business firms' as the empirical basis for his 'theory of oligopoly'. Putting aside the slight misuse of the term 'oligopoly' for this model, which ignores conjectural problems, the sales maximization hypothesis has the virtue that at least one economist believes 'that the typical large corporation . . . seeks to maximize not its profits but its total revenues, which the businessman calls his sales . . . once his profits exceed some vaguely defined minimum level'. As Reid (1981) has pointed out, when Sweezy (1939) developed his version of the kinked demand curve analysis of oligopoly, he did so on the basis of consultancy experience within the business enterprise that might have been just as 'spotty' as Baumol's. That theory, like Baumol's, has had a remarkably long currency in industrial economics. On the survivor principle, Baumol's clearly must have something to recommend it. The specification has a number of merits. Firstly, it runs in terms of well-defined variables. Indeed, the two crucial control variables or instruments in the maximand – output and expenditure on sales promotions and advertising – are amongst the most readily available business statistics within the firm. Secondly, given the assumption that increased advertising will always increase sales volume, the profit constraint will always be binding (i.e. $\Pi = \Pi_0$). And it is the latter property which drives a crucial result of this model concerning the non-neutrality of variations in overhead costs. Thirdly, the dependent variable – sales revenue – in the objective function is highly perceptible and easily measured, irrespective of the number of products being sold by the firm. Buoyant sales confer prestige on the manager, encourage the benevolence of potential lenders, raise the morale of employees and strengthen competitive position in the market place. Given its measurability, perceptibility, and significance to all levels of personnel within the firm, sales probably *is* the best single indicator of what influences its day-to-day functioning. However, what of profit? Baumol admits that 'the determination of the minimum just acceptable profit is a major analytical problem', saying that he can 'only suggest here that it is determined by long-run considerations'. He has in mind that sufficient retentions must be generated to finance expansion plans whilst dividends must be sufficient to make the stock attractive to investors, but never formulates these conditions. Now it is clear that an alternative way of looking at $\Pi \geqslant \Pi_0$ is as a satisficing rule, rather than simply as a constraint on a maximization problem. The relevant question would then be how Π_0, regarded as a goal, might be modified. Behaviourally, a persistent situation in which $\Pi > \Pi_0$ would seem likely to lead an upward revision of Π_0. Whether this occurs or not has something to do with the separation of ownership from control, and the capacity of stockholders to limit by monitoring and incentives the tendency of managers to favour emoluments or perquisites. This issue will be explored further in section 9.4 on principal–agent analysis.

The Marris formulation (9.5)(M) is justified by quite an elaborate psychological and sociological structure in the original formulation. The utility of managers is said to depend upon salaries, favour, status, and job security, in contrast to the utility of owners whose utility depends on profits, capital, market share, and public esteem. At its simplest, this is reduced to saying that owners' utility depends upon the rate of growth of real assets and managers' utility upon the rate of growth of demand for the product and job security. In the steady-state model both growth rates coincide and job security is represented by the valuation ratio. A falling valuation ratio encourages take-over raids, after which top management is likely to be dismissed, and is therefore associated with diminished security and lower utility. There is no doubt that the analysis of Marris (1964) is informed by an enormously detailed knowledge of organization theory, business history, and the sociology of business. In the Marris and Wood (1971) variant, on which we concentrate our attention here, this is reduced to formulating the abstraction of an omniscient, optimizing, collective supermanager.

Williamson (1963), like Marris, drew heavily on the experience and insights of organization theorists in drawing up a list of managerial objectives which included salary, security, power, status, prestige, and professional excellence. In order to connect these motives with behaviour, Williamson introduced the notion of 'expense preference'. Managers have a positive preference for expenditures on staff, emoluments, and discretionary investment. Economists since Marshall in his *Industry and Trade* have noted a preference for staff expansion. Emoluments are a form of economic rent arising from managerial power. Perquisites have the advantage of low perceptibility, and may also be advantageous from a taxation standpoint.

So much for specification of the models. It is to be noted that despite recognizing a number of features of the internal structure of the firm, none of the managerial theorists models the firm in terms of hierarchies or coalitions. The process of moving from individual human motives to a kind of global behaviour characteristic of the firm as a whole is not discussed.

What can one expect, and what does one get, from theories of this sort? Machlup (1967) argued that we are ultimately concerned with how firms respond to changes in conditions. He thought, intuitively, that 'managerialism' would not contribute significantly to our general understanding of these issues. However, it should be observed that the minute one departs from the perfectly competitive situation it becomes very difficult to say anything qualitative about how firms react to changes. Samuelson (1947, p. 42) in his *Foundations of Economic Analysis* pointed out that even the apparently simple problem of concluding how variations in advertising affect the output of a monopolist could not be solved qualitatively; empirical investigation is necessary. Archibald (1961) pressed this point home further by showing that for the Chamberlinian monopolistic competition model there were no conclusions one could draw about the effects of changes in data on the equilibrium price or the size of plant. In a much more general theoretical examination of these problems Archibald (1965) came up with similarly negative conclusions. He considered the case of a multiproduct, multiplant, multimarket firm that had under its control variables such as quantities, qualities, prices, and selling costs. Then the problem is to maximize a function U subject to one or more market constraints; U could be simply net revenue, or any monotonic increasing function of net revenue. Potentially, one can generate a large number of managerial theories of the firm from such a theoretical set-up. Again, he demonstrated the great paucity of qualitative predictions that emerge. It seems clear, therefore, that once one attempts to model any situation involving market imperfections, unambiguous predictions are hard to find. The criticism cannot be directed at managerial models in particular. More to the point is whether there are qualitative predictions that emerge from a managerial model that do not emerge from a neoclassical competitive model.

There is often not a great deal of difference between the conclusions that emerge from each type of model. Solow (1971) set up comparisons between an orthodox neoclassical firm which aimed to maximize its market value, and Williamson–Marris growth models of the firm. A general, but trivial, conclusion was that growth-oriented firms would choose higher rates of growth than profit-oriented firms. But apart from this, both types of firm responded in qualitatively similar ways to changed data like factor prices, the rate of discount, and excise and profit taxes. For the specific formulations given in (9.5) the conclusions are somewhat more cheering. The Baumol model does of course indicate that a sales revenue maximizer will produce more and advertise more than a profit maximizer. But most significant is the conclusion that an increase in fixed costs will lead to a price increase. The received doctrine is that there will be no price or output effect, essentially because marginal costs (which are crucial for the optimality calculation) are unaffected. In the Baumol model, however, the profit constraint is generally binding, and an increase in overheads would mean that the firm no longer earned enough to meet its profit constraint. Output and/or advertising expenditure would have to be reduced in order to earn up to the required level of profit. The most interesting feature of this result is that it is a feature not of the maximization assumption as such but of the profit constraint, which as we observed earlier may be interpreted as a satisficing rule. Yarrow (1976) has shown that the Baumol model is particularly sensitive to variations in the constraint specification.

On an empirical level, a number of attempts have been made to test Baumol's theory. Most have been directed at the assumptions rather than the implications of the theory. Baumol's rationale for the sales revenue maximization hypothesis was that 'executive salaries appear to be more closely correlated with the scale of operations of the firm than with profitability'. Studies by Roberts (1959) and McGuire et al. (1962) confirm a higher correlation between executive incomes and sales than between executive incomes and profits. It was assumed by Baumol that advertising would be increased until the profit constraint was binding. This assumption was tested by Hall (1967) using five-year mean profit rates as a proxy for the profit constraint. No significant correlation was found between sales revenue changes and deviations of actual from desired profit, tending to falsify one of the assumptions of the model. However, one might reasonably question the construction of the proxy for Π_0 and the assumption that it was the same for all firms in a given industry. Beyond the maximum on profit, sales are rising and profit is falling until the profit constraint is binding. Marby and Siders (1966) therefore argued that support for the Baumol model would be indicated if there was a negative correlation between sales and profit. Not surprisingly, as profit has sales incorporated in it by its very definition (and with a positive sign), only significant positive correlations were found. This does not seem to be a valid refutation of the theory. At the moment the theory appears to be neither strongly confirmed nor refuted. One would doubt whether it was ever Baumol's purpose to have his theory treated in this way. He clearly hoped it would help explain the economic world better, but stated with equanimity 'there seems to be no way for it to be tested by statistical or other standard techniques of empirical investigation'. To date, this prediction at least seems to have been validated. Lewellyn (1969), Lewellyn and Huntsman (1970), and Masson (1971) have tended to support the salary–profits correlation, whereas Meeks and Whittington (1975) have produced more evidence in favour of a salary–sales correlation, as well as a devastating critique of Lewellyn and Huntsman. However, none of these studies resolves the crucial issue of causality (maybe good managers improve sales, but will improving sales make a manager good?). Baumol's modest evaluation of the possibilities for undertaking empirical research has proved prophetic.

Williamson (1963) discovered again the limitations on qualitative predictions which may be derived from a utility maximizing model, and had to make special assumptions on second derivatives in order to derive a full set of comparative statics results. In his model the main theorems derivable from a profit maximization hypothesis, with respect to shifts in demand and variations in a sales tax, are preserved. However, new predictions emerged from the effects of lump-sum and profit taxation. These taxes have no consequences for selling expenses and output for a profit maximizing firm. By contrast, in a managerial discretion model, output, selling expenses, and emoluments vary positively with a profits tax, and negatively with a lump-sum tax. These differences can be attributed to the slack that exists in a managerial discretion firm, as contrasted with a profit maximizing firm in which slack is always zero. It is this slack that accommodates in the managerial case to give non-zero effects in the face of changes in lump-sum and profits taxation.

Unfortunately, although the results on profits taxation and lump-sum taxation provide the sharpest means of distinguishing a managerial world from a profit maximizing world, direct tests are difficult to perform. Williamson therefore proposes tests of the type that have been used on the Baumol model. He argues that expenditures which promote managerial satisfaction should be positively correlated with opportunities for managerial discretion. The difficulty with this argument is that it only provides a means of falsifying the managerial discretion model. If no correlation is found then the Williamson model is refuted, whereas if a correlation *is* found then the model is supported but not favoured as a hypothesis over the profit maximizing model. Williamson set up a log-linear cross-sectional regression model in which the compensation of top executives was explained by indices of competition (measured by concentration and entry barriers), tastes of management (measured by composition of the board of directors), and a staff variable (measured by the sum of administrative, general, and selling expenses). The last variable was used as a proxy for the expense incurred in a strictly profit maximizing world. The signs of the parameters for cross-sections of data relating to three separate years were all as predicted by the expense preference hypothesis. The parameters were furthermore statistically significant, barring the composition of the board parameter, which was only significant for one cross-sectional data set. This set of findings does not deny Williamson's model and, whilst consistent with it, is also consistent with a number of other possible models. It is therefore a very weak test of the managerial discretion hypothesis. A similar type of weak test was proposed in which the retained earnings ratio was correlated with managerial taste for discretion (as measured by the composition of the board of directors). The Williamson model is favoured if this correlation is positive, implying that managerial representatives on the board shift dividend policy to their advantage. A number of statistical tests confirmed this result, and Williamson estimated that the retained earnings would increase by 12 per cent if managerial representation on the board of directors were doubled. Finally, Williamson appeals to field work evidence in favour of the managerial discretion model. It would not appear that data were gathered according to any well-articulated field research methodology, as described in chapter 3, but they do provide a unique insight into the internal structure of the firm. The notions of expense preference and discretionary spending were supported by the observations that faced with a fall in profitability, having previously enjoyed a sellers' market for some time, firms would adjust by reducing salaried employment (with personnel, public relations, and R & D experiencing the greater cuts) and by reducing emoluments. One firm reduced overall salaried employment by 32 per cent without changing production, resulting in a more than twofold increase in the return on investment. This suggests that in the buoyant period, managers attended to goals other than profitability. There clearly remains much scope for conducting systematic studies of this sort using field research methods.

Last, we turn to Marris's model. Unlike the other two, it was originally formulated as a growth model. However, Baumol (1962) has shown how his own model may be generalized in this way, and the task has been completed with the Williamson model by Solow (1971). In the latter article it was shown that it was very hard to distinguish observationally between the Marris model and other variants. A principal distinguishing characteristic is that profit maximizing enterprises should have higher profit rates and lower growth rates than growth maximizing (managerial) enterprises. In a classical study Radice (1971) found that, for a sample of 86 UK firms in the food, electrical engineering, and textile industries, profit maximizing (owner-managed) enterprises experienced higher profit rates and higher growth rates than managerial enterprises. Unfortunately these results run up against a statistical 'identification problem' of the sort that was explored in chapter 2. What one is observing is a pair of equilibrium growth and profitability measures, each of which is derived from a maximizing model of the type (9.5)(M). However, over a succession of periods both U and v are likely to be shifting, and a variety of loci can be generated depending on the magnitudes of those shifts rather than on the internal organization of the firm.

One might now ask what direction the managerial theory of the firm will take in the future. It appeared to be the case at one point that the satisficing approach would come to be increasingly influential. That has not come about. Theoretical work on behavioural rules has been limited. Cyert and Kamien (1967) presented a Bayesian analysis of price adjustment based on the simple hypothesis that the firm will raise or lower price by a fixed percentage of its value in the previous period. Demand was assumed subject to a random shock with a known distribution function but an unknown mean. By testing its environment with different prices, the firm could learn about the distribution of demand and hence formulate an appropriate policy for setting an optimal price. Unfortunately, simple though the structure of this problem may be, it requires considerable computational capacity to solve it. To hypothesize such an attribute for an economic agent is a self-contradiction within the behavioural framework.

More significant has been the adaptation of satisficing rules for formulating computer simulation models of the industry and the firm. Important early contributions along these lines include Cyert and March's (1963) model of a department store, Cohen's (1960) model of shoe retailers, shoe manufacturers, and cattlehide leather tanners, and Balderston and Hoggatt's (1962) model of the west coast lumber industry in the US. As Stiglitz and Mathewson (1986, p. xviii) have observed, the contemporary inheritors of the crown of Simon, Cyert, and March are Nelson and Winter (1982; and Nelson, 1986). In their modelling of Schumpeterian competition the firm is characterized by the set of routines it deploys. These are decision rules that have been evolved through past experience, and are the result of search directed at finding better ways of organizing the activities of the firm. The firms that survive and prosper are those that adopt the best routines as applied to choice of production technology, input and output mix, pricing, investment appraisal, personnel selection, R & D, and so on. Such routines are essentially of three types. Firstly, there are 'standard operating procedures' which determine inputs and outputs. Secondly, there are routines that determine investment behaviour. Thirdly, there are routines that involve search behaviour. The statistical model on which Nelson and Winter usually base their simulations is a complex variant of the Markov model introduced in chapter 5 to represent Marshallian views on growth and decay in the industry. Indeed, though we would hesitate to argue with Nelson and Winter's choice of authority, we could argue that their simulations have greater validity as representations of the Marshallian analysis of industrial evolution rather than of the more disruptive Schumpeterian.

In all the discussion of managerialism and satisficing so far, we have not departed from the convenient device of regarding the managerial optimizing or satisficing as being undertaken by one superagent. However, management is a collection of individuals who interact with other collections of individuals within or outside the firm. The firm, viewed in this way, is a coalition of individuals. Aoki (1980) views the firm as an organization of stockholders and employees. The distributive bargaining that takes place between these parties is modelled as a two-person co-operative game. As in all the models developed so far in this chapter, the manager has a key role. In this case he arbitrates between the stockholder and the employees. The decision variables (instruments or controls) are sales price, growth rate, and the stockholders' share in organizational rent. In a model of this sort it can be shown that shifts in the balance of bargaining power have determinate consequences for price and the rate of growth. For example, if employees enjoy enhanced bargaining power, this raises the equilibrium sales price, but beyond a certain point lowers the planned growth rate. Once the internal structure of the firm is probed in this way, and the concept of a single superagent acting as a proxy for a group is abandoned, one is starting to explore an area in which hierarchy and its functions are all important. For a recent attempt to gain insight into growth *and* hierarchy, see Chiang (1986). Hierarchy is the subject matter of the next section.

9.3   MARKETS AND HIERARCHIES

We saw in section 9.1 that firms as organizations could be explained on Coasean lines by arguing that they were more transactionally efficient than the market. That insight has something of a tautological character unless one can explain what it is within the firm that brings about this advantage. Coase himself provided no guidance on this issue, and indeed there was no well-defined economics literature on this subject until academics like Simon and Williamson started to introduce economists to ideas from organization theory. The terminology developed has become complex, and the jargon can on occasion be overwhelming. There is further a relative lack of purely formal reasoning on which one can depend to get a sharply focused idea of what the central issues are. We shall therefore start this section by looking in fairly precise terms at authority and hierarchy, before considering the organizational failure framework.

Coase talked of the entrepreneur allocating by authority within the firm, but did not investigate the nature of this authority. An important contribution to the study of the nature of authority is the work of Simon (1957, chapter 11). He argues that an authority relationship is created between the employer and the employee by the employment contract. Let B denote the boss or employer, and W the worker or employee. Let X denote the set of all possible actions that the worker can undertake on the job, and let x be an element of this set ($x \in X$) – a particular set of clearly defined tasks. Then B *exercises authority over* W if W allows B to select the set of tasks to be performed, $x^\star$. This authority will typically not have an unrestricted domain. Let $A \subset X$ be that subset of tasks which is acceptable to W. Then W will generally only accept the authority of B over him if the chosen set of tasks $x^\star$ lies within the area of acceptance $x^\star \in A$. The employment contract is specified once W has agreed to accept the authority of B, and B has agreed to pay the wage w to W. Let the utility functions of B and W be given by

$$U_1(x, w) = F_1(x) - a_1 w \qquad F_1 \geqslant 0, \quad a_1 > 0$$
$$U_2(x, w) = F_2(x) + a_2 w \qquad F_2 \leqslant 0, \quad a_2 > 0 \tag{9.6}$$

where for simplicity the set of tasks is taken to be one dimensional. Thus B's utility is positive in effort, via the task performed by W, but decreasing in the wage: and W's utility is negative in effort, via the task performed for B, but increasing in the wage. If a contract is not struck between B and W, it is assumed that $U_1 = U_2 = 0$, and when a contract *is* struck it is assumed that neither B nor W is disadvantaged: $U_1 \geqslant 0$, $U_2 \geqslant 0$. If a task x and a wage w exist satisfying these restrictions, the authority relationship is *viable*. Now

$$U_1 \geqslant 0 \quad \Rightarrow \quad F_1 \geqslant a_1 w \qquad \text{and} \qquad U_2 \geqslant 0 \quad \Rightarrow \quad -F_2 \leqslant a_2 w$$

from which

$$a_2 F_1 \geqslant a_2 a_1 w \geqslant -a_1 F_2 \qquad (9.7)$$

Conversely, if $a_2 F_1 \geqslant -a_1 F_2$ holds for the same task x, then a wage w can always be found such that (9.7) is satisfied. Thus (9.7) provides necessary and sufficient conditions for viability of the authority relationship. Note that even though this is an authority relationship (for B is specifying what W will do), it is advantageous to both B and W. Typically, if a viable solution exists, it will not be unique, but will be represented by a region in the wage–task space.

This analysis can be extended by introducing uncertainty. Suppose now that the utilities U_1 and U_2 are not known with certainty at the time B and W negotiate the contract. Let a random state of nature determine what the utilities will be. Then it is useful to distinguish two types of contract – an employment contract and a sales contract. The latter is a simple generalizaton of the non-stochastic case. Without uncertainty, W agrees to undertake specified tasks x^1 for B in return for a specified wage w^1. W is not in an authority relationship with B. When uncertainty is introduced into a sales contract one is dealing with expected utility rather than deterministic utility, but the analysis is otherwise unaltered. B makes a wage offer for specified tasks $x \in X$ independently of the state of nature with the intention of maximizing the expected value of his utility. In an employment contract, by contrast, B adjusts the tasks depending on the state of nature, and has the scope of his authority limited so that $x \in A$. The latter contract involves the exercise of authority, but this has some advantages. In particular B can obtain a greater output on average by adjusting tasks, depending on the state of nature. This removes control from the worker, but promises a higher wage. For a special case, Simon (1957) demonstrated that the employment contract will be preferable to the sales contract, and a statement of this result under general conditions is given by Hess (1983, p. 95).

Of course, if organizations like the firm can provide transactional advantages over the market, this is not to say that they *must* have a structure of authority. However, there appear to be disadvantages in non-authoritarian organizational forms, even though they may offer advantages over markets in handling indivisibilities, mitigating problems of moral hazard and adverse selection (see section 9.4 below), and providing associational benefits. Williamson (1975, pp. 45–9) provides a discussion of these benefits for one such non-authoritarian form – the collective peer group team – but is ultimately more persuaded by the advantages of hierarchy over peer groups. In figure 9.1(a) a four-member peer group case is represented. The four members A, B, C, and D have communication links (represented by straight lines) with all other members, and there is no natural structure of authority. However, systematic monitoring is difficult in peer groups and this can encourage free riders. Furthermore, keeping all channels open to all members imposes strains on the information processing capabilities of members (who are subject to bounded rationality) and diverts resources from productive activities. Agreement on access to

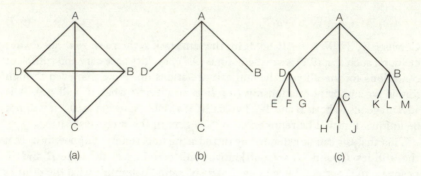

Figure 9.1

indivisible physical assets can also be time consuming and may be frustrating to negotiate, given that such rules, like priority at traffic signals and pedestrian rights of way, are arbitrary but essential to good order. The point is to have rules which are *agreed* upon. The emergence of hierarchy from a peer group is possible if a leader is nominated on a temporary basis as 'peak co-ordinator' on the understanding that the leadership will be rotated. Such a simple hierarchy is illustrated in figure 9.1(b). Members B, C, and D now communicate directly with the 'peak co-ordinator' but not with one another. In terms of the evolution of organizational forms, differences in bounded rationality amongst members of a group may encourage the surrender of peer group democracy in favour of enjoying the productivity gain resulting from having the most able members acting as peak co-ordinators. Once this has happened, hierarchy has been born. This simple form of hierarchy can encourage the development of extended forms of hierarchy. One obvious method of extension is simply to increase the span of control of the peak co-ordinator by adding further members who are subordinate to him but at the same level as the other subordinates. This rapidly runs into problems of bounded rationality. An obvious way of deferring problems of bounded rationality as the organization grows is by serial repro-duction, which is to say that subordinates of the peak co-ordinator in turn acquire further subordinates, for whom they act as peak co-ordinator, and so on. In this way complex hierarchy emerges, as illustrated in figure 9.1(c) where D, C, and B have in turn become peak co-ordinators from the perspective of additional organization members E to M. It is convenient to regard E, F, and G as the 'subordinate' of their 'superior' D, and so on. This form too suffers from drawbacks. As the organization is expanded, superiors are increasingly distanced from the basic data that influence operations, and this information has to be transmitted across hierarchical levels, each of which imposes informa-tional losses. Moving down the hierarchy from the peak co-ordinator are instructions which are aimed at promoting the purposes of the organization. In precisely the same way as information passing up the hierarchy becomes of lesser quality, so too do instructions passed down become progressively degraded, even if subordinates do have the same objectives as their superiors. If they do not, the transmission of instructions is subject to further degradation. The general term for these effects is 'control loss'.

Let us now turn to developing a formal model of control loss along the lines of the work of Williamson (1967). Consider a firm organized on hierarchical lines. At the top of the hierarchy is the entrepreneur or peak co-ordinator whose purpose is to control the number of hierarchical levels in order to maximize the profits of the firm. To do so, he hires administrative employees at various levels of the hierarchy, and workers at the bottom (production) level of the hierarchy. It is assumed that administrative employees and workers are hired at competitive market rates, and that the product of the firm is sold in a competitive market.

Denote the hierarchical levels by the index $h = 0, 1, 2, \ldots, H$, where level $h = 0$ involves production workers, the peak co-ordinator is at the top level $h = H$, and administrative employees are at the intermediate levels. The last named do not have overall responsibility for co-ordination and are not directly involved in production. Their day-to-day administrative activities involve planning, forecasting, accounting, and supervision of their immediate subordinates. If n_h denotes the number of employees at the hth level of the hierarchy, then n_{h-1}/n_h is called the *span of control* s_h, where it will be noted that the more subordinates that must be supervised by their superiors, the greater is the span of control. Williamson assumes a constant span of control s, so the number of workers at the hth hierarchical level can be written

$$n_h = s^{H-h} \quad \text{when } m_H = 1 \tag{9.8}$$

A 'compliance parameter' k determines the fraction of work that a subordinate does to contribute to his superior's objective. Therefore output y_0 is given by

$$y_0 = (ks)^H \quad 0 < k < 1 \tag{9.9}$$

Denote the competitive wage paid to the workers at level 0 by w_0 and the competitive wage paid to salaried workers at the hth hierarchical level by w_h. It will be assumed that the wage paid to each superior is β ($\beta > 1$) times that of his immediate subordinate. Thus the wage at the hth hierarchical level is

$$w_h = w_0 \beta^h \tag{9.10}$$

This assumption, whilst clearly convenient, also has the merit of some empirical support. Profit Π for the peak co-ordinator or entrepreneur is

$$\Pi = py_0 - \Sigma_h w_h n_h \tag{9.11}$$

where p is the price commanded by a unit of output in a competitive market. By substituting (9.8), (9.9), and (9.10) in (9.11), profit may be re-expressed as

$$\Pi = p(ks)^H - \Sigma_h w_0 \beta^h s^{H-h} \qquad (9.12)$$

If H, the number of hierarchies in the firm, is treated as a continuous variable which is under the control of the peak co-ordinator, the optimal (profit maximizing) number of hierarchies is given by solving

$$\max_H \Pi(H) \qquad (9.13)$$

For details of the first-order conditions for this maximization problem the reader is referred to the relevant expression in Williamson (1967, equation 2). That expression involves a term $(\beta/s)^H$. Now $5 < s < 10$ and $1 < \beta < 2$ are plausible ranges for the span of control and wage differential parameters. For H large, the term $(\beta/s)^H$ is vanishingly small, and convergence to zero is rapid (e.g. for $s = 8, \beta = 1.5, H = 4, (\beta/s)^H = 0.001\,23$). This term therefore may be neglected. Then an appropriate expression for the optimal number of hierarchies $H^\star$ is given by

$$H^\star = \left\{ \ln\left[\frac{w_0}{p}\right] + \ln\left[\frac{s}{s-\beta}\right] + \ln\left[\frac{\ln}{\ln(ks)}\right] \right\} \Big/ \ln k \qquad (9.14)$$

Total employment in the firm is the sum of employment in all the hierarchical levels up to the $H^\star$ given by (9.14). Thus

$$\Sigma_h n_h = \Sigma_h s^{H^\star-h} \qquad (9.15)$$

using (9.8). For large corporations this figure typically ranges from 1 to 100 000. This implies an optimal number of hierarchies of between 4 and 7 when (9.15) is solved using plausible values for the span of control and corporate employment. By differentiation of (9.14), comparative statics results can be obtained. The principal results are: $H^\star$ rises as compliance k rises; $H^\star$ rises as span of control s increases; and $H^\star$ falls as the wage differential β between superior and subordinate falls. If there is full compliance, or as Williamson puts it 'no loss of intention between successive hierarchical levels', then $k = 1$ and the optimal $H^\star$ is infinite. This however is a pathological case, and the significant feature of the analysis is that a limit is set on hierarchy. This limit is set by the optimizing conduct of the peak co-ordinator in the face of cumulative control loss between successive hierarchical levels, and does not depend on orthodox arguments usually invoked to impose a theoretical static limit on firm size such as a declining product demand curve and/or a rising factor supply curve.

A managerial variant of this hierarchical control loss model can be developed by appeal to specification (9.5)(W). Write the managerial utility function as

$$U = U(E, \Pi) \qquad (9.16)$$

where E is hierarchical expenses and Π is profit. If management is assumed to have a positive preference for hierarchical expenses, it can be shown that the optimal $H^\star$ for a utility maximizing organization will be larger than for the corresponding profit maximizing organization with the same parameters. This result is consistent with a general conclusion that emerged from section 9.3 to the effect that a managerial firm with expense preference tended to produce more than a profit maximizing firm.

A number of restrictive aspects of the above analysis should be remarked upon. Firstly, the assumption of a fixed span of control might be questioned. Williamson argues that on empirical grounds this is a reasonable assumption, and on theoretical grounds it makes no difference to the conclusions reached. In fact the empirical evidence is somewhat slight, and Williamson's own theoretical accommodation to the possibility of a variable span of control admits only of a difference at the lower level of the hierarchy. Beckmann (1977) in a variable span of control analysis produces the result that no finite optimal number of hierarchies may exist, so the way in which the span of control is specified in hierarchical models is clearly important. Secondly, the analysis ignored interactions between compliance and the span of control. Clearly as span of control increases each supervisor has less time to devote to the supervision of his increased numbers of subordinates, and a decrease in compliance is likely. If this is captured by a general function of the form $k = f(s)$ with $\partial k/\partial s < 0$, no qualitative results can be wrung from the model. However, for the specific form $f(s) = \exp(-gs^2)$ where g is a parameter representing goal inconsistency, Williamson has derived comparative statics properties. Most of these are plausible, barring the result that suggests that the span of control should decrease as output increases. This result is counter-intuitive and also at odds with available evidence. Possibly a respecified $f(s)$ function could correct this anomaly, but one is left with the suspicion of more serious misspecification lurking in the model. The result that an increase in goal consistency leads to an increase in span of control is plausible for large organizations where goal consistency is maintained by rigorous selection and training, and a relatively 'flat' hierarchical structure becomes possible.

The Williamson hierarchical control loss model has been subject to considerable extension and modification, the most significant contributions probably being Mirrlees (1976), Beckmann (1977), and Calvo and Wellisz (1978). We have noted that Beckmann's relaxation of the constant span of control assumption removes the guarantee that the optimal number of hierarchical levels is finite. Beckmann treats managerial control ('supervision') as an intermediate product in the hierarchical firm. Output y_h of supervision at the hth level is regarded as being produced by the labour x_h of managers at that level and the supervisory input y_{h+1} from above:

$$y_h = F_{h+1}(x_h, y_{h+1})$$

At level 0, y_0 is regarded as the final output of the firm, to be sold on a competitive market at the price p, and x_0 is treated as production labour. By successive substitution, y_0 may be written

$$y_0 = F_1(x_0, F_2(x_0, \ldots, F_H(x_{H-1}, x_H)) \ldots)$$

Beckmann chooses F_h to be Cobb-Douglas in form, and develops profit maximization and comparative statics results along the same lines as the Williamson model. Many of the comparative statics results agree with Williamson's conclusions, but a crucial difference between the models is that in Beckmann's case no finite optimal H may exist. Mirrlees (1976) has argued that Williamson's conclusion on the limits to firm size depends on what is essentially an *ad hoc* assumption that compliance is incomplete ($0 < k < 1$). As we have already observed, with complete compliance in Williamson's model the formal proof of loss of control across successive hierarchies collapses. Calvo and Wellisz (1978) have emphasized that the supervision process, rather than incomplete compliance, provides a sounder theoretical explanation for loss of control limitations on firm size. They specify an employee utility function

$$U = u(c) - v(e) \qquad c \geqslant 0, \quad 0 \leqslant e \leqslant 1$$

where U is a concave von Neumann–Morgenstern utility indicator, c is income, and e is effort, with $e = 0$ denoting idleness and $e = 1$ denoting maximum effort. Employees have a probability p of being checked. If they are *not* checked, they are assumed to be working at maximum effort ($e = 1$) and receive a wage of w. If they *are* checked, then they are paid in proportion to their measured effort. Thus for effort e, the employee receives ew. Looked at another way, if the effort is less than maximal there is a positive penalty of $(1 - e)w$. The expected utility for an effort e is therefore defined as

$$z = p[u(we) - v(e)] + (1 - p)[u(w) - v(e)] \qquad (9.17)$$

It is assumed the employee chooses e to maximize this expected utility. The probability of being monitored at the hth level of the hierarchy is assumed to depend upon the span of control, and the effort of the employee is assumed to depend upon the span of control and the wage. For such an organization Calvo and Wellisz (1978) show that no finite optimal H exists. More precisely, they show that if it pays to hire any employee at all, it then follows that the firm's profit could be increased without limit, by increasing the number of hierarchical levels. To emphasize the dependence of the firm size limitation argument on the way in which shirking is handled, Calvo and Wellisz present sufficient conditions for a finite optimal number of hierarchies. They introduce the possibility that subordinates are aware of the periods when they will be monitored. It is assumed that during a proportion x of the work period the employee knows he will not be monitored, and that the firm will pay him wx. For the rest of the time $(1 - x)$ the same monitoring scheme as before pertains. If $\tilde{e}$ is the effort during the time $(1 - x)$, then if the employee *is* checked he will be paid $(1 - x)\tilde{e}w$ giving him an income of $wx + (1 - x)\tilde{e}w$, and if *not* checked he will be treated as though $e = 1$ giving him a wage income of w. An expected utility function is set up analogously to (9.17), and the employee is assumed to choose e to maximize it. In this case it can be shown that the optimal size of hierarchy is finite. Williamson had treated control loss as exogenous, and apparently demonstrated that loss of control due to shirking would limit hierarchy. Calvo and Wellisz showed that this was not necessarily so, and by probing more deeply the informational state of the organization were able to indicate what type of monitoring scheme would lead to diseconomies of administration.

We have formally explored some of the reasons why hierarchy has its limitations. This has emphasized the progressive control loss consequential on extension of the hierarchy. However, Williamson (1971, 1975) has a much richer informal discussion than this of the limitations of hierarchy, and indeed is also critical of Simon's treatment of authority for its narrowness of conception. Taking the latter point first, Williamson would claim that Simon's treatment ignores the full range of sales contracts (specifically, contingent claims and sequential spot contracts), ignores transactional efficiency considerations, and is not well adapted to treating idiosyncratic tasks. Turning now to hierarchy, Williamson deploys the full vocabulary of his organizational failure framework to develop his critique of this organizational form. It is not the purpose of this section to treat this set of arguments in a detailed way, and besides very useful compressed versions are already available in Kay (1982) and Williamson and Ouchi (1983). Here we shall put the matter somewhat tersely.

In essence, Williamson argues that as firms grow and vertical integration is extended, transactional diseconomies are incurred and the advantages naturally deriving from internal organization become impaired. These effects will occur for firms of a given organizational form, and will be ameliorated or reversed if the organizational form is adaptive. The goal distortions that arise when a firm expands include three biases towards internal operations. Firstly, internal sources of supply are controlled by bureaucratic groups whose subgoals are more readily interpreted in terms of membership belief systems than objective profitability. Such groups tend to favour reciprocity relations within the organization rather than market transactions. Secondly, expansion is favoured, not for profitability considerations, but because of its potential for resolving internal conflict. Thirdly, programmes tend to persist because of sunk costs of both the intangible and the pecuniary sort, insulating existing projects from logical economic alternatives. All three biases are buttressed by the communication distortions that an organization may foster (e.g. telling the boss what he wants to hear; reporting only those things that one wants disclosed). The transactional disabilities that Williamson emphasizes are threefold (though bounded rationality and uncertainty might also be significant, if of lesser importance). These are: (a) opportunism, the use of self-disbelieved threats or promises; (b) small numbers, which is a necessary condition for opportunism;

and (c) information impactedness, which occurs when the parties to a transaction are not equally well informed. The difficulty is that these effects will often not show up immediately as vertical integration proceeds and transactions are transferred from the market to the firm. In particular, opportunism, which often takes the form of pursuing a non-profit-oriented subgoal, usually takes some time to take a hold, as it requires the co-operation of a group of managers (e.g. in internal reciprocity relations). Then there are sheer size considerations. We have already mentioned how bounded rationality leads to a finite span of control, and consequential control loss through hierarchical levels. In addition bureaucratic insularity increases as the organization grows, and high-status office holders become insulated from replacement, tending to receive disproportionate rewards of both the pecuniary and non-pecuniary variety. Further, as size increases, atmosphere (attitudinal characteristics that surround the exchange relationship) may deteriorate. As Williamson (1975, p. 128) so aptly put it, 'attitudes of voluntary co-operation are supplanted by the *quid pro quo* orientation'. Finally, as size increases, the promotion ladder of the large firm, which has advantages over the market in terms of long-run incentives, has weaknesses compared with the bonus payments for entrepreneurial activity which can be made without increasing transactions costs in smaller firms. In short, the growth of the firm by radial expansion leads to a variety of organizational failures which can be debilitating for the hierarchical firm.

One response to this might be to return to markets. Williamson would not dismiss this possibility, but rather would argue that it is a matter of striking a balance between organizational failure and market failure. What he offers as an important alternative is the *adaptation of the organizational form*, for recall that all the arguments earlier about the drawbacks of expansion have assumed a constancy of organizational form.

The point of departure for the consideration of organizational alternatives is the so-called 'unitary form' (U-form) enterprise. It is illustrated in figure 9.2. In this hierarchical structure advantage has been taken of the division of labour and economies of scale to set up specialized functional divisions, each being responsible for specific activities like production, sales, and finance. The functional divisions are controlled by a chief executive which corresponds to the peak co-ordinator in the theoretical account of hierarchy given up to this point. Expansion of the U-form leads to problems which have been discussed earlier. Principally, there is cumulative loss of control with its associated efficiency loss and an impaired capacity to take strategic decisions because of the proliferation of subgoals which are not profit oriented. These problems of the U-form enterprise, as the size and complexity of the firm increased, led historically to the development of the multidivisional (M-form) structure. This is illustrated in figure 9.3. In place of the functional divisions of the U-form enterprise there are operating divisions which report back to a general office. Each operating division may be thought of as being a scaled-down version of a

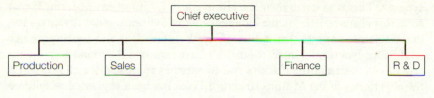

Figure 9.2

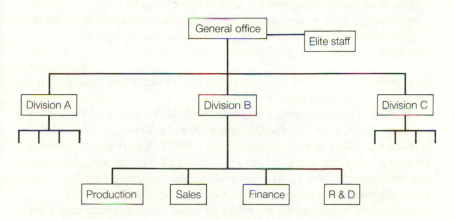

Figure 9.3

specialized U-form enterprise. The divisions work in a semi-autonomous fashion − hence the lack of horizontal linkages in figure 9.3 − and the peak co-ordinator now has the nature of a general office, assisted by an elite staff, which is concerned with formulating strategy. Chandler (1966) particularly emphasized the advantage of the M-form in terms of the activities of the general office, which, freed from the stultifying effects of dealing with an overload of short-term operating and tactical decisions, was able to concentrate effort on long-term planning and appraisal. Williamson (1970) gave a more detailed treatment of the characteristics and advantages of the M-form, which can be summarized as follows: (a) operating decisions are handled by independent divisions; (b) the elite staff attached to the general office assist in the control of divisions by providing advisory and auditing functions; (c) the general office undertakes strategic decisions; (d) the general office is concerned with overall performance rather than the performance of specific divisions; and (e) the M-form is characterized by rationality and synergy. The synergistic aspects of organizational structure were not fully explored by Williamson, but have since been examined in informative detail by Kay (1982), who reaches the conclusion that firms would attempt to combine those activities which would maximize synergy. This is to strengthen the argument in favour of the M-form. It may seem that characteristic (a), the independence of divisions, is not advantageous, but Williamson argues that it cuts off weak interactions and encourages rich (and hence synergistic) interactions. We have now laid the foundation for the crucial conclusion of the markets and hierarchies approach, which is to assert the superiority of the M-form structure. This has been expressed as follows:

The M-form hypothesis
The organization and operation of the large enterprise along the lines of the M-form favour goal pursuit and least-cost behaviour more nearly associated with the neoclassical profit maximization hypothesis than does the U-form organizational alternative. (Williamson, 1975, p. 150)

As a corollary of this, the U-form structure has the characteristics typical of the managerial firm discussed in section 9.2.

Chandler (1966) has traced the spread of the M-form from its beginnings in the early 1920s with Du Pont, General Motors, Standard Oil, and Sears. Imitation was slow at first; however, since World War II it has been widely adopted in the USA, and since the late 1960s in Europe as well. To judge by this evidence, the M-form is a more survivable structure than the U-form. Does this necessarily imply that it is more transactionally efficient?

The M-form hypothesis has been the object of considerable empirical enquiry, important contributions having been made by Armour and Teece (1978), Teece (1981), Thompson (1981), Cable and Dirrheimer (1983), and Cable and Yasuki (1985). Two basic approaches are followed. The first, based on Teece's methodology, directly tests the differential performance between the first firm to adopt the M-form structure and its principal rival in the same industry. The second is based on Cable's methodology, which involves using a linear model of interfirm differences in reported profitability in which explanatory variables are split into those that explain profit maximizing conduct and those that explain managerial conduct.

Teece's method (as in Teece, 1981) involves using a matched-pair comparison between principal firms. It requires identifying the first firm to adopt the M-form structure, and then using a control firm for comparison using selection criteria of product comparability and close competitiveness. Two periods were recognized: (a) when the leading firm was M-form and the control was not; and (b) when both firms were M-form. Performance was measured by rate of return on shareholder equity or rate of return on assets. A difference statistic was constructed with the attribute that the M-form hypothesis would be supported if the performance difference after both firms had become M-form was less than it was when only one was M-form. For 30 US industries reported on by Teece, the M-form hypothesis was supported at the 5 per cent level. Cable's method, as in Steer and Cable (1978), involves estimating the model

$$\Pi_i = f(\mathbf{x}_i) + g(\mathbf{z}_i) + u_i$$

where $f(\mathbf{x}_i)$ denotes the profit maximizing level for the ith firm, $\mathbf{z}_i$ is a vector of variables suggested by managerial theories of the firm, and u_i is a random variable. Profitability Π_i is measured by the price–cost margin, the rate of return on shareholder's equity, or the rate of return on shareholder's equity plus long-term debt. The independent variables chosen include an organizational form dummy, an owner-control dummy, managerial tastes, firm size, and growth. This article was not directed at testing for the efficacy of a specific organizational form, though the M-form was included, and found that organizational form in general had a large and significant impact on profitability for a sample of 82 UK firms over the period 1967–71. Later studies were directed at extending these results to other industrialized nations. Cable and Dirrheimer (1983) adapted the Steer and Cable analysis to test the M-form hypothesis on West German data. The M-form had a negative short-run effect on profitability and a zero long-run effect. Though not ruling out the possibility of a positive long-run effect, Cable and Dirrheimer point to the lack of a trend to M-form in Germany after 1975 as indicative of disenchantment with this organizational form in German business. They are prompted to suggest that institutional and cultural factors may account for the rejection of the M-form hypothesis, citing the prevalence of owner control and of heavy banking involvement in corporate strategy as being of likely significance. An important limitation on the M-form hypothesis suggested by this, is that it is not 'culture free'. This conclusion is reinforced by the findings of Cable and Yasuki (1985) for Japan. There, the trend to M-form has been later and less extensive than in the USA, UK, and West Germany. Cable and Yasuki found that the M-form did not apparently offer any advantages over alternative organizational forms. There is a strong suspicion that whatever the organizational form, managerial interests will dominate for cultural reasons in the case of Japan. The profit motive is not revered in Japan, and growth maximization offers better opportunities for meeting standards of business culture like continuity, growth, frugality, and temperate management. Thus the M-form hypothesis is currently showing evidence of being a much more contingent, context-dependent theory. More recently, Marginson (1985) has also challenged the hypothesis on its own terms (writers on monopoly capitalism would generally start from a different perspective from Williamson, and never regard hierarchy as benign. Most influential of these has been Marglin, 1975, 1984) for its neglect of the development of managerial control loss at the shop floor (factory floor) level. He argues that if management tries to regain control over the work process by shifting bargaining to the divisional level, unions will respond in the same way. Marginson develops a three-equation dynamic recursive model of this process, and concludes that the M-form did indeed shift bargaining away from plant to divisional level. Unions were expected to resist this but such an effect is not shown to be significant, suggesting a move by unions to establish countervailing power at the divisional level.

The markets and hierarchies approach has the M-form hypothesis as its principal result, and it is this which has attracted the most empirical testing. However, as Williamson and Ouchi (1983) point out, the research agenda is much more comprehensive than this. The analysis of clans, non-profit organizations, and public policy towards business using the decision process approach, are other issues requiring full analytical and empirical inquiry. At the root of all this will be the search for transactional efficiency.

9.4 PRINCIPAL–AGENT ANALYSIS

Roman law has handed down to us the concept of agency. It can refer to contractual relationships between many parties, but we shall concentrate on the case in which only two parties are involved. In an agency relationship one party, designated the agent, acts on behalf of another party, designated the principal. An employer and an employee are in a principal–agent relationship, as are: a firm and a supplier; a manufacturer and a salesman; a shareholder and a manager; and (in a non-profit enterprise) a consumer and a supplier. In section 9.3 on markets and hierarchies, the problems considered by Simon (1951) in his discussion of the authority relation between the boss and a worker, and by Calvo and Wellisz (1978) in their discussion of the monitoring of subordinates by superiors, are also examples of principal–agent relationships. Hierarchy, we saw, was concerned with superior–subordinate relationships. As Radner (1985) points out, the principal–agent model provides a very general paradigm for studying superior–subordinate relationships. Mirrlees (1976) was the first to study hierarchy using the principal–agent model, and the origins of modern developments of the theory, without reference to any specific applications, lie in Ross (1974). The literature is specialized and technical, and this section can offer no more than an introduction. A good survey of the theoretical literature is available in Rees (1985), and a useful expository article displaying all the principal results in terms of an Edgeworth–Bowley box diagram is available in Ricketts (1986).

The agent is not fully supervised and has some measure of independence in the way he goes about his activities. The fact that he does so is an aspect of the activities themselves and the opportunity costs of the principal. The agent might be using skills that the principal lacks, and the principal might value his time too highly to engage in the activities himself. A contract is therefore set up between the principal and agent, which specifies the set of activities to be undertaken, and the way in which the agent will be remunerated. Clearly, given the lack of detailed supervision of the agent there is an incentive for him to avoid risk and to shirk on effort. The principal tries therefore to specify in the contract a system of payments which gives the agent an incentive to share risk efficiently and to optimize his effort. In designing such a scheme he has to bear in mind that he cannot directly observe the effort of the agent, may find it difficult to distinguish genuine effort from favourable chance outcomes, and must take into account that the agent will regard the reward system as being part of his own maximization problem.

Before turning to a formal mathematical statement of principal–agent analysis, let us consider a simple example based on the discussion in Hess (1983, chapter 13). In assuming risk neutrality of the agent, it lacks an attribute that would put it into the most interesting category of principal–agent analysis, but it has the advantage of demonstrating how one sets up these problems in formal terms.

Consider a relationship between the manufacturer as principal and the salesman as agent. The venture in which the salesman is engaged involves selling a set of n products produced by the manufacturer. Let the monetary values of amounts sold of each of the products be denoted $v_1, v_2, \ldots, v_n$. There is a different commission rate for each product which specifies the fraction of the value which the salesman may retain, the rest being returned to the manufacturer. Denote these $c_1, c_2, \ldots, c_n$ with $0 < c_i < 1$ for all i. Sales are achieved partly by effort and, as every salesman knows, partly by luck. In principal–agent analysis, this chance aspect to the payoff is a universal feature. Here it is represented by a random variable θ, 'the state of nature'. Effort in this case can be thought of as hours devoted to 'pushing' a certain product line. The relationship of the value of sales achieved for the ith product to the sales effort and the state of nature will be written

$$v_i = v_i(h_i, \theta) \tag{9.18}$$

where h_i represents the time spent trying to sell the ith product and θ is the state of nature. If the salesman has allotted a total of H hours to sales promotion, then

$$\sum_{i=1}^{n} h_i = H \tag{9.19}$$

Assuming that the salesman has a subjective probability distribution over states of nature, the mathematical expectation of his total commission for H hours of effort is

$$
\begin{aligned}
E(\Sigma_i c_i v_i) &= \Sigma_i c_i E(v_i) \\
&= \Sigma_i c_i E\,[\,v_i(h_i, \theta)\,] \qquad \text{from (9.18)} \\
&= \Sigma_i c_i V_i(h_i) \tag{9.20}
\end{aligned}
$$

where $V_i(h_i)$ is the expected value of sales of the ith product if h_i hours are devoted to promoting it. If the salesman is risk-neutral and finds pushing his products irksome, his expected utility from all his effort may be written

$$E(U_A) = \Sigma_i c_i V_i(h_i) - G(H) \tag{9.21}$$

where U_A is the utility of the salesman as 'agent' for the manufacturer. The expression $G(H)$ denotes the disutility of spending H hours in all on sales promotion. The salesman we will suppose may switch his allegiance to another manufacturer should his utility (9.21) fall below a reservation level of $\bar{U}_A$. This value will be market determined, and may depend on factors like the reputation and ability of the salesman. We shall not enquire into these matters, but rather take $\bar{U}_A$ as exogenously determined. The principal – here the manufacturer – has an expected utility function

$$
\begin{aligned}
E(U_p) &= E\left[\Sigma_i v_i - \Sigma_i c_i v_i\right] \\
&= \Sigma_i(1 - c_i)E\left[v_i(h_i, \theta)\right] \\
&= \Sigma_i(1 - c_i)V_i(h_i)
\end{aligned}
\tag{9.22}
$$

where his utility U_p is the value of the outcome from total sales effort less payment to the agent. It is assumed that the principal and the agent have the same subjective probability distribution over θ.

The agent – here the salesman – takes account of the reward system (here the set of commission rates) in determining what is optimal from his standpoint. This is the assumption of 'agent rationality'. If he does so, his problem is to maximize $E(U_A)$. Necessary conditions for doing so are

$$
\frac{\partial}{\partial h_i}\left[\Sigma_i c_i V_i(h_i) - G(\Sigma h_i)\right] = 0
$$

which implies

$$
\begin{aligned}
c_i V_i' - G' &= 0 \\
V_i' &= G'/c_i
\end{aligned}
\tag{9.23}
$$

How does this compare with what will emerge under a Pareto-efficient contract? Efficiency requires that the agency sets commissions and sales effort to solve

$$
\max_{c_i, h_i} E(U_p) = \Sigma_i(1 - c_i)V_i(h_i)
$$

$$
\text{subject to } \Sigma_i h_i = H
\tag{9.24}
$$

$$
E(U_A) = \Sigma_i c_i V_i(h_i) - G(H) = \bar{U}_A
$$

Necessary conditions are that

$$
V_i' = G'
\tag{9.25}
$$

whereas in (9.23) we have

$$
V_i' = G'/c_i > G' \quad \text{for } 0 < c_i < 1
$$

Clearly the agent, in acting from his own standpoint, is not behaving efficiently from the standpoint of the agency.

Suppose now that the manufacturer, as principal, incorporates an 'incentive constraint' into his maximization problem, which recognizes that the agent's sales effort is contingent on the set of commission rates. We will assume that the principal is unable to observe sales effort for a particular commodity, but can monitor total sales effort ('hours on the road'). Then the appropriate maximization problem is

$$\max E(U_p) = \Sigma(1 - c_i) V_i(h_i)$$

subject to

$$h_i: \text{solve max } E(U_A) = \Sigma_i c_i V_i(h_i) - G(H) \tag{9.26}$$

$$\text{subject to } \Sigma_i h_i = H \quad \text{and}$$

$$E(U_A) = \Sigma_i c_i V_i(h_i) - G(H) = \bar{U}_A$$

To solve the maximization problem in (9.26), the manufacturer selects appropriate commission rates c_i and total sales effort H. It is known from the parallel non-stochastic variant of the problem solved by Srinivasan (1981) that the manufacturer can solve this problem with a schedule of *identical* commission rates. If we set $c_i = c^*$ a constant for $i = 1, 2, \ldots, n$, the agent's (salesman's) expected utility is

$$E(U_A) = c^* \Sigma_i V_i(h_i) - G(H^*) \tag{9.27}$$

where H^* is controlled by the principal. Maximizing (9.27) is equivalent to maximizing $\Sigma_i V_i(h_i)$. Now from the Pareto-efficient case considered under (9.24), the maximand is

$$\Sigma_i(1 - c_i) V_i(h_i) = \Sigma_i V_i(h_i) - \Sigma_i c_i V_i(h_i)$$
$$= \Sigma_i V_i(h_i) - G(H) - \bar{U}_A$$

from the second constraint. For given H and exogenous $\bar{U}_A$ this too is equivalent to maximizing $\Sigma_i V_i(h_i)$. Therefore, if the principal controls total sales effort and sets a uniform commission rate, he will provide the agent with an appropriate incentive to behave efficiently, without having to monitor the allocation of sales effort on the various products.

The above is an attempt to introduce the formal framework of principal–agent analysis in the context of an example which will appeal to an industrial economist. However, the linear structure of the model, and particularly its assumption of a risk-neutral agent, limit the insights it can give into the general principal–agent problem.

Now let us turn to a more abstract treatment of principal–agent analysis. The agent has to undertake an act α chosen from an action set. The consequence, or payoff, from this depends not only on the act itself, but also upon the state of nature, described by the stochastic variate θ. The action is usually thought of in terms of effort, and the payoff is a wealth variable from which the principal derives utility. In turn, the principal makes a payment to the agent, from which the agent derives utility. All this activity is governed by a contract which specifies the purpose for which the agent is acting, the way in which he will be rewarded, and possibly the way in which actions and states of nature determine outcomes. The principal is motivated by a desire for the agent to behave optimally with respect to risk-bearing and action. Principal–agent analysis is concerned with ways in which contracts can be designed to bring this about.

The principal and agent are assumed to have non-convex von Neumann–Morgenstern utility functions, which will be denoted U_p and U_A. For an action α chosen from the set of possible actions and a state of the world θ, the outcome (consequence, payoff, or reward) is given by the wealth variable x, where

$$x = x(\alpha, \theta) \qquad x_\alpha \geqslant 0, \quad x_{\alpha\alpha} \leqslant 0 \quad x_\theta > 0 \tag{9.28}$$

Given the interpretation of α as effort, the restrictions in (9.28) indicate that effort has a positive but diminishing marginal product (or, strictly speaking, non-negative and non-increasing). If we assume that the greater is θ, the better is the state of the world, then the last restriction in (9.28) follows. The principal's utility function is defined by

$$U_p = U_p(x - y) \qquad U_p' > 0, \quad U_p'' \leqslant 0 \tag{9.29}$$

where $(x - y)$ is the outcome x less the payment y to the agent. The agent's utility function is

$$U_A = U_A(y, \alpha) \qquad \begin{array}{ll} U_{A_y} > 0, & U_{A_{yy}} \leqslant 0 \\ U_{A_\alpha} < 0, & U_{A_{\alpha\alpha}} > 0 \end{array} \tag{9.30}$$

where y is the sum the agent receives from the principal and α is effort. The contract specifies a *fee schedule*, which in general states what the agent receives, depending upon the outcome, the state of the world, the level of effort, and so on. A crucial assumption of the principal–agent literature is that the fee schedule depends on variables which both the principal and agent can observe. For simplicity, we will assume that the outcome x is the only variable they both observe. Then the fee schedule is

$$y = y(x) \tag{9.31}$$

The linear fee schedule $y = \gamma x + \beta$ is one that has received a lot of attention in the literature. It often makes sense empirically (e.g. wage contracts often have a fixed payment plus a bonus which is proportional to performance). Further, it is closely related to Pareto-efficient fee schedules under interesting theoretical conditions (see Ross, 1974, pp. 221–4). The agent may be able costlessly to observe an information variable z which gives at least some information about the state of nature and will influence his effort according to $\alpha = \alpha(z)$. This can be regarded as a decision rule. The motivation of the agent is to choose an α that maximizes

$$E\{U_A(y, \alpha)\} = E\{U_A[y(x[\alpha(z), \theta]), \alpha(z)]\} \tag{9.32}$$

The motivation of the principal is to choose a contract which best promotes his interest in that it maximizes

$$E\{U_p(x - y)\} = E\{U_p[x[\alpha(z), \theta] - y(x[\alpha(z), \theta])]\} \qquad (9.33)$$

where his choice is exercised by selecting a particular fee schedule. For both (9.32) and (9.33) expectations are defined over the principal's and the agent's subjective distribution of θ, which is assumed identical for each party. The agent is assumed to have an alternative occupation open to him which offers the reservation utility of $\bar{U}_A$. Now the optimal agency relationships would specify a fee schedule y and decision rule α which maximized $E(U_p)$ subject to the incentive constraint of α maximizing $E(U_A)$ and the reservation utility constraint $E(U_A) \geqslant \bar{U}_A$. If *any* y and α could be used, maximization of $E(U_p)$ subject to $E(U_A) \geqslant \bar{U}_A$ would lead to a Pareto-efficient contract. It would be a first-best solution. However, the introduction of the incentive constraint turns it into a second-best solution, in a way entirely analogous to the second-best solutions of chapter 7.

The question that now arises is whether it is possible to devise a contract that will *induce* efficiency. Optimal risk-sharing will certainly follow if the agent's action is fixed at $\alpha = \alpha^0$. Then $E(U_p)$ for $\alpha = \alpha^0$ is maximized over y subject to $E(U_A) \geqslant \bar{U}_A$ for $\alpha = \alpha^0$. Then the principal's and agent's marginal rates of substitution of wealth between any two states of the world are equal. If α is at least observable, then $E(U_p)$ is maximized over y and α subject to $E(U_A) \geqslant \bar{U}_A$. For the latter case, the agent is paid according to $y^\star(\theta)$ for taking action $\alpha^\star$, where $(y^\star, \alpha^\star)$ are solutions to the constrained maximization problem of the previous sentence. There is an incentive for the agent to cheat, for he will be guaranteed $y^\star$ and may be tempted to choose an effort level $\alpha' < \alpha^\star$. But we have said that in this formulation the principal observes α. Thus if $\alpha' < \alpha^\star$ is observed *ex post*, then $y' < y^\star$ will be paid, with y' being set sufficiently low to force the agent to choose $\alpha^\star$. This is known as a forcing contract.

The general case in which the principal can only observe x and knows nothing about α and θ is complex. The literature on principal–agent analysis shows that in this situation there will generally be a departure from optimal risk-sharing. This prompts the question: can extra information improve the situation? It can be shown, as in Rees (1985, pp. 22–4), that it is always optimal to incorporate into a contract any variable which costlessly provides information about α and which depends on θ, except when the agent is risk-neutral.

Two types of models have dominated principal–agent literature – those concerned with moral hazard, and those concerned with adverse selection. Both these ideas have been informally incorporated into the markets and hierarchies framework of section 9.3, to explain the advantages of organizations over markets. *Moral hazard* is a type of principal–agent problem in which the agent is the insured party and the action α that he may take to safeguard against loss cannot be observed by the principal, the insurer. An agency usually responds to the moral hazard problem by offering the agent incomplete insurance coverage, leaving him bearing some risk, and providing some incentive to exercise care. This assumes identical agents. If they are distinct, then the problem the principal faces is in discovering the type of person who is seeking insurance. *Adverse selection* occurs when the agent has an incentive to misrepresent knowledge he has of his personal circumstances. Thus an agent who knows he is a bad insurance risk may conceal this private information when seeking insurance cover. In Williamson's framework information impactedness (the existence in exchange of informational differentials concerning true conditions) and opportunism (the making of false promises) result in adverse selection. A more concrete example of this is provided by Weitzman's (1976) discussion of the Soviet incentive model, as expounded by Rees (1985). In the original scheme, enterprises were set output targets, and were paid a bonus if they were bettered. This provided enterprises with an incentive to under-represent their true potential at the time when information was being gathered to determine targets. The *ex post* achievement of higher levels of production could then be attributed to chance or increased effort rather than to false initial information. Whether the proposed Soviet scheme for providing an incentive to report honestly is actually valid is a matter of some dispute, but it is suggestive of the sort of application that would interest industrial economists.

Principal–agent analysis is an area of advanced economic theory which has been very highly developed, based on a number of assumptions which require relaxation. Firstly, the assumption that principal and agent hold identical beliefs about the state of the world (represented by the density function $f(\theta)$) seems very rigid. Secondly, the costs of acquiring knowledge about α and θ are ignored. What results there *are* suggest that conclusions are sensitive to violation of this zero-cost assumption. Thirdly, there is typically no discussion of how reservation utilities for the agent are determined. In the way most models are set up, the principal enjoys all the gains from trade and the agent is held at this reservation utility level. Discussion of the circumstances under which the agent can share some of the gains is necessary, as is the possibility of making reservation utilities endogenous.

9.5 CONCLUSION

The organizational view of the firm offers a wide range of insights into the nature of hierarchy. It is remarkable how often profit maximization, cost minimization, and efficiency continue to assert their significance, whatever the perspective. Until now, these have been regarded as theoretical constructs which enable predictions to be made. What the organizational approach shows is that they can be objects of analysis in their own right. Rather than postulating cost minimization, one can now ask what mechanisms might best facilitate it.

Amid this welter of theoretical activity, what is apparently required now is more empirical analysis. It seems likely that the case study approach of chapter 3 is well fitted to the empirical analysis of alternative institutional forms and mechanisms.

Part V
Conclusion

10

Theories of industrial organization

The avowed purpose of this book has been to stimulate the reader into reappraising the manner in which the analysis of industrial organization may be conducted. In particular it has taken the most established approach in the literature – the structure–conduct–performance paradigm – and presented a number of coherent alternatives.

The alternatives have had varied characteristics. They range from the atheoretical (as in the case study approach) to the purposively theoretical (as in contestability analysis). Some are by nature empirically oriented (such as the structural modelling approach), whilst others emphasize *a priori* rather than inductive knowledge (as in the Austrian approach). Some are largely positivist in intention (as is the Marshallian), whilst others have prescription as their main purpose (as with the workably competitive approach). This is all to suggest that there are no *obvious*, preferable, logical alternatives to the structure–conduct–performance approach, because what one regards as an alternative depends on the purpose at hand.

Furthermore, before one turns to any alternative theory as a panacea, it is necessary to affirm that the structure–conduct–performance approach is enormously flexible, and in some measure can accommodate elements of any of the other approaches expounded above. Let us consider five examples.

Firstly, the case study method was the one initially proposed by Mason for looking at the industry or firm. On the basis of his experience with case studies, he proposed the structure, conduct, and performance categories, and hoped that future industrial economists would examine individual cases using this framework. That this has not happened on a large scale is more a reflection of the drift of academic fashion than of any inherent incompatibility between the case study method and the SCP approach.

Secondly, early statistical interpretations of the SCP approach, particularly emphasizing the structure and performance dimensions, derive from Bain (1951). These lacked a coherent theory of conduct, gave no consideration to the problem of aggregation, and ignored issues of causality and simultaneity. Today, industrial economists familiar with the econometric arts are now developing SCP models which rival those formulated in earlier decades by teams of professional econometricians, statisticians, and computer scientists. For example, Geroski (1982) develops a model in which *structure* is characterized by a *k*-firm dominant group surrounded by a competitive fringe, *conduct* entails price-setting to maximize profits by the dominant group and price-taking to maximize profits by the fringe, and *performance* is measured by departures of the price–cost margin from its theoretical norm. Causality tests are performed, and the model is estimated as a simultaneous equation system. 'Industrial econometrics' has begun to be absorbed into the SCP paradigm.

Thirdly, the workable competition literature derives from the US Sherman Act of 1890 and the judicial interpretation that surrounded it, and subsequent antitrust, monopolies and mergers, and restrictive practices legislation in America, Great Britain, and elsewhere. The theory has typically not been of the abstruse variety, as it must be directly related to enforceable law applied to detectable misdemeanours. As Sosnick (1958) has shown, this theory may readily be interpreted within an SCP framework. As our own elaboration in chapter 7 was intended to suggest, it can be further developed in an analytical style compatible with contemporary standards.

Fourthly, even highly abstract theoretical schools like the Austrian, which make little appeal to empirical data and avoid the logical machinery of mathematics, can be interpreted in terms of structure, conduct, and performance dimensions. In this case, structure would not be confined to characteristics of a single industry, for, as Kirzner (1973, pp. 119–25) indicates, this would be to deny the role of the entrepreneur in linking up markets. Monopoly would be an aspect of structure, though Austrians use it in a narrower sense than in the orthodox literature. In an Austrian world, conduct is competitive, though in the sense of a profit-seeking rivalrous process rather than the equilibrating of profit maximization. Performance in the Austrian framework would not be evaluated by using Paretian criteria, but rather, as Kirzner (1973, p. 235) puts it, by 'the degree to which currently known information is optimally deployed'.

Finally, in the markets and hierarchies approach market structure is generally oligopolistic, with firms of different organizational form (e.g. U-form, M-form, H-form) being in competition. Conduct is driven by the behavioural assumptions of bounded rationality and self-interest. The way it manifests itself through the overt behaviour of firms depends, as chapter 9 has indicated, on the nature of hierarchy, authority, contractual form, monitoring, and other factors within the organization called the firm. Performance is judged by the extent to which the firm as an organization economizes on transactions costs, broadly interpreted. By implication, the performance of the industry can be judged in terms of the performance of the firms that make it up. For example, given widespread evidence on the relative transactional efficiency of the M-form over the U-form, an industry-wide shift from the latter to the former would be held to imply an improvement in industry performance.

As these examples indicate, it is possible to interpret many of the distinct theories of industrial organization expounded in earlier chapters within a sufficiently flexibly interpreted structure–conduct–performance framework. Does this therefore draw us to the inevitable conclusion that the SCP paradigm provides us with a kind of overarching theory? The author would suggest a gentle negative. The selection of the five examples was an intellectual exercise of the sort that could have been repeated with most, if not all, of the approaches to industrial organization that have been expounded in this book. Perhaps most obviously the transactional (or markets and hierarchies) and Austrian (or property-rights/competitive-process) approaches could lay claim to being all-embracing theories. Certainly proponents of these theories argue in this way, but it is comforting to observe that it appears respectable in methodological circles to welcome the proliferation of theories. Many look to Lakatos's (1970) methodology of scientific research programmes to provide guidance on the critical evaluation of competing theories. From the viewpoint of this book on theories of industrial organization, four significant points emerge from methodological writings in this vein.

Firstly, in evaluating a theory one is not making a judgement of a theory at one time, but rather making a judgement on a sequence of evolving theories as they develop through time. Thus the SCP approach is a theory which has evolved from its case study origins with Mason, through the statistical work of Bain, to the econometric estimation of Geroski. One is evaluating this sequence rather than the stages symbolized by Mason, Bain, and Geroski alone. Similarly, the Marshallian theory is a sequence from Marshall, through Andrews and Richardson, to Newman, Wolfe, Loasby, and (arguably) Nelson and Winter.

Secondly, falsification has a lesser role than Popperians would have claimed. An important purpose of the study of Reid (1981) on the persistence of the kinked demand curve theory of oligopoly was to enquire into how a theory which had been refuted in the leading journals by eminent authorities could nevertheless continue to have wide currency over forty years later. It is clear that on the one hand few tests indicating falsification are decisive, and on the other that a theory is not readily abandoned if there is no suitable replacement for it. In the case of the kinked demand curve, tests of the theory which proved negative were not judged decisive by the economics profession, and furthermore economics desperately lacked (and lacks) *any* good theory of oligopoly. In a similar way, the economics profession appears convinced by Williamson's argument that the M-form is superior to the U-form in a transactional sense. Earlier studies by Armour and Teece (1978) and Steer and Cable (1978) favoured the M-form hypothesis for the USA and the UK. The study by Cable and Dirrheimer (1983) provided strong negative evidence but was greeted with equanimity, and we were advised (p. 61) that 'the German results should not be interpreted as either casting doubt on earlier findings or refuting the M-form hypothesis in general'. More recently, Cable and Yasuki (1985) turned their attention to Japanese enterprises and again found no positive effect from the M-form. Unperturbed, they reported (p. 417) that 'the negative M-form results for Japan, like those for Germany, do not necessarily detract from earlier positive results for the UK and US, or refute the M-form hypothesis in general'. The problem is clearly that tests are never clear cut (for 'accounting quirks' and 'cultural factors' can subvert the test methodology), and alternatives to the M-form hypothesis which are intellectually persuasive do not exist.

Thirdly, internal criticism of a theory is more powerful than external criticism. The external critic is inclined to start from the position that his theory is correct, and therefore finds other theories – from his standpoint – either unintelligible or false. A follower of the SCP approach who thought of structure in terms of concentration, conduct in terms of profit maximization, and performance in terms of deviations from marginal cost pricing, would find – as an external critic – the Austrian position incomprehensible. It has been the experience of the author to witness this as a member of seminar or conference audiences, and no doubt some readers have had the same experience. However, external criticism is based on an alternative standpoint, and not surprisingly is calculated to encourage rejection of distinct theories. Internal criticism is more compelling if it leads to a powerful critique, but is obviously more intellectually demanding, and can cause cognitive problems for even very intelligent individuals who have totally internalized a particular perspective.

Finally, if competition among theories is to be welcomed, it should be no surprise to economists that methodologists can also favour some protection of theories! Alternative theories are a stimulus to general scientific advance, and the dominance of any single theory can be an impediment to further progress. 'Theoretical pluralism', wrote Lakatos (1970, p. 155), 'is better than theoretical monism.' The structure–conduct–performance approach is clearly dominant, but rival theories still attract attention, with the market and hierarchies approach being perhaps the most significant alternative. It is hoped that one role of this book will be to provide some coverage of, and internal as well as external criticism of, theories of industrial organization which are not currently dominating the professional literature of industrial economics. As Lakatos (1970, p. 157) has put it: 'We must not discard a budding research programme simply because it has so far failed to overtake a powerful rival . . . As long as a budding research programme can be rationally reconstructed as a progressive problem shift, it should be sheltered for a while from a powerful established rival.' May at least some of these theories find temporary shelter within these covers.

References

Adams, E. (ed.) 1961: *The Structure of American Industry.* New York: Macmillan.

Adelman, I.G. 1958: A stochastic analysis of the size distribution of firms. *Journal of the American Statistical Association,* 53, 893–904.

Alchian, A.A. and Demsetz, H. 1972: Production, information costs, and economic organization. *American Economic Review,* 62, 777–95.

Andrews, P.W.S. 1949: *Manufacturing Business.* London: Macmillan.

Andrews, P.W.S. 1951: Industrial analysis in economics. Chapter 4 of Wilson, T. and Andrews, P.W.S. (eds) 1951: *Oxford Studies in the Price Mechanism.* Oxford: Clarendon Press.

Andrews, P.W.S. 1964: *On Competition in Economic Theory.* London: Macmillan.

Andrews, P.W.S. and Brunner, E. 1975: *Studies in Pricing.* London: Macmillan.

Ansoff, H.I. 1965: *Corporate Strategy.* London: Penguin.

Aoki, M. 1980: A model of the firm as a stockholder–employee cooperative game. *American Economic Review,* 70, 600–10.

Aoki, M. 1983: Managerialism revisited in the light of bargaining-game theory. *International Journal of Industrial Organization,* 1, 1–22.

Appelbaum, E. and Lim, C. 1985: Contestable markets under uncertainty. *Rand Journal of Economics,* 16, 28–40.

Archibald, G.C. 1961: Chamberlin versus Chicago. *Review of Economic Studies,* 24, 9–28.

Archibald, G.C. 1965: The qualitative content of maximizing models. *Journal of Political Economy,* 73, 27–36.

Armour, H.O. and Teece, D.J. 1978: Organizational structure and economic performance: a test of the multidivisional hypothesis. *Bell Journal of Economics,* 9, 106–22.

Arrow, K.J. 1951: *Social Choice and Individual Values.* New York: Wiley.

Bailey, E.E. 1981: Contestability and the design of regulatory and antitrust policy. *American Economic Review,* 71, 178–83.

Bailey, E.E. and Friedlander, A.F. 1982: Market structure and multiproduct industries. *Journal of Economic Literature*, 20, 1024–48.

Bailey, E.E., Kaplan, D.P. and Sibley, D.S. 1983: On the contestability of airline markets: some further evidence. In Finsinger, J. 1983: *Economic Analysis of Regulated Markets*. London: Macmillan, 48–64.

Bailey, E.E. and Panzar, J.C. 1981: The contestability of airline markets during the transition to deregulation. *Journal of Law and Contemporary Problems*, 44, 125–45.

Bain, J.S. 1951: Relation of profit-rate to industry concentration: American manufacturing 1936–1940. *Quarterly Journal of Economics*, 65, 293–324.

Bain, J.S. 1956: *Barriers to New Competition*. Cambridge, Mass.: Harvard University Press.

Bain, J.S. 1959: *Industrial Organization*. New York: Wiley.

Balderston, F.E. and Hoggatt, A.C. 1962: *Simulation of Market Processes*. Berkeley: Institute of Business and Economic Research.

Barback, R.H. 1964: *The Pricing of Manufactures*. London: Macmillan.

Barnard, C.I. 1938: *The Functions of the Executive*. Cambridge, Mass.: Harvard University Press.

Baumol, W.J.L. 1958: On the theory of oligopoly. *Economica*, 25, 187–98.

Baumol, W.J.L. 1959: *Business Behaviour, Value and Growth*. New York: Macmillan.

Baumol, W.J.L. 1962: On the theory of expansion of the firm. *American Economic Review*, 52, 1078–87.

Baumol, W.J.L. and Quandt, R.E. 1964: Rules of thumb and optimally imperfect decisions. *American Economic Review*, 54, 23–46.

Baumol, W.J.L. 1982: Contestable markets: an uprising in the theory of industry structure. *American Economic Review*, 72, 1–15.

Baumol, W.J.L. and Bradford, D.E. 1970: Optimal departures from marginal cost pricing. *American Economic Review*, 60, 265–83.

Baumol, W.J.L., Panzar, J.C. and Willig, R.D. 1982: *Contestable Markets and the Theory of Industry Structure*. New York: Harcourt, Brace, Jovanovich.

Baumol, W.J.L., Panzar, J.C. and Willig, R.D. 1983: Contestable markets: reply. *American Economic Review*, 73, 491–6.

Baumol, W.J.L., Panzar, J.C. and Willig, R.D. 1986: On the theory of perfectly contestable markets. In J.E. Stiglitz and G.F. Mathewson (eds) 1986: *New Developments in the Analysis of Market Structure*. London: Macmillan, 339–65.

Beckmann, M.J. 1977: Management production functions and the theory of the firm. *Journal of Economic Theory*, 14, 1–18.

Bergson, A. 1938: A reformulation of certain aspects of welfare economics. *Quarterly Journal of Economics*, 52, 310–34.

Berle, A.A. and Means, G.C. 1932: *The Modern Corporation and Private Property*. New York: Macmillan.

Boadway, R. and Harris, R. 1977: A characterization of piecemeal second best policy. *Journal of Public Economics*, 8, 169–90.

Böhm-Bawerk, E. von 1888: *The Positive Theory of Capital*, translated by W. Smart (1891). New York: Steckert.

Boswell, J. 1973: *The Rise and Decline of Small Firms*. London: George Allen and Unwin.

Brock, W.A. 1983: Contestable markets and the theory of industry structure: a review article. *Journal of Political Economy*, 91, 1055–66.

Brown, C.V. and Jackson, P.M. 1986: *Public Sector Economics*, 3rd edn. Oxford: Basil Blackwell.

Brozen, Y. 1977: Introduction to K.W. Clarkson, *Intangible Capital and Rates of Return*. Washington: American Enterprise Institute.

Brozen, Y. 1982: *Concentration, Mergers and Public Policy*. New York: Macmillan.

Burnham, J. 1941: *The Managerial Revolution: What is Happening in the World*. New York: John Day.

Cable, J. and Dirrheimer, M.J. 1983: Hierarchies and markets: an empirical test of the multidivisional hypothesis in West Germany. *International Journal of Industrial Organization*, 1, 43–62.

Cable, J. and Yasuki, H. 1985: Internal organization, business groups and corporate performance: an empirical test of the multidivisional hypothesis in Japan. *International Journal of Industrial Organization*, 3, 401–20.

Caldwell, B.J. 1982: *Beyond Positivism*. London: George Allen and Unwin.

Calvo, G. and Wellisz, S. 1978: Supervision, loss of control and the optimum size of the firm. *Journal of Political Economy*, 86, 943–52.

Caves, R.E. 1972: *American Industry: Structure, Conduct, Performance*, 3rd edn. Englewood Cliffs, N.J.: Prentice-Hall.

Chamberlin, E.H. 1933: *The Theory of Monopolistic Competition*. Cambridge, Mass.: Harvard University Press.

Chamberlin, E.H. 1962: *The Theory of Monopolistic Competition*. Cambridge, Mass.: Harvard University Press.

Chandler, A. 1966: *Strategy and Structure*. New York: Doubleday.

Chang, S.H. 1986: Cost savings, wages and the growth of the firm. *Economic Journal*, 96, 798–807.

Chou, T.C. 1984: A simultaneous equation analysis of trade, concentration and profitability: the case of Taiwan. Paper delivered at 11th annual conference of European Association for Research in Industrial Economics, Fontainebleau.

Clark, J.M. 1940: Towards a concept of workable competition. *American Economic Review*, 30, 241–56.

Clark, J.M. 1955: Competition: static models and dynamic aspects. *American Economic Review*, 45, 450–62.

Clark, J.M. 1961: *Competition as a Dynamic Process*. Washington DC: Brookings Institution.

Clarke, P. and Davies, S.W. 1982: Market structure and price–cost margins. *Economica*, 49, 277–87.

Coase, R.H. 1937: The nature of the firm. *Economica*, 4, 386–405.

Cohen, K.J. 1960: *Computer Models of the Shoe, Leather, Hide Sequence*. Englewood Cliffs, N.J.: Prentice-Hall.

Comanor, W.S. and Wilson, T.A. 1967: Advertising, market structure and performance. *Review of Economics and Statistics*, 49, 423–40.

Commons, J.R. 1934: *Institutional Economics*. Madison: University of Wisconsin Press.

Coursey, D., Isaac, R.M. and Smith, V.L. 1984: Natural monopoly and contested markets: some experimental results. *Journal of Law and Economics*, 27, 91–114.

Cowling, K.G. 1976: On the theoretical specification of industrial structure–performance relationships. *European Economic Review*, 8, 1–14.

Cowling, K.G. and Waterson, M. 1976: Price–cost margins and market structure. *Economica*, 43, 267–74.

Cowling, K.G. and Mueller, D. 1978: The social costs of monopoly power. *Economic Journal*, 88, 727–48.

Cowling, K.G., Stoneman, P., Cubbin, J., Cable, T., Hall, G., Domberger, S. and Dutton, P. 1980: *Mergers and Economic Performance*. Cambridge: Cambridge University Press.

Cowling, K.G. 1982: *Monopoly Capitalism*. London: Macmillan.

Cyert, R.M. and March, J.G. 1963: *A Behavioural Theory of the Firm*. Englewood Cliffs, N.J.: Prentice-Hall.

Cyert, R.M. and Kamien, M.I. 1967: Behavioural rules and the theory of the firm. In A. Phillips and O.E. Williamson (eds), *Prices: Issues in Theory, Practice and Public Policy*. Pittsburgh: University of Pennsylvania Press, 1–10.

Davies, G. and Davies, J. 1984: The revolution in monopoly theory. *Lloyds Bank Review*, 153, 38–52.

Davies, S.W. 1985: Multinationals in UK manufacturing: research design; data collection methodology. University of East Anglia, UK, Economics Research Centre working paper no. 6.

Davies, S.W. and Lyons, B.R. 1982: Seller concentration: the technological explanation and demand uncertainty. *Economic Journal*, 92, 903–19.

Davis, O.A. and Whinston, A.B. 1965: Welfare economics and the theory of the second best. *Review of Economic Studies*, 32, 1–14.

Demsetz, H. 1973: Industry structure, market rivalry, and public policy. *Journal of Law and Economics*, 16, 1–9.

Diamantopoulos, A. and Kay, N.M. 1986: Modelling corporate strategy: the role of environmental uncertainty and corporate strategy choice. Heriot-Watt University, UK, working paper 1986/19.

Dorfman, R. and Steiner, P.O. 1954: Optimal advertising and optimal quality. *American Economic Review*, 44, 826–36.

Drucker, P. 1946: *Concept of the Corporation*. New York: John Day.

Dusansky, R. and Walsh, J. 1976: Separability, welfare economics and the theorem of second best. *Review of Economic Studies*, 43, 49–52.

Edwards, R.S. and Townsend, H. (eds) 1961: *Studies in Business Organization*. London: Macmillan.

Eichner, A.S. 1976: *The Megacorp and Oligopoly*. Cambridge: Cambridge University Press.

Encaoua, D. and Jacquemin, A. 1980: Degree of monopoly, indices of concentration and threat of entry. *International Economic Review*, 21, 87–105.

Evans, D.S. and Heckman, J.J. 1984: A test for subadditivity of the cost function with an application to the Bell system. *American Economic Review*, 74, 615–23.

Ferguson, C.E. 1964: *A Macroeconomic Theory of Workable Competition*. Durham, North Carolina: Duke University Press.

Fog, B. 1960: *Industrial Pricing Policy*. Amsterdam: North Holland.

Forchheimer, K. 1908: Theoretisches zum unvollständigen Monopole. *Schmollers Jahrbuch*, 32, 1–12.

Francis, A. 1983: Markets and hierarchies: efficiency or domination?. Chapter 5 in A. Francis, J. Turk and P. Willman (eds), *Power, Efficiency and Institutions: A Critical Appraisal of the 'Markets and Hierarchies' Paradigm*. London: Heinemann, 105–16.

Frisch, R. 1950: Alfred Marshall's theory of value. *Quarterly Journal of Economics*, 64, 495–524.

Fröbel, R., Heinrichs, J. and Kreye, O. 1980: *The New International Division of Labour*. Cambridge: Cambridge University Press.

Gabel, H.L. 1979: A simultaneous equation analysis of the structure and performance of the United States petroleum refining industry. *Journal of Industrial Economics*, 28, 89–104.

Gee, J.M.A. 1983: Marshall's view on 'short period' value formation. *History of Political Economy*, 15, 181–205.

Geroski, P.A. 1982: Interpreting a correlation between market structure and performance. *Journal of Industrial Economics*, 30, 319–26.

Geroski, P.A. 1982: Simultaneous equations models of the structure–performance paradigm. *European Economic Review*, 19, 145–58.

Geroski, P.A. 1983: Some reflections on the theory and application of concentration indices. *International Journal of Industrial Organization*, 1, 79–94.

Glaser, B.G. and Strauss, A.L. 1967: *The Discovery of Grounded Theory: Strategies for Qualitative Research*. New York: Aldine.

Golbe, D.L. 1986: Safety and profits in the airline industry. *Journal of Industrial Economics*, 34, 305–18.

Gordon, R.A. 1945: *Business Leadership in the Large Corporation*. Washington DC: Brookings Institution.

Goudie, A.W. and Meeks, G. 1985: Individual economic agents in a macro-economic model: UK companies in Cambridge M.D.M. *Journal of Policy Modelling*, 7, 289–309.

Greer, D.F. 1971: Advertising and market concentration. *Southern Economic Journal*, 38, 19–32.

Guesnerie, R. 1980: Second-best pricing rules in the Boiteaux tradition. *Journal of Public Economics*, 13, 51–80.

Hague, D.C. 1971: *Pricing in Business*. London: George Allen and Unwin.

Hall, M. 1967: Sales revenue maximization: an empirical examination. *Journal of Industrial Economics*, 15, 143–56.

Hall, R.L. and Hitch, C.J. 1939: Price theory and business behaviour. *Oxford Economic Papers*, 2, 12–45. Reprinted in T. Wilson and P.W.S. Andrews (eds) (1951), *Oxford Studies in the Price Mechanism*. Oxford: Clarendon Press.

Hannah, L. and Kay, J.A. 1977: *Concentration in Modern Industry*. London: Macmillan.

Harberger, A.C. 1954: Monopoly and resource allocation. *American Economic Review*, 44, 77–87.

Harrison, G.W. and McKee, M. 1985: Monopoly behaviour, decentralized regulation and contestable markets: an experimental evaluation. *Rand Journal of Economics*, 16, 51–69.

Hart, P.E. 1962: The size and growth of firms. *Economica*, 29, 29–39.

Hart, P.E. and Morgan, E. 1977: Market structure and economic development in the United Kingdom. *Journal of Industrial Economics*, 25, 177–93.

Hause, J.C. 1977: The measurement of concentrated industrial structure and the size distribution of firms. *Annals of Economic and Social Measurement*, 6, 73–107.

Hausman, J. 1978: Specification tests in econometrics. *Econometrica*, 46, 697–720.

Heath, J.B. 1961: Restrictive practices and after. *Manchester School*, 29, 173–202.

Hess, J.D. 1983: *The Economics of Organization*. Amsterdam: North Holland.

Hicks, J.R. 1935: Annual survey of economic theory – monopoly. *Econometrica*, 3, 1–20. Reprinted in G.J. Stigler and K.E. Boulding (eds) (1952), *Readings in Price Theory*. Chicago: Irwin.

Hirschman, A.O. 1970: *Exit, Voice and Loyalty*. Cambridge, Mass.: Harvard University Press.

Holler, M.J. 1985: The theory of contestable markets: comment. *Bulletin of Economic Research*, 37, 65–7.

Intriligator, M.D. 1978: *Econometric Models, Techniques and Applications*. Englewood Cliffs, N.J.: Prentice-Hall.

Intriligator, M.D., Weston, J.F. and De Angelo, H. 1975: An econometric test of the structure–conduct–performance paradigm in industrial organization. Paper presented at the Econometric Society Third World Congress, Toronto.

Jacobsen, L.R. 1986: Entrepreneurship and competitive strategy in the new small firm: an empirical investigation. University of Edinburgh, Department of Economics, Ph.D. thesis.

Jensen, M.C. and Meckling, W. 1976: Theory of the firm: managerial behaviour, agency costs and ownership structure. *Journal of Financial Economics*, 3, 304–60.

Jewitt, I. 1981: Preference structure and piecemeal second best policy. *Journal of Public Economics*, 16, 215–31.

Joskow, P.L. and Klevorick, A.K. 1979: A framework for analyzing predatory pricing policy. *Yale Law Journal*, 89, 213–70.

Kahn, A.E. 1953: Standards for antitrust policy. *Harvard Law Review*, 28.

Kahn, R.F. 1935: Some notes on ideal output. *Economic Journal*, 45, 25–6.

Kaldor, N. 1934: The equilibrium of the firm. *Economic Journal*, 44, 66–76.

Kalecki, M. 1937: The principle of increasing risk. *Economica*, 4, 440–7.

Kalecki, M. 1939: *Essays in the Theory of Economic Fluctuations*. London: George Allen and Unwin.

Kamerschen, D. 1966: An estimation of 'welfare losses' in the American economy. *Western Economic Journal*, 4, 221–36.

Kaplan, A.D.H., Dirlam, J.B. and Lanzillotti, R.E. 1958: *Pricing in Big Business*. Menasha, Wisconsin: Brookings Institution.

Kay, N.M. 1982: *The Evolving Firm: Strategy and Market Structure in Industrial Organization*. London: Macmillan.

Kessides, I. 1982: *Towards a Testable Model of Entry: A Study of the US Manufacturing Industries*. Princeton University, unpublished thesis.

Kihlstrom, R.E. and Laffont, J.J. 1979: A general equilibrium entrepreneurial theory of firm formation based on risk aversion. *Journal of Political Economy*, 87, 719–48.

Kirzner, I.M. 1973: *Competition and Entrepreneurship*. Chicago: University of Chicago Press.

Kirzner, I.M. 1979: *Perception, Opportunity and Profit*. Chicago: University of Chicago Press.

Econometric analysis Klein, L.R. 1950: *Economic Fluctuations in the United States, 1921–1941*. New York: Wiley.

Klein, L.R. (ed.) 1969: *Essays in Industrial Econometrics*, vols I and II. Pennsylvania: Graphic Printing.

Knight, F.H. 1921: *Risk, Uncertainty and Profit*. Boston: Houghton Mifflin.

Lakatos, I. 1970: Falsification and the methodology of scientific research programmes. In I. Lakatos and A. Musgrave (eds), *Criticism and the Growth of Knowledge*. Cambridge: Cambridge University Press, 91–116.

Lawson, T. 1985: Uncertainty and economic analysis. *Economic Journal*, 95, 909–27.

Leibenstein, H. 1973: Competition and X-efficiency. *Journal of Political Economy*, 81, 765–77.

Lerner, A.P. 1934: The concept of monopoly and the measurement of monopoly power. *Review of Economic Studies*, 1, 157–75.

Lewellyn, W. 1969: Management and ownership in the large firm. *Journal of Finance*, 24, 299–322.

Lewellyn, W. and Huntsman, B. 1970: Managerial pay and corporate performance. *American Economic Review*, 60, 710–20.

Liebhafsky, H.H. 1971: *American Government and Business*. New York: Wiley.

Lintner, J. 1956: Distribution of incomes and dividends among corporations, retained earnings and taxes. *American Economic Review*, 46, 97–113.

Lipsey, R.G. and Lancaster, K.J. 1956: The general theory of second best. *Review of Economic Studies*, 24, 11–32.

Littlechild, S.C. 1979: An entrepreneurial theory of games. *Metroeconomica*, 31, 143–65.

Littlechild, S.C. and Owen, G. 1980: An Austrian model of the entrepreneurial market process. *Journal of Economic Theory*, 23, 361–79.

Littlechild, S.C. 1981: Misleading calculations of the social cost of monopoly power. *Economic Journal*, 91, 348–63.

Loasby, B.J. 1978: Whatever happened to Marshall's theory of value? *Scottish Journal of Political Economy*, 25, 1–12.

Loeb, M. and Magat, W.A. 1979: A decentralized method for utility regulation. *Journal of Law and Economics*, 22, 399–404.

Lofland, J. 1971: *Analyzing Social Settings: A Guide to Qualitative Observation and Analysis*. Belmont, Ca.: Wadsworth.

Lunn, J. 1986: An empirical analysis of process and product patenting: a simultaneous equation framework. *Journal of Industrial Economics*, 34, 319–30.

McGuire, J.W., Chiu, J.S.Y. and Elbing, A.O. 1962: Executive incomes, sales, and profits. *American Economic Review*, 52, 753–61.

Machlup, F. 1967: Theories of the firm: marginalist, behavioural, managerial. *American Economic Review*, 57, 1–33.

Mackintosh, A.S. 1963: *The Development of Firms*. Cambridge: Cambridge University Press.

McManus, M. 1959: Comments on 'The general theory of the second-best'. *Review of Economic Studies*, 26, 209–24.

Mann, H.M. 1971: The interaction of barriers and concentration: a reply. *Journal of Industrial Economics*, 19, 291–3.

Marby, B.D. and Siders, D.L. 1966: An empirical test of the sales maximization hypothesis. *Southern Economic Journal*, 367–87.

Marginson, P. 1985: The multidivisional firm and control over the work process. *International Journal of Industrial Organization*, 3, 37–56.

Marglin, S. 1975: What do bosses do? In A. Gorz (ed.), *The Division of Labour*. Hassocks: Harvester Press.

Marglin, S. 1984: Knowledge and power. In F.H. Stephen (ed.), *Firms, Organization and Labour*. London: Macmillan.

Markham, J.W. 1950: An alternative approach to the concept of workable competition. *American Economic Review*, 40, 349–61.

Marris, R. 1964: *The Economic Theory of Managerial Capitalism*. London: Macmillan.

Marris, R. and Wood, A.J.B. (eds) 1971: *The Corporate Economy*. London: Macmillan.

Marshall, A. 1899: *Economics of Industry*, 3rd edn. London: Macmillan.

Marshall, A. 1919: *Industry and Trade*. London: Macmillan.

Marshall, A. 1961: *Principles of Economics*, variorum edition. London: Macmillan, for the Royal Economic Society.

Martin, S. 1979: Advertising, concentration and profitability: the simultaneity problem. *Bell Journal of Economics*, 10, 639–47.

Mason, E.S. 1939: Price and production policies of large-scale enterprise. *American Economic Review (Papers and Proceedings)*, 29, 61–74.

Mason, E.S. 1949: The current state of the monopoly problem in the United States. *Harvard Law Review*, 62, 1265–85.

Masson, R. 1971: Executive motivation, earnings and consequent equity performance. *Journal of Political Economy*, 79, 1278–92.

Meeks, G. and Whittington, G. 1975: Director's pay, growth and profitability. *Journal of Industrial Economics*, 24, 1–14.

Menger, C. 1871: *Principles of Economics*, translated and edited by J. Dingwall and B.F. Hoselitz (1950). Glencoe, Illinois: Free Press.

Miles, M.B. and Huberman, A.M. 1984: *Qualitative Data Analysis*. London: Sage.

Mirrlees, J. 1971: An exploration in the theory of optimum income taxation. *Review of Economic Studies*, 38, 175–208.

Mirrlees, J. 1976: The optimal structure of incentives and authority within an organization. *Bell Journal of Economics*, 7, 105–31.

Miyazaki, H. 1982: A Marshallian theory of the firm. Research paper no. 28. Workshop on Factor Markets, Stanford University, Sept. 1982.

Miyazaki, H. 1984: Internal bargaining, labour contracts, and the Marshallian theory of the firm. *American Economic Review*, 74, 381–93.

Näslund, B. 1977: *An Analysis of Economic Size Distributions*. Berlin: Springer-Verlag.

Nelson, R.R., Winter, S.G. and Schuette, H.L. 1976: Technical changes in an evolutionary model. *Quarterly Journal of Economics*, 90, 90–118.

Nelson, R.R. and Winter, S.G. 1978: Forces generating and limiting competition under Schumpeterian competition. *Bell Journal of Economics*, 9, 524–48.

Nelson, R.R. and Winter, S.G. 1982: *An Evolutionary Theory of Economic Change*. Cambridge, Mass.: Harvard University Press.

Nelson, R.R. 1986: Evolutionary modelling of economic change. In J.E. Stiglitz and F. Mathewson (eds), *New Developments in the Analysis of Market Structure*. London: Macmillan, 450–74.

Newman, P. 1960: The erosion of Marshall's theory of value. *Quarterly Journal of Economics*, 74, 587–600.

Newman, P. and Wolfe, J.N. 1961: A model for the long-run theory of value. *Review of Economic Studies*, 29, 51–66.

Nowotny, E. and Walther, H. 1978: *Die Wettbewerbintensität in Österreich: Ergebnisse der Befragungen and Interviews*. Vienna: Orac Verlag.

Oughton, C. 1985: Multinationals in UK manufacturing: selection of a sample of case studies. University of East Anglia, UK, Economics Research Centre working paper no. 5.

Pagoulatus, E. and Sorensen, R. 1981: A simultaneous equation analysis of advertising, concentration and profitability. *Southern Economic Journal*, 47, 728–41.

Peltzman, S. 1977: The gains and losses from industrial concentration. *Journal of Law and Economics*, 20, 229–63.

Penrose, E.T. 1952: Biological analogies in the theory of the firm. *American Economic Review*, 42, 804–19.

Penrose, E.T. 1959: *The Theory of the Growth of the Firm*. Oxford: Basil Blackwell.

Phillips, A. 1962: *Market Structure, Organization and Performance*. Cambridge, Mass.: Harvard University Press.

Phillips, A. 1972: An econometric study of price-fixing, market structure and performance in British industry in the early 1950s. In K.G. Cowling (ed.), *Market Structure and Corporate Behaviour*. London: Gray-Mills, 177–92.

Phillips, A. 1976: A critique of empirical relations between market structure and profitability. *Journal of Industrial Economics*, 24, 241–9.

Pigou, A.C. (ed.) 1925: *Memorials of Alfred Marshall*. London: Macmillan.

Porter, M. 1980: *Competitive Strategy*. New York: Free Press.

Porter, M. 1985: *Competitive Advantage*. New York: Free Press.

Prais, S.J. 1974: A new look at the growth of industrial concentration. *Oxford Economic Papers*, 26, 273–88.

Radice, H. 1971: Control type, profitability and growth in large firms. *Economic Journal*, 81, 547–62.

Radner, R. 1985: The internal economy of large firms. *Economic Journal* (supplement), 96, 1–22.

Ramsey, F.P. 1927: A contribution to the theory of taxation. *Economic Journal*, 37, 47–61.

Rees, R. 1985: The theory of principal and agent, parts I and II. *Bulletin of Economic Research*, 37, 3–26 and 75–95.

Reid, G.C. 1975: An analytical study of price leadership. University of Edinburgh, Department of Economics, Ph.D. thesis.

Reid, G.C. 1977: Comparative statics of the partial monopoly model. *Scottish Journal of Political Economy*, 24, 153–62.

Reid, G.C. 1979: An analysis of the firm, market structure and technical progress. *Scottish Journal of Political Economy*, 26, 15–32.

Reid, G.C. 1980: The dominant firm with convex technology. *Managerial and Decision Economics*, 1, 112–16.

Reid, G.C. 1981: *The Kinked Demand Curve Analysis of Oligopoly*. Edinburgh: Edinburgh University Press.

Reid, G.C. 1986: Methodological and empirical issues in the application of field research techniques to the business enterprise. University of Edinburgh, Department of Economics, discussion paper 1986:1.

Richardson, G.B. 1960: *Information and Investment*. Oxford: Oxford University Press.

Ricketts, M. 1986: The geometry of principal and agent: yet another use for the Edgeworth box. *Scottish Journal of Political Economy*, 33, 228–48.

Robbins, L. 1928: The representative firm. *Economic Journal*, 38, 387–404.

Roberts, D.R. 1959: *Executive Compensation*. Glencoe, Illinois: Free Press.

Robertson, D.H. 1959: Some Marshallian concepts. *Economic Journal*, 69, 382–4.

Robinson, J. 1933: *The Economics of Imperfect Competition*. London: Macmillan.

Rosen, S. 1972: Learning by experience as joint production. *Quarterly Journal of Economics*, 86, 366–82.

Ross, S.A. 1974: On the economic theory of agency and the principle of similarity. In M.S. Balch, D.L. McFadden and S.Y. Wu (eds), *Essays on Economic Behaviour under Uncertainty*. Amsterdam: North Holland, 215–37.

Rothbard, M.N. 1962: *Man, Economy and State*. Los Angeles: Nash.

Samuelson, P.A. 1947: *Foundations of Economic Analysis*. Cambridge, Mass.: Harvard University Press.

Santoni, G. and Church, A. 1972: A comment on the general theorem of the second best. *Review of Economic Studies*, 39, 527–30.

Saving, T.R. 1970: Concentration ratios and the degree of monopoly. *International Economic Review*, 11, 139–46.

Sawyer, M.C. 1982: On the specification of structure–performance relationships. *European Economic Review*, 18, 295–306.

Saxton, C.C. 1942: *The Economics of Price Determination*. London: Oxford University Press.

Scherer, F.M. 1979: *Industrial Market Structure and Economic Performance*, 2nd edn. Chicago: Rand McNally.

Schroeter, J.R. 1983: A model of taxi service under fare structure and fleet size regulation. *Bell Journal of Economics*, 14, 81–96.

Schumpeter, J.A. 1942: *Capitalism, Socialism and Democracy*. London: George Allen and Unwin.

Schwartz, M. and Reynolds, R.J. 1983: Contestable markets: an uprising in the theory of industry structure: comment. *American Economic Review*, 73, 488–90.

Schwartzman, D. 1960: The burden of monopoly. *Journal of Political Economy*, 68, 627–30.

Sharkey, W.W. 1982: *The Theory of Natural Monopoly*. Cambridge: Cambridge University Press.

Shaw, R.W. and Sutton, C.J. 1976: *Industry and Competition: Industrial Case Studies*. London: Macmillan.

Shepherd, W.G. 1972: The elements of market structure. *Review of Economics and Statistics*, 54, 25–37.

Shepherd, W.G. 1984: Contestability vs. competition. *American Economic Review*, 74, 572–87.

Shove, G.F. 1930: The representative firm and increasing returns. *Economic Journal*, 40, 94–116.

Shove, G.F. 1942: The place of Marshall's *Principles* in the development of economic theory. *Economic Journal*, 52, 284–329.

Shubik, M. 1961: Objective functions and models of corporate optimization. *Quarterly Journal of Economics*, 75, 345–75.

Shubik, M. 1982: *Game Theory in the Social Sciences*. Cambridge, Mass.: MIT Press.

Shubik, M. 1984: *A Game Theoretic Approach to Political Economy*. Cambridge, Mass.: MIT Press.

Simon, H.A. 1951: A formal theory of the employment relationship. *Econometrica*, 19, 293–305.

Simon, H.A. 1952: A comparison of organization theories. *Review of Economic Studies*, 20, 40–48.

Simon, H.A. 1957: *Models of Man*. New York: Wiley.

Simon, H.A. 1959: Theories of decision-making in economics and behavioural science. *American Economic Review*, 49, 253–83.

Simon, H.A. 1961: *Administrative Behaviour*, 2nd edn. New York: Macmillan.

Simon, H.A. 1982: *Models of Bounded Rationality*. Vol. 1: *Economic Analysis and Public Policy*. Vol. 2: *Behavioural Economics and Business Organization*. Cambridge, Mass.: MIT Press.

Smirlock, M., Gilligan, T. and Marshall, W. 1984: Tobin's q and the structure–performance relationship. *American Economic Review*, 74, 1051–60.

Smith, A. 1776: *An Inquiry into the Nature and Causes of the Wealth of Nations*. Glasgow Edition, R.H. Campbell, A.S. Skinner and W.B. Todd (eds) (1976). Oxford: Oxford University Press.

Solow, R. 1971: Some implications of alternative criteria for the firm. In R. Marris and A.J.B. Wood (eds), *The Corporate Economy*. London: Macmillan, 318–42.

Sosnick, S.H. 1958: A critique of concepts of workable competition. *Quarterly Journal of Economics*, 72, 380–423.

Spence, M. 1983: Contestable markets and the theory of industry structure: a review article. *Journal of Economic Literature*, 21, 981–90.

Spence, M. 1986: Cost reduction, competition and industry performance. In J.E. Stiglitz and G.F. Mathewson (eds) (1986), *New Developments in the Analysis of Market Structure*. London: Macmillan, 475–515.

Sraffa, P. 1926: The laws of returns under competitive conditions. *Economic Journal*, 36, 535–50.

Sraffa, P. 1930: Increasing returns and the representative firm: a criticism. *Economic Journal*, 40, 89–93.

Srinivasan, V. 1981: Equal commission rate policy for a multiproduct salesforce. *Management Science*, 27, 731–56.

Steer, P.S. and Cable, J.R. 1978: Internal organization and profit: an empirical analysis of large UK companies. *Journal of Industrial Economics*, 27, 13–30.

Steindl, J. 1945: *Small and Big Business*. Oxford University: Oxford University Institute of Statistics monograph.

Steindl, J. 1965: *Random Processes and the Growth of Firms: A Study of the Pareto Law*. London: Griffin.

Stigler, G.J. 1940: Notes on the theory of duopoly. *Journal of Political Economy*, 48, 521–41.

Stigler, G.J. 1968: *The Organization of Industry*. Homewood, Illinois: Irwin.

Stiglitz, J.E. and Mathewson, F. (eds) 1986: *New Developments in the Analysis of Market Structure*. London: Macmillan.

Strickland, A.D. and Weiss, L.W. 1976: Advertising, concentration and price–cost margins. *Journal of Political Economy*, 84, 1109–21.

Strotz, R.H. 1960: Interdependence as a specification error. *Econometrica*, 28, 428–41.

Swann, D., O'Brien, D.P., Maunder, W.P.J. and Howe, W.S. 1974: *Competition in British Industry: Restrictive Practices Legislation in Theory and Practice*. London: George Allen and Unwin.

Sweezy, P. 1939: Demand under conditions of oligopoly. *Journal of Political*

Economy, 47, 568–73.

Taussig, F.W. 1921: Is market price determinate? *Quarterly Journal of Economics*, 35, 394–411.

Teece, D.J. 1981: Internal organization and economic performance: an empirical analysis of the profitability of principal firms. *Journal of Industrial Economics*, 30, 173–200.

Telser, L.G. 1972: *Competition, Collusion and Game Theory*. Chicago: Aldine-Atherton.

Thompson, S. 1981: Internal organization and profit: a note. *Journal of Industrial Economics*, 30, 201–11.

Tsurumi, H. 1969: An econometric study of oligopolistic competition among American automobile firms, together with a forecast exercise. In L.R. Klein (ed.), *Essays in Industrial Econometrics*, vol. I. Pennsylvania: Graphic Printing, 29–92.

Varian, H.R. 1984: *Microeconomic Analysis*, 2nd edn. New York: Norton.

Vickers, J. and Yarrow, G. 1985: *Privatization and the Natural Monopolies*. London: Public Policy Centre.

Viner, J. 1931: Cost curves and supply curves. *Zeitschrift fur Nationalökonomie*, 3, 23–46. Reprinted in K.E. Boulding and G.J. Stigler (eds), *Readings in Price Theory*. London: George Allen and Unwin.

Von Neumann, J. and Morgenstern, O. 1944: *Theory of Games and Economic Behaviour*. Princeton: Princeton University Press.

Waterson, M. 1984: *Economic Theory of the Industry*. Cambridge: Cambridge University Press.

Weiss, L.W. 1969: Advertising, profits and corporate taxes. *Review of Economics and Statistics*, 51, 421–30.

Weitzman, M.L. 1976: The new Soviet incentive model. *Bell Journal of Economics*, 7, 251–7.

Weitzman, M.L. 1983: Contestable markets: an uprising in the theory of industry structure: comment. *American Economic Review*, 73, 486–7.

Whitaker, J.K. 1982: The emergence of Marshall's period analysis. *Eastern Economic Journal*, 8, 15–29.

Wied-Nebbeling, S. 1975: *Industrielle Preissetzung*. Tübingen: Mohr (Paul Siebeck).

Williamson, O.E. 1963: Managerial discretion and business behaviour. *American Economic Review*, 53, 1032–57.

Williamson, O.E. 1964: *The Economics of Discretionary Behaviour*. Englewood Cliffs, N.J.: Prentice-Hall.

Williamson, O.E. 1967: Hierarchical control and optimum firm size. *Journal of Political Economy*, 75, 123–38.

Williamson, O.E. 1968: Economies as an antitrust defense: the welfare trade-offs. *American Economic Review*, 58, 18–36.

Williamson, O.E. 1970: *Corporate Control and Business Behavior*. Englewood Cliffs, N.J.: Prentice-Hall.

Williamson, O.E. 1971: Managerial discretion, organization form and the multidivision hypothesis. In R. Marris and A.J.B. Wood (eds), *The Corporate Economy*. London: Macmillan, 343–86.

Williamson, O.E. and Bhargava, N. 1972: Assessing and classifying the internal structure and control apparatus of the modern corporation. In K.G. Cowling (ed.), *Market Structure and Corporate Behaviour*. London: Gray-Mills.

Williamson, O.E. 1975: *Markets and Hierarchies*. New York: Free Press.

Williamson, O.E. and Ouchi, W.G. 1983: The markets and hierarchies programme of research: origins, implications, prospects. In A. Francis, J. Turk and F. Willman (eds), *Power, Efficiency and Institutions*. London: Heinemann, 13–34.

Williamson, O.E. 1986: Vertical integration and related variations on a transaction-cost economic theme. In J.E. Stiglitz and G.F. Mathewson (eds) (1986), *New Developments in the Analysis of Market Structure*. London: Macmillan, 149–74.

Wolfe, J.N. 1955: The industry and the representative firm. *Economic Journal*, 65, 712–14.

Wolfe, J.N. 1964: The representative firm. *Economic Journal*, 64, 337–49.

Worcester, D.A. 1957: Why 'dominant firms' decline. *Journal of Political Economy*, 65, 338–46.

Wu, D.M. 1973: Alternative tests of independence between stochastic regressors and disturbances. *Econometrica*, 41, 733–50.

Wu, D.M. 1974: Alternative tests of independence between stochastic regressors and disturbances: finite sample results. *Econometrica*, 42, 529–46.

Yarrow, G.K. 1976: On the predictions of the managerial theory of the firm. *Journal of Industrial Economics*, 24, 267–79.

Index